FORMATION AND INTERTEXTUALITY
IN ISAIAH 24–27

Society of Biblical Literature

Ancient Israel and Its Literature

Thomas C. Römer, General Editor

Number 17

FORMATION AND INTERTEXTUALITY
IN ISAIAH 24–27

Edited by

J. Todd Hibbard and Hyun Chul Paul Kim

Society of Biblical Literature
Atlanta

Library of Congress Cataloging-in-Publication Data

Formation and intertextuality in Isaiah 24–27 / edited by J. Todd Hibbard and Hyun Chul Paul Kim.
     p. cm. — (Society of biblical literature ancient Israel and its literature ; no. 17)
    Includes bibliographical references and index.
    Summary: The formation and interpretation of Isaiah 24-27, the "Isaiah Apocalypse," are important for understanding Isaiah's compositional history, emerging religious thought in the Persian Period, and scribal techniques for late biblical materials. The volume explores these and other issues and outlines new directions--Provided by publisher.
    ISBN 978-1-58983-886-4 (paper binding : alk. paper) — ISBN 978-1-58983-887-1 (electronic format) — ISBN 978-1-58983-888-8 (hardcover binding : alk. paper)
    1. Bible. Isaiah, XXIV–XXVII—Criticism, interpretation, etc. 2. Bible. Isaiah, XXIV–XXVII—Criticism, Textual. 3. Intertextuality in the Bible. I. Hibbard, James Todd, editor. II. Kim, Hyun Chul Paul, editor.
    BS1515.52.F67 2013
    224'.1066—dc23   2013027657

Printed on acid-free, recycled paper conforming to
ANSI/NISO Z39.48-1992 (R1997) and ISO 9706:1994
standards for paper permanence.

BS1515.52 FOR

Dedicated to the recently retired first-generation scholars of
the Formation of the Book of Isaiah Group at SBL

Contents

Abbreviations

1QIsa^a	Qumran Isaiah^a Scroll
AB	Anchor Bible
ABD	*The Anchor Bible Dictionary.* Edited by David Noel Freedman. 6 vols. New York: Doubleday, 1992.
ABRL	Anchor Bible Reference Library
ACEBTSup	Amsterdamse Cahiers voor Exegese en Bijbel zijn tradities Supplement Series
AOAT	Alter Orient und Altes Testament
ANET	*Ancient Near Eastern Texts Relating to the Old Testament.* Edited by James B. Pritchard. 3rd ed. Princeton: Princeton University Press, 1969.
AnOr	Analecta orientalia
AuOr	*Aula orientalis*
ArBib	The Aramaic Bible
ATD	Das Alte Testament Deutsch
AUM	Andrew University monographs
BASOR	*Bulletin of the American Schools of Oriental Research*
BDB	Brown, Francis, Samuel R. Driver, and Charles A. Briggs. *A Hebrew and English Lexicon of the Old Testament.* Oxford: Clarendon, 1907.
BETL	Bibliotheca ephemeridum theologicarum lovaniensium
BGBE	Beiträge zur Geschichte der biblischen Exegese
BH	Biblical Hebrew
BHS	*Biblia Hebraica Stuttgartensia.* Edited by Karl Elliger and Wilhelm Rudolph. Stuttgart: Deutsche Bibelgesellschaft, 1983.
b. Ḥul	Babylonian Talmud, tractate *Ḥullin*
Bib	*Biblica*
BibInt	Biblical Interpretation
BKAT	Biblischer Kommentar, Altes Testament

BMes	Bibliotheca mesopotamica
BN	*Biblische Notizen*
BRGA	Beiträge zur Religionsgeschicte des Altertums
BWA(N)T	Beiträge zur Wissenschaft vom Alten (und Neuen) Testament
BZ	*Biblische Zeitschrift*
BZAW	Beihefte zur Zeitschrift für die alttestamentliche Wissenschaft
CAT	*The Cuneiform Alphabetic Texts from Ugarit, Ras Ibn Hani and Other Places.* Edited by Manfried Dietrich, Oswald Loretz, and Joaquin Sanmartín. ALASPM 8. Münster: Ugarit-Verlag, 1997.
CBET	Contributions to Biblical Exegesis and Theology
CBH	Classical Biblical Hebrew
CBSC	Cambridge Bible for Schools and Colleges
CC	Continental Commentaries
CEB	Common English Bible
ConBOT	Conectanea Biblica Old Testament Series
CTA	*Corpus des tablettes en cunéiformes alphabétiques découvertes à Ras Shamra-Ugarit de 1929 à 1939.* Edited by Andrée Herdner. Mission de Ras Shamra 10. Paris: Geuthner, 1963.
CTH	*Catalogue des Textes Hittites.* Edited by Emmanuel Laroche. EeC 75. Paris: Klincksieck, 1971.
DDD	*Dictionary of Deities and Demons in the Bible.* Edited by Karel van der Toorn, Bob Becking, and Pieter W. van der Horst. 2nd ed. Leiden: Brill, 1999.
EBC	Expositor's Bible Commentary
EBib	Etudes bibliques
EBH	Early Biblical Hebrew
ECC	Eerdmans Critical Commentary
EeC	Etudes et commentaires
ELB	Elberfelder 1905 (German) Bible
ESV	English Standard Version
ET	English Translation
ETL	*Ephemerides theologicae lovanienses*
ExpTim	*Expository Times*
FAT	Forschungen zum Alten Testament
FOTL	Forms of the Old Testament Literature

GNB	Good News Bible
GNT	Good News Translation
HALOT	Koehler, Ludwig, Walter Baumgartner, and Johann J. Stamm. *The Hebrew and Aramaic Lexicon of the Old Testament*. Translated and edited under the supervision of M. E. J. Richardson. 4 vols. Leiden: Brill, 1994–1999.
HBS	Herders Biblische Studien
HKAT	Handkommentar zum Alten Testament
HO	Handbuch der Orientalistik
HS	*Hebrew Studies*
HSAT	Die Heilige Schrift des Alten Testamentes
HSM	Harvard Semitic Monographs
HTKAT	Herders theologischer Kommentar zum Alten Testament
HTS	Harvard Theological Studies
HUCA	Hebrew Union College Annual
ICC	International critical commentary on the Holy Scriptures of the Old and New Testaments
IH	Israelian Hebrew
IEJ	*Israel Exploration Journal*
Int	*Interpretation*
JAOS	*Journal of the American Oriental Society*
JBL	*Journal of Biblical Literature*
JPOS	*Journal of the Palestine Oriental Society*
JNSL	*Journal of Northwest Semitic Languages*
JSOT	*Journal for the Study of the Old Testament*
JSOTSup	Journal for the Study of the Old Testament Supplement Series
JTS	*Journal of Theological Studies*
KAT	Kommentar zum Alten Testament
KBo	*Keilschrifttexte aus Boghazköi*. WVDOG 30, 36, 68–70, 72–73, 77–80, 82–86, 89–90. Edited by Hans Gustav Güterbock and Heinrich Otten. Berlin: Mann, 1916–1970.
KHC	Kurzer Hand-Commentar zum Alten Testament
KTU	*Die keilalphabetischen Texte aus Ugarit*. Edited by Manfried Dietrich, Oswald Loretz, and Joaquin Sanmartín. AOAT 24.1. Neukirchen-Vluyn: Neukirchener, 1976.
KUB	*Keilschrifturkunden aus Boghazköi*
LBH	Late Biblical Hebrew

LDBT	Young, Ian, and Robert Rezetko. *Linguistic Dating of Biblical Texts*. Bible World. 2 vols. London: Equinox, 2008.
LEI	Leidse Vertaling
LHBOTS	Library of Hebrew Bible Old Testament Series
LUÅ	Lunds universitets årsskrift
LXX	Septuagint
MH	Mishnaic Hebrew
MT	Masoretic Text
NAB	New American Bible
NABre	New American Bible, revised edition
NASB	New American Standard Bible
NJB	New Jerusalem Bible
NJPS	*Tanakh: The Holy Scriptures: The New JPS Translation according to the Traditional Hebrew Text*
NCB	New Century Bible
NET	New English Translation
NETS	*A New English Translation of the Septuagint and Other Greek Translations Traditionally Included under that Title*. Edited by Albert Pietersma and Benjamin G. Wright. New York: Oxford University Press, 2007.
NIV	New International Version
NLT	New Living Translation
NVBS	New Voices in Biblical Studies
OAN	oracles against the nations
OAT	Alter Orient und Altes Testament
Or	*Orientalia*
OTL	Old Testament Library
OTM	Old Testament Message Series
OTWSA	*Ou-Testamentiese Werkgemeenskap in Suid-Afrika.*
OtSt	*Oudtestamentische Studiën*
PredOT	De Prediking van het Oude Testament
QD	Quaestiones disputatae
QH	Qumranic Hebrew
RB	*Revue biblique*
RBL	*Review of Biblical Literature*
RevExp	*Review and Expositor*
RHPR	*Revue d'histoire et de philosophie religieuses*
RSV	Revised Standard Version
SAOC	Studies in Ancient Oriental Civilizations

SB	Sources bibliques
SBH	Standard Biblical Hebrew
SBL	Society of Biblical Literature
SBLAIL	Society of Biblical Literature Ancient Israel and Its Literature
SBLDS	Society of Biblical Literature Dissertation Series
SBLRBS	Society of Biblical Literature Resources for Biblical Study
SBLSymS	Society of Biblical Literature Symposium Series
SBLWAW	Society of Biblical Literature Writings from the Ancient World
SEÅ	*Svensk exegetisk årsbok*
SEL	*Studi epigrafici e linguistici*
SHR	Studies in the History of Religions (supplement to Numen)
SHCANE	Studies in the History and Culture of the Ancient Near East
TA	*Tel Aviv*
Tg. Ps.-J.	*Targum Pseudo-Jonathon*
Tg. Isa.	*Targum Isaiah*
T-I	Trito-Isaiah, Isaiah 56–66
TZ	*Theologische Zeitschrift*
UBL	Ugaritisch-biblische Literatur
UCOP	University of Cambridge Oriental Publications
UF	*Ugarit-Forschungen*
VIHA	*Veröffentlichungen des "Instituts für Historische Anthropologie*
VT	*Vetus Testamentum*
VTSup	Supplements to Vetus Testamentum
WBC	Word Bible Commentary
WVDOG	Deutsche Orient-Gesellschaft: Wissenschaftliche Veroffentlichung
ZAW	*Zeitschrift für die alttestamentliche Wissenschaft*
ZUR	Zürcher Bibel

INTRODUCTION

J. Todd Hibbard and Hyun Chul Paul Kim

The book of Isaiah provides readers with a colorful tapestry of images, rich poetic language, and a deep well of theological insights. Among the prophetic books, it offers the widest window into the social and political world of Israel and Judah during many of the turbulent times of the first millenium B.C.E. Its compositional arc is, in the view of critical scholarship, a long one, stretching from the eighth century B.C.E. to fifth or fourth centuries B.C.E. (or beyond). Though the longstanding division of the book into three major sections—Proto-, Deutero-, and Trito-Isaiah—has proved useful for understanding much about the contexts of the book's composition and development, scholars have also insisted that this division does not correspond neatly to the chronology of the book's development in every respect. Moreover, in recent years, studies that approach the book synchronically or canonically have arisen, complementing the previous diachronic orientations to the book, as well as scholarship devoted to the book's reception and interpretation. The result is that the present state of Isaiah scholarship is extremely diverse in the questions it pursues and the methods used to pursue them.

The large size of the book of Isaiah prompts scholars frequently to focus attention on smaller units within the book. Isaiah 24–27, sometimes (mis-)labeled as the "Isaiah Apocalypse," is one such unit that has attracted attention, at least since the early twentieth century. These chapters are preceded by a collection of oracles focused on foreign entities (Isa 13–23) and followed by a section whose nucleus is thought to be related to the crises of the late eighth century B.C.E. during the reign of Hezekiah (Isa 28–33). Accounting for their position in the book is only one of the issues confronting exegetes. Indeed, these four short chapters present the reader with many questions. To what do the several references to an anonymous city refer (24:10, 12; 25:2; 26:1, 5; 27:10)? Do these chapters offer the first reference to resurrection in the Hebrew Bible (26:19)? How do these chapters anticipate apocalyptic? To what does the broken "everlasting covenant" refer (24:5)? How should the imagery of Yhwh swallowing death (25:8) be interpreted? What is the relationship between these chapters and Canaanite myth? What are the circumstances of their composition? Who wrote them? What is their relationship to the surrounding material? Are the chapters a unified composition? Is there evidence of redaction in the section? Do the chapters present a unified message? These and many other questions have been addressed through the years but, owing to their unresolved status, remain open.

This volume explores several of these issues with the hope that some light will be shed on the critical interpretive issues. The present collection of essays continues the long tradition of published volumes emanating from the Society of Biblical Literature's Formation of the Book of Isaiah Group (now Section). Three earlier collections have established this group as a home for productive and creative scholarship on Isaiah, and it is our hope that this volume continues in that vein. The most recent contribution, *The Desert Will Bloom: Poetic Visions in Isaiah*,[1] focused on Isaiah's poetic dimensions, explicitly keying on the book's use of language and poetry. Prior to that publication, the collective dialogues of the group resulted in *"As Those Who are Taught": The Interpretation of Isaiah from the LXX to the SBL*.[2] This volume was oriented toward the theme of the reading process, the interactions between text and reader. It explored concrete examples of ways in which the book has been interpreted from the ancient to the modern period. The first volume offered by the group, *New Visions of Isaiah*,[3] was also driven by questions about how the reading process influenced interpretation. The volume's essays variously considered the location of meaning—did such reside in the text, the author, or the reader? Additionally, the volume was deeply interested in the differences between synchronic and diachronic readings. Though each of these volumes was

---

1. A. Joseph Everson and Hyun Chul Paul Kim, eds., *The Desert Will Bloom: Poetic Visions of Isaiah* (AIL 4; Atlanta: Society of Biblical Literature, 2009).

2. Claire Mathews McGinnis and Patricia K. Tull, eds., *"As Those Who are Taught": The Interpretation of Isaiah from the LXX to the SBL* (SBLSymS 27; Atlanta: Society of Biblical Literature, 2006).

3. Roy F. Melugin and Marvin A. Sweeney, *New Visions of Isaiah* (JSOTSup 214; Sheffield: Sheffield Academic Press, 1996; repr., Atlanta: Society of Biblical Literature, 2006).

driven by questions rooted in a different time than we now inhabit, the volumes retain their importance for helping set the agenda in Isaiah studies even today.

The present volume builds on these earlier contributions, but differs in one important respect. Unlike these earlier collections which contained essays that ranged over the whole of Isaiah, this volume is restricted to issues arising in one relatively small section of the book. In this sense, this volume charts a different course than these earlier publications. Whereas the earlier volumes were more methodologically homogeneous—at least in the questions they addressed—in exploring a range of texts in Isaiah, this volume poses assorted questions using diverse methodologies to the same section of Isaiah. That does not mean, however, that the issues addressed in these essays do not have importance for reading other portions of the book or the book as a whole (whether synchronically or diachronically). To the contrary, it is hoped that these collected essays demonstrate specifically how reading a small section can be enriching and illuminating in understanding the whole of the book of Isaiah in light of its rich literary complexity, ancient traditions, and thematic messages. The following essays, composed by scholars with diverse methodological expertise (a team of seasoned and up-and-coming scholars across the two continents), are examples of a concerted effort for such an interpretive endeavor.

Several of the articles in this volume had their origin in a 2011 Formation of the Book of Isaiah Group meeting in San Francisco devoted to the study of Isa 24–27. Others were commissioned specifically for this project. Taken together, they demonstrate the exciting and creative research that is being conducted on this small unit in Isaiah at the present moment.

Christopher Hays takes up the challenge of dating Isa 24–27, no small task since these four chapters have generated the greatest range of compositional dates in the entire book (ranging from the eighth century B.C.E. to the second century B.C.E.). Several difficulties confront the exegete in assigning dates to these chapters, not least the lack of historical referents in Isa 24–27. Hays's approach to the question is based on a diachronic approach to Hebrew linguistics. He asks where the language of Isa 24–27 should be situated within the broader development of Hebrew in first millennium B.C.E. His cautious conclusions are provisional but offer the promise of reframing the question of Isa 24–27's date in a helpful and constructive manner.

In an essay that examines important themes and their function in Isa 24–27 as a whole, Hyun Chul Paul Kim identifies three key elements of these chapters. First, he notes the presence of the older ancient Near Eastern *Chaoskampf* and examines how this theme is used in these chapters as a polemic against tyrants and empires. Second, he notes how the antiempire theme is combined with a distinction betweeen the righteous and the wicked in these chapters. These two elements are part of Isa 24–27's role as a literary hinge between Isa 13–23 and 28–35 in his view. Finally, he notes that the anonymous city may have both Zion and Babylon in view in a way that allows the reader to draw open-ended conclusions about the future.

Micaël Bürki offers a new angle into the old problem of the identity or identities of the anonymous city or cities repeatedly mentioned in Isa 24–27. This has proven to be one of the issues generating the most interest among scholars, as they attempt to identify the nameless city. This scholarly detective work has frequently been carried out in service of attempting to date the material in this section. Bürki's essay notes the contrasting images of the cities in the section and identifies it as a key structural feature of this material. Additionally, he argues that the images of the city in Isa 24–27 should be read in light of the preceding oracles against the nations (Isa 13–23), which might help shed light at least on the identity and meaning of the Moabite city in Isa 25.

Wilson de A. Cunha explores the royal dimensions of Isa 24:21–23 and 27:12–13. His essay argues that these two passages should be read as thematically linked. Isaiah 24:21–23 depicts judgment on those entities that challenge Yhwh's reign while asserting the fact of Yhwh's reign. Isaiah 27:12–13 completes the idea by suggesting that gathered exiles who come to worship Yhwh as part of the restoration offer a demonstration of that rule. The latter completes the thought of the former in his view.

Using the insights of comunication analysis, Archibald L. H. M. van Wieringen examines Isa 24:21–25:12. In his view, this text unit is the first part of two elaborations on 24:1–20. His essay notes the presence of different speakers in the text, the interaction of which propels the unit forward. He also draws attention to what he calls the "text-internal" reader and analyzes her/his experience of reading the text.

The festive banquet scene of Isa 25:6–8 is the focus of two essays in the volume. Beth Steiner argues that this scene is the climactic image of Isa 24–27 and owes much to the mythological portraits of gardens and banquets in the cultures surrounding Israel. Of particular importance is her insistence that the meal is associated with Yhwh's enthronement. Paul Kang-Kul Cho and Janling Fu's contribution also examines this passage, but from a slightly different angle. They are intrigued by the image of

Yhwh swallowing up death, not least because in the Canaanite materials of Ugaritic origin, Mot (Death) is the great "swallower." Their essay looks at textual and thematic issues that clarify these actions in Isa 25.

Two essays in the volume explore the related themes of death and resurrection. Three passages from Isa 24–27 that deal with living and dying—25:8, 26:14, and 26:19—are of interest to Annemarieke van der Woude. Also using the insights of communication analysis, she highlights how each passage presents death, which includes for her what is not contrary to death in these passages. It is her contention that the meaning of death is clarified through an analysis that includes noting what it stands in opposition to. Finally, she attends to the spatial dimension of death in these passages as well. In a related but methodologically very different piece, Stephen Cook argues that Isa 26:19 espouses the idea of individual resurrection, an argument that challenges the more widespread view that the verse speaks of the dead living and corpses rising as a metaphor of national restoration. His interpretation sees the verse as integral to the entire lament (26:11–19), but contrasting especially to verse 14's insistence that Judah's foreign overlords will not rise.

Building on the hypothesis that Isa 24–27 is a Persian period text, J. Todd Hibbard's essay explores possible connections between Isa 24–27 and Isa 56–66, much of which is also thought to have been composed in the Persian period. He examines elements of Isa 24 and 26 in particular and places them in relationship with passages in Trito-Isaiah that use similar language or express similar ideas. His provisional conclusion is that certain texts in Isa 24–27 counter or respond to texts in Isa 56–66, primarily because of disappointment over the lackluster restoration effort.

John Willis examines the complicated chapter of Isa 27 and seeks to unravel some of its interpretive difficulties. He offers a close reading of the text that highlights the chapter's structure, imagery, and language. Key for his interpretation of the passage is the vineyard of 27:2–5.

Finally, in an essay that covers all of Isa 24–27, Carol Dempsey examines the literary and poetic features of these chapters. She argues that these chapters possess an internal unity whose poetry "tells a story" about destruction *and* salvation. The chapters' themes fit well with what precedes (Isa 13–23) and what follows (Isa 28–33) in her view. Her essay concludes with some interesting hermeneutical considerations about the text's portrayal of God with which modern readers of the text must wrestle.

In sum, the essays of this volume reveal the richness and diversity of this short section of Isaiah. Indeed, though these essays are methodologically diverse and entertain a variety of critical questions, exegetes of these chapters will undoubtedly identify issues that were left unexplored by this modest volume. Perhaps this may call for another volume on Isa 24–27!

We dedicate this volume to the (somewhat) recently retired professors and scholars of the first generation of the Formation of the Book of Isaiah Group: Willem A. M. Beuken, Edgar W. Conrad, A. Joseph Everson, Chris Franke, Rolf Rendtorff, Patricia K. Tull, Gary Stansell, †John D. W. Watts, and Roy D. Wells. Their high-quality scholarship and mutual open-mindedness have set a model example of how scholarship can be both profound and fun. We are grateful for their academic excellence in vigorously paving the way of Isaiah scholarship in the last decades. We are equally grateful for their humility and gentle encouragement to junior scholars. Their love for this great prophet Isaiah has indeed become manifest as an exegetical feast provided by our God (Isa 25:6). The next generation of Isaiah scholarship is indebted to their legacy and hopeful of following in their path.

The Date and Message of Isaiah 24–27 in Light of Hebrew Diachrony*

Christopher B. Hays

The problem of the composition and redaction of Isa 24–27 has haunted scholars of the book throughout the past century and more. These chapters resist traditional methods for locating texts historically. With their imagery of God overcoming death and raising the dead, they are especially significant to our understanding of Judean religion and its heirs, Judaism and Christianity. Yet, disinterred from historical context, they drift unmoored.

It is time to renew the study of Isa 24–27 in light of the outpouring of recent scholarship on linguistic dating of texts in the Hebrew Bible. There has not been a dedicated study of the language of Isa 24–27 focused on diachrony since that of George Buchanan Gray in his 1912 commentary.[1] At that time, the knowledge of Semitic languages and understanding of linguistic dating were far less well developed. Even now, the language may not provide a firm date for these chapters, but I do anticipate it will help to establish a credible time horizon for these texts on a more empirical basis than has been possible through other methods.

It became clear to me when I began to work on Isa 24–27 that the question of its date had been neglected in recent years and that the common opinions of many scholars and students were based on outdated scholarship (see below). In the years since, I have regularly taught historical Hebrew grammar and have returned to these chapters as a test case for linguistic dating. That latter conversation has heated up significantly; as a result, some of the research needed to support my own has

---

* This essay is dedicated to the memory of my teacher John H. Hayes. I would like to thank Scott B. Noegel for reading and commenting on it.

1. George Buchanan Gray, *A Critical and Exegetical Commentary on the Book of Isaiah, I–XXXIX* (ICC; New York: Scribner's Sons, 1912), 463–72.

now been carried out, with the effect of changing our understanding of
the language of postexilic prophetic books such as Haggai and Isa 40–66.
I present here some opening reflections on this project, along with some
preliminary results.

1. METHODS

Many other methods have previously been brought to bear on the date of
Isa 24–27 without generating consensus.

First, these chapters are nearly bereft of proper nouns and clear historical references. There is not a single personal name, and apart from Jerusalem, Judah, and Zion, the only proper nouns are Egypt and Assyria (27:13),
which are paired as bookends of the region,[2] and the Moabites (25:10), who
were longstanding rivals to Israel and Judah in the Iron Age Levant.

Second, there are no loanwords in the text significant to dating, such
as Persian[3] or Greek. One term (טל in 26:19) appears to reflect an Aramaized spelling, but one that was attested in Judah in the preexilic period.[4]

Third, the idea of God's overcoming death and raising the dead was
once fitted to an evolutionary scheme by a past generation of scholars who
thought it must reflect late (probably Hellenistic) ideas about resurrection.[5] This view can now be set aside in light of the widespread references

---

2. A similar bookending effect is achieved with Egypt and Assyria in texts from
a wide range of periods, e.g., Isa 7:18; 11:11, 16; 19:23–24; Jer 2:18; Lam 5:6; Hos 7:11;
11:11; 12:1; Mic 7:12; Zech 10:10.

3. רזי in 24:16 is not likely related to Persian *rāza* ("secret"), which later came into
Babylonian Aramaic (רָזָא); see Michael Sokoloff, *A Dictionary of Jewish Babylonian
Aramaic of the Talmudic and Geonic Periods* (Ramat-Gan: Bar Ilan University Press,
2002), 1067. There is no indication in the passage that the speaker is keeping a secret,
and no such noun is attested in any of the northwest Semitic dialects of the biblical
period. See, e.g., the comments of Hans Wildberger, *Isaiah 13–27* (trans. Thomas H.
Trapp CC; Minneapolis: Augsburg Fortress, 1997), 491, 493. On the lack of significance for dating, see Ronald Hendel, "Unhistorical Hebrew Linguistics: A Cautionary
Tale," n.p. Online: *www.bibleinterp.com/opeds/hen358022.shtml.*

4. In Aramaic, טל(ל) (cognate with Heb. צל) means "shadow, shade," and, by
metaphorical extension, "protection." The name of the Judean queen Hamital (חמיטל
/ המוטל = "my father-in-law is protection"; 2 Kgs 23:31; 24:48; Jer 52:1) contains the
Aramaized form of the word, and so suggests that there were by-forms in use in Judah
during the preexilic period.

5. For example: Rudolf Smend, "Anmerkungen zu Jes. 24–27," *ZAW* 4 (1884):
161–224.

to gods raising the dead in the ancient Near East, from Marduk to Baal—a motif that dates minimally to the Bronze Age.[6]

Fourth, the earlier assignation of Isa 24–27 to the Hellenistic genre of apocalyptic has now been widely recognized as faulty. Even many of the early modern German scholars on whose work the past consensus was built recognized this.[7] There remains the claim that these chapters are "eschatological," a view that I have contested.[8] This is a topic that will benefit from further analysis, but at best these chapters contain features that were incorporated into later apocalyptic literature.

Fifth and finally, the most recent monographic studies of these chapters have largely focused on intertextual method.[9] As I have pointed out elsewhere, such studies speak of Isa 24–27 as "alluding to" and "building on" various exilic and postexilic texts, but they have presumed the historical order of texts without demonstrating it.[10]

2. Divergent Opinions

Since William R. Millar's literary and thematic study (1976), many recent commentators have followed him in placing much of Isa 24–27 in the sixth century.[11] Millar's method was to show the text's formal similarities with Semitic poetry as far back as Ugarit in terms of both prosody and themes. Hebrew prosody broke down in the postexilic period, as the

---

6. See references to resurrection/revivification in the index of Christopher B. Hays, *Death in the Iron Age II and in First Isaiah* (FAT 79; Tübingen: Mohr Siebeck, 2011), 443.

7. William R. Millar, *Isaiah 24–27 and the Origin of Apocalyptic* (HSM 11; Missoula, Mont.: Scholars Press, 1976), 3.

8. Wilhelm Rudolph, *Jesaja 24–27* (BWA[N]T 62; Stuttgart: Kohlhammer, 1933), 58: "Die Kapitel sind durch und durch eschatologisch." See Hays, *Death in the Iron Age II*, 318–23.

9. E.g., J. Todd Hibbard, *Intertextuality in Isaiah 24–27: The Reuse and Evocation of Earlier Texts and Traditions* (FAT 2/16; Tübingen: Mohr Siebeck, 2006).

10. Hays, *Death in the Iron Age II*, 316–17.

11. Millar places the text in "the last half of the sixth century B.C." (*Isaiah 24–27*, 120). Dan G. Johnson proposes a preexilic section in 587 and a larger exilic section (*From Chaos to Restoration: An Integrative Reading of Isaiah 24-27* [JSOTSup 61; Sheffield: JSOT Press, 1988], 16–17). Marvin Sweeney tentatively suggests the late sixth century (*Isaiah 1–39 with an Introduction to Prophetic Literature* [FOTL 16; Grand Rapids: Eerdmans, 1996], 320). Blenkinsopp suggests a date shortly after 539 (*Isaiah 1–39* [AB 19B; New York: Doubleday, 2003], 348).

relatively prosaic form of Haggai, Malachi, and Zechariah shows, whereas Millar finds that much of Isa 24–27 adheres to good, classical form.[12] His thematic arguments cannot be presented in detail here, but motifs such as feasting with God (25:6) and the divine victory over the sea monsters (27:1), which had been identified by earlier scholars as apocalyptic, can be clearly seen to have deep and ancient roots in West Semitic mythology.

While Millar's contributions remain significant, one must acknowledge the imprecision of his methods. He was working at Harvard when the study of archaic poetry, especially under Frank Moore Cross, was ascendant. For all the contributions made by Cross and his school, the idea that poetry can be reliably typologized on the basis of its meter is not widely followed today. In the case at hand, Millar fails to deal with the fact that the meter of sections of earlier prophetic books is inconsistent as well. The project of identifying editorial interventions on the basis of meter is highly speculative. Millar's discussion of thematic affinities is even less precise. He usefully demonstrates the antiquity of certain themes, but as many of them appear in the Levant from the Late Bronze Age into the Common Era, that alone is not helpful. Therefore, Millar's study is not especially cogent on the matter of a specific date, even to the century. What it did do was to reopen the field, so that it even became possible again to argue for an eighth-century date on historical-critical grounds—as, for example, John Hayes has done.[13]

From the Continental side, these chapters have received very different treatment; there, the assumption of very late composition has been the norm. Hans Wildberger, in his massive commentary, does not argue the date himself at all, but rather cites the slim 1933 study by Wilhelm Rudolph as the definitive word.[14] It cannot bear that weight; Rudolph's conclusions were based largely on the overstated claim that the chapters are "apocalyptic" in nature and "eschatological through and through."[15]

---

12. He places 26:11–27:6 in a later period on the basis of its less classical prosody, however.

13. John H. Hayes and Stuart A. Irvine, *Isaiah the Eighth-Century Prophet: His Times and Preaching* (Nashville: Abingdon, 1987), 294–320. Scott B. Noegel concludes in this way as well: "Dialect and Politics in Isaiah 24–27," *AuOr* 12 (1994): 177–92 (191–92).

14. Rudolph, *Jesaja 24–27*.

15. Ibid., 58.

These claims still need to be addressed more fully in another venue, but they are not terribly strong.

In general, one does not discern much recent intellectual ferment in Europe surrounding these chapters. Konrad Schmid writes in the new *T&T Clark Handbook of the Old Testament* that "it remains doubtful whether any portions of chs. 24–27 originated before the Diadochan era," that is, the third century.[16] The support cited for this claim is the 1973 commentary of Otto Kaiser, which spends pages mulling over the possibility of a location in mid-second century. The section receives similar treatment from Jacques Vermeylen.[17]

Since, as Kaiser acknowledged, the book of Isaiah ended up copied with only minor textual variants in the Great Isaiah Scroll from Qumran (dated to about 125 B.C.E.), this theory asks us to believe that the scroll reached its canonical form in Jerusalem and was almost immediately transmitted to the Dead Sea area. Although this would have been, therefore, a period in which major additions to Isaiah were still possible, by chance (!) this was the very last edition of the book, so that the form of the Masoretic version is identical to the Qumran and LXX versions. We are also to believe that there is *no sign* of this late fluidity in Isaiah in the versions—as there is (amply) in the case of LXX and MT Jeremiah. This strains credulity. It suits the data much better to conclude that the book reached its present form significantly earlier and had a fixed canonical form well before it was brought to Qumran and translated into Greek. The question to be settled is whether it more likely achieved that form somewhere in the sixth and fifth centuries or in the fourth and third.

3. Linguistic Dating

Here linguistic dating can be of service. While it does not offer the precision of Carbon-14 or even paleography, when two camps are divided by centuries, there it has potential. This is not the place to review the history of the study of Hebrew diachrony, from the early rabbis who recognized

---

16. Jan Christian Gertz et al., *T&T Clark Handbook of the Old Testament: An Introduction to the Literature, Religion, and History of the Old Testament* (London: T&T Clark, 2012), 414.

17. Jacques Vermeylen, *Du prophète Isaïe à l'apocalytique: Isaïe, I–XXXV, miroir d'un demi-millénaire d'expérience religieuse en Israël* (2 vols.; EBib; Paris: Gabalda, 1977–1978), 1:352–63.

the difference between biblical and Mishnaic Hebrew;[18] to early critical scholars such as Hugo Grotius, F. H. Wilhelm Gesenius, and Franz Delitzsch, who noticed the variations in the Hebrew of different books; to the more recent debates between Avi Hurvitz and Robert Polzin over the date of the Priestly source. Detailed histories of scholarship are available, so I focus on the most recent debates. The topic has been heating up for more than a decade, seemingly sparked by the claims of "minimalist" biblical scholars who proposed that nearly the entire Bible was composed in the postexilic period. That conclusion seemed incompatible with the previous scholarship on Hebrew diachrony—for example, Delitzsch had said in his 1877 commentary that "if the book of Qoheleth were of old Solomonic origin, then there would be no history of the Hebrew language."[19] In these earlier works, differences in language were explained largely in terms of diachronic change.

The publication by Ian Young and Robert Rezetko of the two-volume *Linguistic Dating of Biblical Texts* (2008, hereafter *LDBT*) has presented a unified case against such diachronic theories and thus against the method of linguistic dating itself. The crux of the case is that the linguistic features that many previous scholars had taken to be indicators of lateness (or earliness) were invalid as markers, since many of them could be found in both early and late texts. After surveying previous scholarship, they conclude that Early Biblical Hebrew (EBH) and Late Biblical Hebrew (LBH) cannot be placed on even a relative timeline because they were "co-existing styles."[20] In their view, this coexistence could be explained in various ways—the primary options are dialectical and sociolectical variation—but not as diachronically significant.

The response to *LDBT* has been swift. It has appeared in various venues, but the volume *Diachrony in Biblical Hebrew*, edited by Cynthia Miller-Naudé and Ziony Zevit, gathered a number of scholars who

---

18. See b. Ḥul. 137b: "The language of Torah is its own (language), and the language of the Sages is its own (language)" (לשון תורה לעצם ולשון חכמים לעצם). Cited in Mark Rooker, *Biblical Hebrew in Transition: The Language of the Book of Ezekiel* (Sheffield: JSOT Press, 1990), 26 n. 11.

19. Franz Delitzsch, *Commentary on the Song of Songs and Ecclesiastes* (Leipzig: Dörffling & Franke, 1875; repr., Edinburgh: Clark, 1877; repr., Grand Rapids: Eerdmans, 1982), 190.

20. Ian Young and Robert Rezetko, *Linguistic Dating of Biblical Texts* (BibleWorld; 2 vols.; London: Equinox, 2008), 2:70, 141.

argue in favor of linguistic dating. One of the most significant contributions was by Robert Holmstedt, who demonstrated that the *expectations* of the authors of *LDBT* were incorrect: linguistic change does not occur systematically in real languages; changes occur in the individual grammar of speakers and are only gradually diffused more widely. For example, a speaker and his grandparent live and use a language concurrently but in different ways. Therefore, *LDBT* was correct that many classical features of Biblical Hebrew (BH) coexisted with the later features that eventually replaced them, but the distribution of these features was still susceptible to diachronic mapping. Drawing on standard works in historical linguistics that are removed from the ideological debate about BH, Holmstedt shows that one should expect earlier features to be replaced by later features gradually, with the rise of late features forming an S-curve when graphed over time.[21]

The model Holmstedt described may need to be modified slightly to account for certain facts (1) that in BH we are dealing with written texts rather than spoken language; (2) that writing represents language only imperfectly; and (3) that attention to the historical/sociological realities of normative scribal schools may in fact allow us to speak of "periods" of the language rather than only diverse idiolects of specific writers.[22] For example, Classical Biblical Hebrew (CBH) may reflect the norms of the preexilic royal Jerusalem chancellery and may have broken down in the postexilic period because there was no longer any social structure to support it. Because of social pressures, the written form of languages is less fluid than the spoken form—and this is all the more true in societies where writing is a technology limited to a minority. Therefore, scholars focused on sociolinguistics in ancient Judah can still take periodization quite seriously.[23]

In spite of their differences, Zevit rightly credits the authors of *LDBT* for their extensive catalogue of features that have been identified as diachronically significant.[24] Their charts include eighty-eight grammatical

---

21. Robert Holmstedt, "Historical Linguistics and Biblical Hebrew," in *Diachrony in Biblical Hebrew* (ed. Cynthia Miller-Naudé and Ziony Zevit; Winona Lake, Ind.: Eisenbrauns, 2012), 97–125 (101–4).

22. William S. Schniedewind, "Steps and Missteps in the Linguistic Dating of Biblical Hebrew," *HS* 46 (2005): 377–84 (381).

23. Frank Polak, "Sociolinguistics: A Key to the Typology and the Social Background of Biblical Hebrew," *HS* 47 (2006): 115–62.

24. Ziony Zevit, "Not So Random Thoughts Concerning Linguistic Dating and

features and 372 lexical items gathered from twelve books and articles, from Arno Kropat's 1909 study of the Chronicler's Hebrew to the 2006 edition of the Joüon-Muraoka grammar. Because the methodology of each previous study varied, the data is incomplete and inconsistent. Zevit suggests mapping the occurrences of all biblical occurrences of all these features in a systematic way so that they can be analyzed. One can expect an ongoing debate about the chronological significance of the variations in linguistic features, not least because, as Holmstedt has pointed out, we are working towards a "relative chronology of both linguistic features *and* ancient texts."[25] It is not ideal to have to work on an equation with multiple variables, but each one depends on the other, so there is no alternative.

The charts are blunt instruments, and it would be desirable to have them reedited for various reasons: they overlap (some of the same features are covered under both grammar and lexicon), and they occasionally misrepresent the underlying sources.[26] They also include features that are not found in BH at all (e.g., ones only found in Qumranic Hebrew [QH] or Mishnaic Hebrew [MH]). It might be useful to argue against the most extreme late dates for Isa 24–27 to show that it includes forms that might have differed in QH,[27] but it would be more useful to generate more detailed charts classifying features as LBH, QH, MH, *et cetera*, so that terms such as סף and קנה are not listed as "Early Biblical Hebrew" when in fact they are simply BH. The very term EBH is problematic, since most scholars agree that we are dating relatively. The term "Classical Biblical Hebrew" is preferable. CBH is a form of the language that was normalized in the preexilic period, but which postexilic authors strove to emulate to a greater or lesser degree.

Diachrony in Biblical Hebrew," in *Diachrony in Biblical Hebrew* (ed. Cynthia Miller-Naudé and Ziony Zevit; Winona Lake, Ind.: Eisenbrauns, 2012), 455–88 (483).

25. Holmstedt, "Historical Linguistics and Biblical Hebrew," 119.

26. For example, *LDBT* identifies a "decrease of paragogic āh (הָ‑) on first person imperfect and *waw*-consecutive verbs (i.e., lengthened imperfect, 'pseudo cohortative')" as an LBH feature (see literature cited in *LDBT* 2:168, grammatical feature #32). This is potentially confusing: whereas the "long imperfect" is rare in Chronicles, it is common at Qumran. I do not mean to say that the authors of *LDBT* are unaware of the facts, only that the method of presentation has limited clarity.

27. For example, Isa 24:7 uses אנח in the N versus an HtD stem in QH; Isa 26:17 uses הרה versus QH מלאה; Isa 26:9 uses קרב (singular) versus the QH-attested plural. (These features and their references are listed in *LDBT* as lexical features 25, 189, and 310, respectively.)

Another shortcoming of the existing lists of "late" features for the purpose of analyzing Isa 24–27 is that the previous scholarship on diachrony in BH has focused mostly on prose. As anyone who has read the Bible in Hebrew can attest, this sort of analysis is more difficult for poetic texts, since poetry does not follow many of the same grammatical and syntactical rules as prose does, and poetry also more often uses uncommon lexicon. For example, noun patterns ending in ־וּת have been classified as an LBH marker,[28] and the uncommon term גֵּאוּת occurs in 26:10. It occurs roughly half a dozen other times in BH, all in poetry; and since four of those are in Isa 9:7, 12:5, and 28:1, 3, it is in no way a clear marker of lateness.

A further example of the need to adjust one's methods for poetic texts is the decline of the direct object marker את in LBH in favor of verbs with an attached pronominal suffix.[29] Shalom Paul, in a study of late forms in Isa 40–66, includes the high ratio of pronominally suffixed verbs to occurrences of את as a marker of lateness, but it is not. As is well known, a decreased use of prose particles, including את, is characteristic of Hebrew poetry in general.[30] As a means of studying the phenomenon, I looked at suffixed and unsuffixed occurrences of את in Isaiah and the Psalms. If a decline in usage was characteristic of later forms, it should be discernible, much as the rise of the use of the relative pronoun שׁ־ for אֲשֶׁר is in the Psalms. However, there is no discernible diachronic pattern in Psalms or Isaiah. As expected, the occurrences of את are highest in Isa 36–37, prose passages imported from 2 Kings. Other chapters that show middling increases in occurrences of את include Isa 8–9, 19, and 65–66. In the case of late chapters such as Isa 65–66, the rise in use of the direct object marker probably reflects the breakdown of poetic form in the postexilic period—the opposite of what diachronic patterns for prose lead us to expect.

A central question of any diachronic investigation is when Hebrew authors ceased to be able to re-create CBH. In a recent book review, Christoph Levin issued a broadside: "The development of the Hebrew language has, generally speaking, no more than marginal importance for the history of Hebrew literature," because "Old Testament Hebrew is characterized by an astonishing uniformity. It is for the most part impossible to distinguish

---

28. See literature cited in *LDBT* 2:172, grammatical feature 55.
29. See literature cited in *LDBT* 2:174, grammatical feature 65.
30. C. L. Seow, *A Grammar of Biblical Hebrew* (Nashville: Abingdon, 1995), 157.

linguistic stages in its historical development … [over] almost a thousand years."[31] Levin holds that LBH only emerged two centuries after the exile, which is when he places the composition of Chronicles-Ezra-Nehemiah. By contrast, Hurvitz has recently reasserted his longstanding conclusion that "there is not even one literary composition dated by consensus to exilic/post-exilic times whose linguistic profile coincides with that of Standard Biblical Hebrew [SBH]."[32]

It would be surprising if Levin's claim were correct, not only because diachrony has been widely observed in BH, but also because it would be highly unusual for a language to remain unchanged. For example, Levin calls SBH "the 'church Latin,' so to speak, of the theological seminary attached to the Second Temple"—but diachrony can be observed in church Latin as well![33]

Claims that CBH continued unchanged well into the Persian Period have been based particularly on the idea that postexilic prophetic books such as Haggai, Zechariah, and Isa 40–66 were composed in good CBH.[34] Indeed, that claim was until very recently a linchpin in the arguments against linguistic dating; but closer recent analyses contradict it. William Schniedewind was correct to consider it an "oft-repeated misconception … that later writers could accurately imitate earlier linguistic exemplars. To be sure, there are examples of later scribes imitating earlier style, but these imitations are always just that—imitations. Ancient scribes did not have the historical or linguistic tools to imitate earlier text-artifacts with complete precision."[35]

On that topic, a trio of recent linguistic studies of postexilic prophetic works requires attention: First, in his study of LBH in Isa 40–66, Paul adduced dozens of features of lexicon, syntax, and grammar—many

---

31. I am referring to Christoph Levin's review of Richard M. Wright, *Linguistic Evidence for the Pre-exilic Date of the Yahwistic Source*, published in *RBL* (2006) at: http://www.bookreviews.org/pdf/4860_5055.pdf. I do not cite Levin to disagree with his assessment of the book under review but as a leading European scholar whose opinions I take to be both influential and representative.

32. Avi Hurvitz, "The Recent Debate on Late Biblical Hebrew: Solid Data, Experts' Opinions, and Inconclusive Arguments," *Hebrew Studies* 47 (2006): 207.

33. Polak, "Sociolinguistics," 123–24.

34. Martin Ehrensvärd, "Linguistic Dating of Biblical Texts," in *Biblical Hebrew: Studies in Chronology and Typology* (ed. Ian Young; London: T&T Clark, 2003), 175–77.

35. Schniedewind, "Steps and Missteps," 382–83.

of which have multiple occurrences—showing that Isa 40–66 certainly derived from a period when the language was changing. Even Second Isaiah, which is usually taken to derive from right around the end of the exile, is rife with unusual verb forms that were foreign to CBH but characteristic of Aramaic and Rabbinic Hebrew. Paul identified thirty-two late features in Isa 40–55 alone.[36] In short, the indications are remarkably strong that the author(s) of the postexilic portions of Isaiah were no longer writing CBH.

Haggai provides the ground for another important test sounding in early postexilic prophecy; the book's emphasis on the completion of the temple (probably in 515 B.C.E.) indicates that it derives from the years immediately following the return from exile. A recent dissertation by Seoung-Yun Shin, written under Hurvitz, concluded that Haggai, Zechariah, and Malachi belong to the LBH stratum.[37] But whereas there were many identifiable later features in Zechariah and Malachi, Shin identified only two features with potential diachronic significance in Haggai.[38] The first is LBH dating formulae;[39] the second is the *hapax legomenon* מלאכות for a "message" from the Lord in Hag 1:13. מלאכות may indeed be a late usage under Aramaic influence, since CBH has an ample store of terms for divine messages. This by itself would be thin evidence, but later work has bolstered the case. Paul added the use of the infinitive absolute as a finite verb (Hag 1:6, 9) and unusual (apparently late) uses of עור (Hag 1:14) and עמד (Hag 2:5).[40] Even more recently, Gary Rendsburg has produced a more extensive survey, adding nine more specific features that

---

36. Shalom Paul, "Signs of Late Hebrew in Isaiah 40–66," in *Diachrony in Biblical Hebrew* (ed. Cynthia Miller-Naudé and Ziony Zevit; Winona Lake, Ind.: Eisenbrauns, 2012), 293–300 (passim). This number can be further subdivided into twenty-six in Isa 40–48 and six in 49–55.

37. Seoung-Yun Shin, "A Lexical Study on the Language of Haggai-Zechariah-Malachi and Its Place in the History of Biblical Hebrew" (Ph.D. diss., Hebrew University, 2007).

38. Furthermore, Shin identifies four features in the corpus where Haggai, Zechariah, and Malachi use SBH forms rather than possible LBH forms. Two of these four occur in Haggai. Haggai uses SBH יהושע (1:1; 2:2) instead of LBH ישוע and SBH מן ומעלה ... (2:15, 18) instead of LBH מן ... ולמעלה.

39. The formula ב־ ... יום לחדש is typologically earlier, whereas the formulae ב־ ... לחדש (Hag 2:1, 20) and ביום ... לחדש (Hag 1:1, 15) are typologically later.

40. Paul, "Signs of Late Hebrew," 294, 297.

indicate lateness,[41] as well as statistical analysis based on Frank Polak's work. Although the features that mark Haggai's language as late are somewhat less striking than those in Zechariah, it demonstrates ample variance from CBH.

4. Preliminary Survey of Isaiah 24–27

In analyzing the language of Isa 24–27, I take the lists compiled from previous scholarship as a starting point—that is, the complete lists from *LDBT*, plus the additional features identified in postexilic prophetic books by Shin, Paul, and Rendsburg. The purpose is to inventory all *possible* late features, which then need to be reanalyzed case-by-case. I see no value in enumerating CBH features, because one can assume that the author was trying to write CBH. The only value for dating is to find where a late author erred because of the influence of the language spoken around him.

It would be quite difficult to make a case that the Hebrew of Isa 24–27 is typologically late. None of the significant late features Paul identifies in Isa 40–66 are present in 24–27,[42] nor are any of the features identified by Shin or Rendsburg in the Minor Prophets.[43] Out of the 372 lexical items in *LDBT*, I find two that could possibly argue for a late date:

---

41. Gary A. Rendsburg, "Late Biblical Hebrew in the Book of Haggai," in *Language and Nature: Papers Presented to John Huehnergard on the Occasion of his 60th Birthday* (ed. Rebecca Hasselbach and Na'ama Pat-El; SAOC 67; Chicago: Oriental Institute, 2012), 329–44. The features are: (1) הן as "if" (Hag 2:12); (2) עד in place of CBH עוד (Hag 2:19); (3) the idiom שׂים לב על versus CBH שׂים לב ל־ (Hag 1:5, 7); (4) הרבה as a substantive (Hag 1:6, 9); (5) פחה as a term for native governor (Hag 1:1, 14; 2:2, 21); (6) עמד in the sense of "abide, endure" (Hag 2:5); (7) an increase in the use of the phrase היכל יהוה (Hag 2:15, 18); (8) the expression (כה) אמר יהוה צבאות (Hag 1:2, 5, 7; 2:6, 7, 9, 11); and (9) the common LBH formula המלך X (1:1, 15).

42. I contest the relevance of the two features of Isa 24–27 included in Paul's list of late features. One is the use of pronominally suffixed verb forms as opposed to verb + marker of the definite direct object + pronominal suffix, for the reasons that are described above in this essay. The second is the use of the plural form עולמים (26:4). (This feature is also listed in *LDBT*.) Isaiah 24:5, 25:2 use the singular (עולם); Isa 26:4 has the plural (צור עולמים). The plural does occur in late texts such as 2 Chr 6:2; Dan 9:24; Ps 145:13; Eccl 1:10; Isa 45:17 (2x); and 51:9. This might have relevance, but the plural also appears in 1 Kgs 8:3; Pss 61:5; 77:6, 8; it may not be a strong marker.

43. I am setting aside for now the statistical methods for grammar and syntax that Rendsburg draws from Polak—computations such as the number of nouns per verb. The relevance of such methods for poetry is not clear.

(1) The possible use of preposition עַל for אֶל in 24:22, in the phrase עַל־בּוֹר ... וְאֻסְּפוּ אֲסֵפָה ("and they shall be gathered together ... to the pit").[44] Although אסף can take עַל as its preposition in the sense of "gather to" (2 Sam 17:11; 2 Kgs 22:20; Amos 3:9), it more commonly takes אֶל in CBH.[45] The construction with אֶל is very common in burial formulae such as, "he was gathered to his people" (וַיֵּאָסֶף אֶל־עַמָּיו; Gen 25:8, etc.), which are relevant here.

(2) The use of אוֹרָה ("light") in 26:19, although the meaning of the phrase is contested.

There are six other features found in Isa 24–27 that increase in frequency in late Hebrew texts; for example, the one occurrence of the 1cs pronoun is אֲנִי rather than אָנֹכִי. With such a small sample size, such changes are not relevant. By contrast, at least fifty lexical features of Isa 24–27 map on the CBH side of the chart.[46] Such a preponderance is not determinative for dating, but it shows that the sample size is large enough to generate significant data.

Again, closer study is necessary. As an example of this need, we might take the term מַסְגֵּר ("prison") in Isa 24:22. It also occurs in Isa 42:7 and Ps 142:8, as well as in Mishnaic Hebrew and Jewish Aramaic. An alternate form, מִסְגֶּרֶת, appears in Ps 18:46, 2 Sam 22:46, and Mic 7:17, which supplies a possible "CBH" alternative to an apparently LBH term. However, a closer analysis of the term shows that *msgr* appears in a monarchic-period Judean seal: *l'zryhw š'r hmsgr* ("[Belonging] to Azariah the porter of the prison").[47] Since this must be an official seal, one can only conclude that biforms were in use in the preexilic period and that the distribution in BH is haphazard (not terribly surprising for such a small sample).

---

44. I omit the MT's אָסִיר, following 1QIsaᵃ and LXX. Unless otherwise noted, all biblical translations are my own.

45. I have excluded instances of אסף עַל that express "gather against."

46. The feature numbers (from *LDBT* 2:179–214): 7, 24, 25, 27, 37, 44, 48, 54, 66, 74, 88, 93, 95, 106, 109, 112, 115, 126, 131, 133, 142–44, 152, 155, 161, 167, 172, 179, 189–90, 225, 248, 258, 261, 265, 271, 309–10, 318, 333, 339, 343, 346–47, 349, 351, 361, 367.

47. Nahman Avigad, "Hebrew Seals and Sealings and Their Significance for Biblical Research," in *Congress Volume: Jerusalem, 1986* (ed. John A. Emerton; VTSup 40; Leiden: Brill, 1988), 7–16 (10).

Turning to grammar and syntax, I would isolate five grammatical features for discussion. Remarkably, I find only two out of eighty-eight that have potential significance for typological lateness:[48]

(1) The increase in the use of the D passive verbal pattern *mequṭṭāl* is characteristic of late texts,[49] and Isa 24–27 has four such forms that are unique in BH or are mostly attested in late texts. Interestingly, they occur in close proximity in two places: מְמֻחָיִם and מְזֻקָּקִים in Isa 25:6[50] and מְנֻפָּצוֹת and מְשֻׁלָּח in 27:9–10.[51]

(2) The preference for plural forms of certain nouns,[52] namely, אֱמֻנִים ("a righteous nation that keeps faithfulness[es]," 26:2), which elsewhere occurs only in Prov 13:17; 14:5; 20:6; and בִּינוֹת ("a people without understanding[s]," 27:11), a *hapax legomenon* in the plural.[53]

By contrast, two other features of Isa 24–27 would map as typologically early, both relating to passive verb forms:

(3) LBH shows a tendency to replace Gp forms with *niphals*, reflecting the archaism and rarity of the Gp. However, there

---

48. There are a number of features for which the increase or decrease has been identified as a diachronic (late) marker that occur in Isa 24–27, but not in a significant density. For example, the increased use of a personal pronoun as emphatic subject of a finite verb (*LDBT* grammatical feature 67), and this occurs in Isa 24:14 and 27:12, but no one would attempt to typologize the language on that basis.

49. See literature cited in *LDBT* 2:168, grammatical feature #35.

50. מחה is a *hapax legomenon*; זקק appears in the same Dp participle pattern in Ps 12:7, 1 Chr 29:4, 28:18.

51. מְנֻפָּצוֹת is the only Dp occurrence of the root in BH. שלח occurs ten times in Dp; the only other Dp participle is in Isa 16:2, where it refers to scattered nestlings. The forms in 25:6 are relatively esoteric and do not have obvious "early" alternatives in BH. By contrast, the forms in 27:9–10 could have been expressed in other ways.

52. See literature cited at *LDBT* 2:169, grammatical feature #42. These specific plural terms have not previously been identified as diachronically significant.

53. Perhaps this should be repointed בִּינוֹת, an abstract form that would have a cognate in Targumic Aramaic. See Marcus Jastrow, *A Dictionary of the Targumim, the Talmud Babli and Yerushalmi, and the Midrashic Literature* (New York: Judaica, 1996), 163.

are two or three Gp forms in Isa 24–27.[54] Such forms decrease greatly in the books that are generally agreed to be postexilic.

(4) LBH prefers active impersonal constructions to passive ones, yet there are a number of uncommon passive forms in Isa 24–27 that could have been expressed impersonally: הַדּוּשׁ (25:10); יוּשַׁר (26:1); יֻחַן (26:10); יְכֻפַּר (27:9); תְּלֻקְּטוּ (27:12).

There are no Gp forms other than participles in Haggai, Zechariah, or Malachi.[55] It would take further analysis to determine whether the passive-versus-impersonal distribution is significant.

Fifth and finally, a decrease in the occurrence of the paragogic *nun* on imperfect forms is generally thought to be characteristic of late texts.[56] The paragogic *nun* is not found at all in 24–27, except three times in the space of nine verses in chapter 26.[57] Two of them are pausal imperfect forms and thus normal in classical Hebrew: יֶחֱזָיֻן in 26:11 and יְקוּמֻן in 26:19. This would be characteristic of an early text. However, צָקֻון in 26:16 is not regular; the paragogic *nun* should not appear on a perfect. It does so on only two other occasions in BH.[58] This misuse of the *nun* suggests that perhaps we are dealing instead with late-but-archaizing editorial activity.[59] Therefore, linguistic analysis might confirm common scholarly conclusions about the complexity of the formation of Isa 24–27, if indeed the language of those chapters is not uniform. Interestingly, Gray noted, "All

---

54. הָרֻג (27:7); אֻסְּפוּ (24:22; although pointed as *pual*, it expresses the passive of the *qal*, not the *piel*); and possibly סֻגְּרוּ in this same verse: not clearly the passive of the *piel*. This last case is complicated and depends on the meaning of the root; see Christopher B. Hays, "Damming Egypt / Damning Egypt: The Paronomasia of *skr* and the Unity of Isa 19:1–15," *ZAW* 120 (2008): 612–16.

55. There are three non-participial passives of לקח in Isa 40–66 (49:24, 25; 52:5) that have been seen as Gp by some, but they are more often analyzed as *pual* or *hophal* (so BDB and *HALOT*).

56. See literature cited in *LDBT* 2:167, grammatical feature #31.

57. All three are present in 1QIsa[a] as well. These verses are not preserved in 1QIsa[b].

58. Deuteronomy 8:3, 16: both with ידע—perhaps reflecting a reanalysis of the initial *yod* as an imperfect preformative?

59. On failed attempts at archaizing, see Avi Hurvitz's study, "Originals and Imitations in Biblical Poetry: A Comparative Examination of I Sam 2:1–10 and Ps 113:5–9," in *Biblical and Related Studies Presented to Samuel Iwry* (ed. Ann Kort and Scott Morschauser; Winona Lake, Ind.: Eisenbrauns, 1986), 115–21.

that is peculiar in the use of the particles is confined to the song in 26:1–19,"[60] and Scott Noegel identified a particularly large number of Israelian Hebrew (IH) features in chapter 26.[61]

One significant further task is to determine whether dialectical and diachronic analysis may be compatible. Rendsburg's well-known identification of IH clearly depends on the identification of early texts linked to the northern kingdom, which ceased to exist in 721 B.C.E.[62] As noted above, Noegel has argued that certain sections of Isa 24-27 show numerous features identified as IH. He suggests that these chapters may be an example of prophetic "code-switching," that is, taking on the linguistic characteristics of another language or dialect when one addresses another people group.[63]

5. Preliminary Findings

It must be emphasized again that this is little more than a progress report; any conclusions drawn at this point are provisional. The task remains to inventory and analyze the language of Isa 24-27 item by item. However, the number of late features in Isa 24-27 identified so far is quite low, and one has not yet encountered a single one of the sort of obvious neologisms that characterize the works of the middle to late Persian Period.

A nakedly quantitative approach is poorly suited to linguistic data[64] (mostly because some features are much more significant than others). However, the analysis of the data available thus far shows that, however one counts, the rate of "late" features per word in Isa 24-27 is less than that of Isa 40-55, Haggai, Zechariah, and Malachi. These findings are also only a few pieces of the puzzle; it remains to be seen whether such an analysis, carried out over the whole Bible and beyond, would yield comprehensible results.

---

60. Gray, *Book of Isaiah*, 466.

61. Noegel, "Dialect and Politics," 177–92.

62. For summary and further literature: Gary A. Rendsburg, "A Comprehensive Guide to Israelian Hebrew: Grammar and Lexicon," *Orient* 38 (2003): 5–35.

63. Noegel, "Dialect and Politics," 191–92; Rendsburg, " A Comprehensive Guide to Israelian Hebrew," 7.

64. Ziony Zevit, "Symposium Discussion Session: An Edited Transcription," *HS* 46 (2005): 371.

If the final results remain consistent with these preliminary findings, then linguistic data practically rules out a Hellenistic date for Isa 24–27. That would take us into the period of the Qumran Psalms and the Great Isaiah Scroll, when there is no sign that CBH was being effectively emulated any longer.[65] Furthermore, the comparison with Haggai and Isa 40–66 at least *suggests* that Isa 24–27 is typologically prior to those compositions.

I have not yet found anything to contradict the opinion that I expressed in *Death in the Iron Age II*: while certain thematic considerations mark Isa 24–27 as later than the time of Isaiah ben Amoz, the most plausible date is in the late seventh century, in the time of Josiah. Although it will remain possible to hypothesize certain later interpolations, the linguistic and formal data point to the century between the late seventh and late sixth centuries as the most plausible horizon for the composition of most of this hotly contested pericope.

To put together some of the data laid out above into a hypothetical synthesis: In addition to generally classical language and prosody of Isa 24–27, one finds in these chapters numerous Israelian Hebrew features, suggesting an address to northerners, as well as a call to "those who were lost in the land of Assyria and those who were driven out to the land of Egypt" to "come and worship the LORD on the holy mountain at Jerusalem" (27:13). This must come from either the time of the second temple (i.e., after 515) or from that of the first temple. If the linguistic data make a post-515 date unlikely, then what about the seventh century? The Assyrian depredations of the eighth and seventh centuries B.C.E. certainly scattered northerners to Assyria (2 Kgs 17:6) and Egypt,[66] and it was a project of the

---

65. Jan Joosten has characterized the Qumran scribes knowledge of Hebrew as "rather heterogeneous": BH elements transmitted by an authentic tradition, elements that have undergone a semantic development, BH words or expressions that were reinterpreted, features of LBH, items due to Aramaic influence, elements of spoken Hebrew dialects, et cetera. See Jan Joosten, "The Knowledge and Use of Hebrew in the Hellenistic Period Qumran and Septuagint," in *Diggers at the Well: Proceedings of a Third International Symposium on the Hebrew of the Dead Sea Scrolls and Ben Sira* (ed. Takamitsu Muraoka and John F. Elwolde; Leiden: Brill, 2000), 115–30 (129).

66. Although the account of the fall of Samaria in 2 Kgs 17 does not mention northern refugees fleeing to Egypt, it is almost certain that this happened. Jeroboam of Israel fled to Egypt when threatened politically (1 Kgs 12:2), as did Hadad of Edom. A more general flight to Egypt took place from Judah to Egypt upon the Babylonian destruction (2 Kgs 25:26), and still more fled there after the murder of Gedaliah (Jer 41–44). These numerous and widespread events surely point to the general presence

kings of Judah to gather up wave after wave of refugees.[57] (In postexilic period, by contrast, northerners were stridently excluded from the temple [Ezra 4:1–4].)[68] Perhaps, then, the Israelian song of Isa 26 was sung to northerners. Perhaps it is a promise to ordain peace (26:12) for those who had experienced war, to expand the boundaries of Judah to make room for refugees, enlarging the nation (26:15), in sum, to raise up a moribund people to new life (26:19), much as Hosea described (Hos 6:1–3) and as Ezekiel prophesied to the Judeans themselves in more baroque manner (Ezek 37). The grouping of these texts as descriptions of national restoration is well established;[69] the question is where Isa 26 fits into the timeline.

The theory that Isa 24–27 was composed in the Hellenistic period is fundamentally *homiletical*; that is to say, we can imagine the text speaking to situations at that time, just as we know the Bible has spoken to situations ever since. But in light of the data, we cannot suppose that it was composed at that time. It will be salutary for scholars to set aside the least likely historical periods for the text's composition and focus on locating it where it belongs: namely, as one of the preexisting pieces that were gathered together by postexilic prophets in the book called Isaiah.[70]

---

of expatriate Israelites in Egypt. See further: Garrett Galvin, *Egypt as a Place of Refuge* (FAT 2/51; Tübingen: Mohr Siebeck, 2011).

67. William S. Schniedewind, *How the Bible Became a Book* (Cambridge: Cambridge University Press, 2004), 66–73.

68. It must be admitted that in the postexilic layers of Isaiah, specifically, there is evidence of a much more inclusive view of "foreigners," e.g., Isa 56:6–8.

69. Hays, *Death in the Iron Age II*, 335. See also the comments of John J. Collins, who places Isa 26 at the end of the Exile: *Daniel* (Hermeneia; Minneapolis: Fortress, 1993), 395.

70. I allude to Hugh G. M. Williamson's *The Book Called Isaiah: Deutero-Isaiah's Role in Composition and Redaction* (Oxford: Clarendon, 1994). Although Williamson does not share my assessment of these chapters, it seems to me that they could easily be made to fit into his *Fortscheibungshypothese*.

CITY, EARTH, AND EMPIRE IN ISAIAH 24–27[*]

Hyun Chul Paul Kim

The primary thesis of this study is as follows. Even though it is a collection of numerous loose pieces, Isa 24–27 as a composite whole displays key thematic and compositional functions in its present form.[1] First, echoing the ancient Near Eastern *Chaoskampf* traditions, the text depicts polemics against the empires and tyrants. The unknown identity of the city and double meanings of the earth/land signify the ongoing political struggles toward the culminating and impending historical future with YHWH's victory and kingship.

Second, key intertextual allusions highlight the place and function of this text as a hinge between chapters 13–23 and 28–33. On the one hand, the antiempire polemics pick up the comparable motifs against many nations in chapters 13–23. On the other hand, the antiwicked polemics between the righteous and the wicked (possibly within the rebuilding community) paves a thematically coherent way into chapters 28–33.

Third, with regard to the redactional formation, the prophetic indictment against Jerusalem may have been conjoined by the announcement of the demise of Babylon (the "Babylon redaction"). At the same time, neither Zion nor Babylon are specifically stated—except in 24:23 and 27:13 for Zion (see 26:1 for "Judah"), which are located in the "on that day" sections and most likely later additions. This anonymity seems deliber-

---

* An earlier version of this paper—which was funded by the Professional Development Fund from Methodist Theological School in Ohio (MTSO)—was presented at the International Meeting of the SBL, Amsterdam, Netherlands, 24 July 2012.

1. Marvin A. Sweeney, *Isaiah 1–39 with an Introduction to Prophetic Literature* (FOTL 16; Grand Rapids: Eerdmans, 1996), 316: "Despite the shifts in form or genre that have caused many scholars to conclude that these chapters are fragmentary, the present analysis of the structure and genre of chs. 24–27 demonstrate a high degree of coherence and unity of purpose."

ate, through which the text offers messages that are relevant to the exilic and postexilic audiences (the "anonymization redaction"), both reflecting on the past (e.g., 587 and 539 B.C.E.) and hoping into the future (beyond Babylon), with the open-ended implications.

1. Ancient Near Eastern Mythology

Isaiah 24–27, among other sections in the book of Isaiah, is replete with vivid religiopolitical polemics against the overpowering empires. In these polemics, the text employs many common motifs of the ancient Near Eastern mythology and cosmogony. In particular, the *Chaoskampf* motif is here reconceptualized in the prophetic polemics against the oppressive hegemony, especially through the tension between the good/righteous and evil/wicked in the anonymous cities, earth/land, and empires.[2]

These chapters incorporate notable phrases and themes from the Creation Epic (*Enuma Elish*) and Poems about Baal and Anat (Baal Epic), accentuating the intentional, subversive polemics against the propaganda and ideology of the pervasive neighboring worldviews. Identifying the exact *Sitz im Leben* of each of these known ancient documents remains disputable, as John Day elucidates:

> The striking parallelism between the relatively late text in Is. 27:1 and the Ugaritic texts almost a millennium earlier is a reminder that the closeness of the language of Old Testament texts to that of the Ugaritic texts is not necessarily an indication of an early date for the Old Testament passages in question.[3]

Also, some of the pertinent occurrences in Isaiah appear to be redactional additions. Nonetheless, comparing the parallel references can illuminate

---

2. Dan G. Johnson, *From Chaos to Restoration: An Integrative Reading of Isaiah 24–27* (JSOTSup 61; Sheffield: JSOT Press, 1988), 98: "The *Chaoskampf* is the overriding theme which ties the composition together. With its pattern of threat/battle, victory, and restoration, it lent itself particularly well to the prophet's deep conviction that destruction was not the final word from [Yhwh]; that the encroachment of chaos was only transitory and would soon give way to the triumph of [Yhwh]."

3. John Day, *God's Conflict with the Dragon and the Sea: Echoes of a Canaanite Myth in the Old Testament* (UCOP 35; Cambridge: Cambridge University Press, 1985), 142.

helpful insights on the religiopolitical polemics inherent in the Isaianic texts.

First of all, the initial verse already provides a subtle hint of the motifs of the creation of the world and its reversal into chaos:

Enuma Elish IV.102–103, 137
It cut through her insides, splitting the heart, Having thus subdued her, he extinguished her life.... He split her {=Tiamat}[4] like a shellfish into two parts. (*ANET*, 67)

Isa 24:1
Now the Lord is about to lay waste the earth and make it desolate [or "split it open"[5]], and he will twist its surface and scatter its inhabitants.[6]

After his valiant defeat of Tiamat, in *Enuma Elish*, Marduk splits up her dead body and creates the sky and earth from it. It is Marduk's defeat and splitting up of his rival god that leads to the creation of the world. Admittedly, it is not Marduk but YHWH who through the divine utterance vanquishes any chaotic forces and creates the world (Gen 1:1–2, "darkness covered the face of the deep [תהום]"). Now YHWH is said to empty out and split up the earth, as if reversing the creation and its orderliness. Thus, Isaiah reasserts that YHWH is the one who will disturb the sinful world and punish the rebellious forces.

Second, in the first of the seven "on that day" passages in Isa 24–27, YHWH is portrayed as taking control of the celestial constellations and thereby resuming the rightful position as the true divine King in Zion:

Enuma Elish V.1–2, 12, 19–20
He {=Marduk} constructed stations for the great gods, / Fixing their astral likenesses as constellations.... / The Moon he caused to shine, the night (to him) entrusting.... / When the sun [overtakes] thee at the base of heaven, / *Diminish* [thy crown] and retrogress in light. (*ANET*, 67–68)

---

4. In order to distinguish the original emendations in *ANET*, which are marked by [square brackets] and (round brackets), I am using {curly brackets} for my insertions into the ancient Near Eastern texts.

5. Joseph Blenkinsopp, *Isaiah 1–39: A New Translation with Introduction and Commentary* (AB 19; New York: Doubleday, 2000), 349.

6. Unless otherwise noted, all translations of biblical texts are from the NRSV.

Baal Epic
Baal goes up in the mou[ntain], / Dagon's Son in the s[ky]. /Baal sits
upon [his th]rone, Dagon's Son upon [his se]at. (*ANET*, 142)

Isa 24:21-23
On that day the Lord will punish the host of heaven in heaven, and on
earth the kings of the earth. They will be gathered together like prisoners
in a pit; they will be shut up in a prison, and after many days they will be
punished. Then the moon will be abashed, and the sun ashamed; for the
Lord of hosts will reign on Mount Zion and in Jerusalem, and before his
elders he will manifest his glory.

According to the *Enuma Elish*, Marduk fixed the stars and installed the
moon and the sun(-god), which were considered the objects of worship
in ancient religious culture.[7] The Isaianic text, however, proclaims that it
is YHWH who made those celestial bodies and that they are mere creatures
subjected to the divine rule and punishment. Furthermore, this Isaianic
text juxtaposes another popular Canaanite mythology, the Baal Epic. In
the battles of the gods, Baal eventually ascends to Mount Zaphon, taking
the throne. In contrast, it is YHWH in the Isaianic text who, after subdu-
ing the hosts of the heaven and the kings of the earth, will reissue the
divine reign in Mount Zion over the whole world (see 24:18–22).[8] YHWH's
supreme authority over all objects of worship and human rulers is heightened by the repeated occurrences of the verb "to punish" (literally, "to
visit") throughout this section (24:21–22; 26:14, 16, 21; 27:1, 3; see also
10:3, 12; 13:4, 11; 23:17; 29:6).[9]

---

7. Blenkinsopp, *Isaiah 1–39*, 356: "Worship of sun, moon, and other celestial
bodies was widespread in antiquity and quite familiar in Iron Age Israel (e.g., Deut
4:19; 17:3; Jer 8:2; 19:3; Zeph 1:5). The idea of hostile and malevolent celestial powers
is also rooted in ancient cosmogonies and theogonies that narrate the theme of celestial rebellion (e.g., *Enuma Elish*, Hesiod)."

8. John Day addresses another key connection between Isa 24:18b–19 and the
Baal Epic (*CTA* 4.vii.25-32 [= *KTU* 1.4.vii.25-32). Both texts display not only the
motif of the theophany and the earth, but especially the motif of the kingship of the
deity, which is closely associated with "Baal's opening a window in his palace" in the
Baal Epic and now YHWH opening the windows of heaven (*God's Conflict with the
Dragon and the Sea*, 146).

9. For the intertextual echoes of the Flood accounts of Genesis in Isa 24 and 26,
see Ulrich F. Berges, *The Book of Isaiah: Its Composition and Final Form* (trans. Millard
C. Lind; Sheffield: Sheffield Phoenix Press, 2012), 163–78; trans. of *Das Buch Jesaja:*

Third, the famous banquet passage, which seems to be a more integral subunit than the "on that day" passages, alludes to both the *Enuma Elish* and the Baal Epic.[10] Here again, the juxtaposition of two different mythological documents displays how these traditions were prevalent in ancient Mesopotamia both across the geography and throughout time periods:[11]

Baal Epic, *KTU* 1.5 ii.2–6; 1.5 vi.8–19; 1.6 ii.21–23; 1.6 iii.1–3;
One lip to earth and one to heaven, / [He stretches his to]ngue to the stars. / Baal enters his mouth, / Descends into him like an olive-cake, / Like the yield of the earth and trees' fruit…. / We came upon Baal / Fallen on the ground: / Puissant Baal is dead, / The Prince, Lord of Earth, is perished…. / I {=Mot} did *masticate* Puissant Baal. / I made him like a lamb in my mouth; / Like a kid in my gullet he's crushed…. / [That Puissant Baal had died], / That the Prince [Lord of Earth] had perished. And behold, alive is [Puissant Baal]! And behold, existent the Prince, Lo[rd of Earth]! (*ANET*, 138–40)

Baal Epic, *KTU* 1.3 iv.21–25 (cf. 27–31)
[An]swers the Maiden [An]ath, / Replies [Yabamat] Liimmim: / "I'll *take* war *away* [from the earth, / Banish] (all) *strife* from the soil,… / I'll *take* war *away* from the earth, etc." (*ANET*, 137)

Enuma Elish VI.69, 71–75
All of them gathered, … / The gods, his fathers, at his banquet he seated:

Komposition und Endgestalt (HBS 16; Freiburg: Herder, 1998) and J. Todd Hibbard, *Intertextuality in Isaiah 24–27: The Reuse and Evocation of Earlier Texts and Traditions* (Tübingen: Mohr Siebeck, 2006), 56–69, 159–67.

10. According to Willem A. M. Beuken, the correlations between 25:1–5 and 25:6–8 are integral. In fact, the redactional seams that join 24:14–20, 21–23, and 25:1–5, 6–8, 9–10a run coherently as a unified whole in the course of prophetic anticipation and fulfillment ("The Prophet Leads the Readers into Praise: Isaiah 25:1–10 in Connection with Isaiah 24:14–23 Seen against the Background of Isaiah 12," in *Studies in Isaiah 24–27: The Isaiah Workshop–De Jesaja Werkplaats* [ed. Hendrik Jan Bosman and Harm van Grol; Leiden: Brill, 2000], 121–56).

11. Interestingly, a similar juxtaposition of same two mythologies can be seen in Jer 50–51, in its polemic against Babylon. See Martin Kessler, *Battle of the Gods: The God of Israel Versus Marduk of Babylon: A Literary/Theological Interpretation of Jeremiah 50–51* (Assen: Van Gorcum, 2003), 125: "Its language [e.g., 51:34–40] is reminiscent of the cosmic battle between creation and chaos, the tale of *Enuma Elish* where Marduk kills Tiamat, the abyss, or the myth of Baal where he conquers Yamm, the sea. The people of Zion are asked to intone a call for YHWH to avenge what was done to them, which in turn is followed by a promise oracle which seals Babylon's fate."

/ "This is Babylon, the place that is your home! / Make merry in its pre-
cincts, occupy its broad [places]." / The great gods took their seats, / They
set up festive drink, sat down to a banquet. (*ANET*, 69; see also 134)

Isa 25:6-8
On this mountain the Lord of hosts will make for all peoples a feast of
rich food, a feast of well-aged wines, of rich food filled with marrow, of
well-aged wines strained clear. And he will destroy on this mountain
the shroud that is cast over all peoples, the sheet that is spread over all
nations; he will swallow up death forever. Then the Lord GOD will wipe
away the tears from all faces, and the disgrace of his people he will take
away from all the earth, for the Lord has spoken.

Blenkinsopp cogently elucidates the parallels: "*Enuma Elish* (3:129–
38) and the Ugaritic Baal texts (51 IV 35–59) also speak of banquets following the victory and accession to the throne of Marduk and Baal, respectively, and there can be no doubt that this association of ideas was quite
familiar."[12] At the same time, the differences or reconceptualizations are
noticeable. Just as the divine purpose of creating humanity in the image
of God markedly differs from the creation of humanity for the relief of the
gods in *Enuma Elish*, so the invitees of the banquet are different—the great
gods in *Enuma Elish* as opposed to "all peoples" and "all nations" in Isaiah
(see 2:2–4).[13] Likewise, contrary to Babylon as the place of the feast, the
Isaianic text announces YHWH's own mountain, much the same way the
location of YHWH's enthronement adopts but shifts from Mount Zaphon
to Mount Zion.[14]

---

12. Blenkinsopp, *Isaiah 1–39*, 358.

13. John Day's observation of parallelism is insightful: "It has hitherto remained
unnoted that 'the seventy sons of Asherah' invited to the feast, corresponding to the
totality of the divine pantheon, account for the universality of the banquet in Is. 25:6,
where '*all* peoples' come" (*God's Conflict with the Dragon and the Sea*, 149). Now, the
Isaianic text further makes a shift from the celestial to terrestrial realm. Furthermore,
on the intertextual echo of the covenant meal at Sinai, including the "seventy of the
elders of Israel" (Exod 24:1, 9), see Hibbard, *Intertextuality in Isaiah 24–27*, 77–83:
"In this case, a tradition about a covenant meal between God and Israel has been
reworked so that the meal now points to a new kind of relationship between God and
humankind generally" (80).

14. From another angle, the shift moves from Mount Sinai to Mount Zion. See
Berges, *Book of Isaiah*, 170–71: "The meal of Yhwh with Moses and the elders (cf. Isa.
24.23), which sealed the communion of Israel with its God (Exod. 24.9–11), is here

Moreover, as is well attested in other studies, the Isaianic text makes a sharp contrast between Baal's impotence and YHWH's omnipotence. To the exiles, Baal's incapacity before Mot, the ruler of the netherworld, may have engendered the idea that YHWH too was defeated by the chaotic forces. However, the Isaianic text proclaims otherwise, with countering depictions. In the Canaanite myth, Baal was indeed defeated and even consumed by Mot in his mouth. By contrast, in Isaiah such chaotic forces have no power or control. Rather, it was YHWH who whistled for the superpower empire like Assyria as YHWH's own tool to chastise Israel (10:5–6). Whereas Baal was swallowed by Mot (cf. Jer 51:34, 44), the prophet declares that YHWH will surely swallow up Mot forever. As Dan G. Johnson avers, "It acts as a polemic against the Canaanite religion."[15] YHWH will assuredly claim victory over Mot, much the same way Baal becomes alive again. Indeed, YHWH will nullify the ferocious devourer and revive the dead: "Your dead shall live, their corpses shall rise…. For your dew is a radiant dew, and the earth will give birth to those long dead [literally, 'the fallen shades']" (Isa 26:19; cf. 26:14; 14:9).[16]

Additionally, rather than Maiden Anat, Baal's sister, who declares to "take away" war and strife "from the earth," it is YHWH who himself will "take away" reproach "from all the earth." Here, in Anat's reply to Baal's command to hasten to Mount Zaphon, the expressions from Harold L. Ginsberg's translation (*ANET*, 137) appear to suggest a striking parallel with Isa 25:8. On the other hand, however, Mark S. Smith and Wayne T. Pitard recently offered a different rendition: "And Adolescent [A]nat an[swered], / [The In-law] of the Peoples replied: / 'I myself will offer [in the ea]r[th] war, / [Pu]t in the dust lo[v]e; / I will pour [peace] amid the earth, / Tran[quili]ty ami[d the fie]lds.'" (CAT 1.3 IV 21–25).[17] The expres-

---

extended to all nations, i.e., to the righteous of all nations. Sinai is not [*sic*] longer the place of meeting with God, but rather, Zion."

15. Johnson, *From Chaos to Restoration*, 65: "This imaginative depiction of Mot swallowing Baal very likely provides the backdrop for the statement in 25:8a." See also Blenkinsopp, *Isaiah 1–39*, 359.

16. For the mythological overtones of the "radiant dew" (CAT 1.3.i.22–25), in addition to the dangerous forces of the "land of the dead" as the "land of no return" (CAT 1.4.viii.14–24; 1.6.ii.19–23), see Mark S. Smith and Wayne T. Pitard, *The Ugaritic Baal Cycle II: Introduction with Text, Translation and Commentary of KTU/CAT 1.3–1.4* (VTSup 114; Leiden: Brill, 2009), 119–20, 719–23.

17. Smith and Pitard, *Ugaritic Baal Cycle II*, 278–79. See also Mark S. Smith, *The Ugaritic Baal Cycle I: Introduction with Text, Translation and Commentary of KTU 1.1–*

sions do not match closely, as this rendering rather mirrors Baal's earlier message (CAT 1.3 IV 8–10). Nonetheless, at the least, the motif of setting peace and placing tranquility on the earth coheres well with the comparable motif in Isa 25:7–8. Thus, it seems evident that the polemical inversion is heightened by the Isaianic text's personification of the divine compassion and mercy, especially to the poor and needy (25:4), as if reaching to "wipe away the tears from all faces, and the disgrace of his people" (25:8).

Fourth, even though the following verse as one of the "on that day" passages appears to be an insert (forming a bracket with 27:12–13), its place is significant in the present form. In YHWH's culminating second speech to Job, YHWH mentions the divine power over mythological forces, such as Behemoth and Leviathan (Job 40:15, 25 [ET 41:1]; see also Job 7:12; Ps 74:13–15; Isa 51:9–10; Gen 1:21). Similarly, the culminating segment in Isa 24–27 pronounces YHWH's complete annihilation of Leviathan and the dragon:

Baal Epic, *KTU* 1.3 iii.41–42; 1.5 i.1–3
I {=Anath} did crush the crooked serpent, / Shalyat [*šlyṭ*] the seven-headed,… / If thou {=Baal} smite Lotan, the serpent slant, / Destroy the serpent tortuous, / Shalyat (*šlyṭ*) of the seven heads. (*ANET*, 137–38)

Isa 27:1
On that day the Lord with his cruel and great and strong sword will punish Leviathan the fleeing serpent, Leviathan the twisting serpent, and he will kill the dragon that is in the sea.

This verse undoubtedly portrays YHWH, instead of Baal, as the most powerful God over against the most insurmountable forces and symbols of the ancient world.[18] Here a double meaning seems to be intended. On the one hand, YHWH will finish off the most formidable chaotic forces in the celestial realm, as it was commonly understood in the ancient religious culture. On the other hand, however, these mythological figures can sym-

---

1.2 (VTSup 55; Leiden: Brill, 1994), 202–9. My appreciation to Paul K. Cho for helping me locate the Ugaritic texts and informing me that the same passage is repeated elsewhere in CAT 1.1.ii.19–20; 1.3.iii.14–17; and 1.3.iv.8–10.

18. For an extensive analysis regarding the identity of these mythological figures (e.g., Yamm, Nahar, Leviathan, Dragon, Rahab, Tehom, etc.), see Smith and Pitard, *Ugaritic Baal Cycle II*, 247–65. See also Hans Wildberger, *Isaiah 13–27* (trans. Thomas H. Trapp; Minneapolis: Fortress, 1997), 579.

bolically represent the menacing empires in the political realm, which are denounced and denied of their power by the righteous God.

Finally, the concluding "on that day" passage of this section echoes the Baal Epic through which Yʜwʜ's assured victory over Assyria and Egypt is reaffirmed:

> Baal Epic, *KTU* 1.2 iv.27, 30
> Baal would rend, would smash Yamm, / Would annihilate Judge Nahar.…
> / For our captive is Prin[ce Yamm], / Our captive is Judge Nahar. (*ANET*, 131)

> Isa 27:12–13
> On that day the Lord will thresh from the channel of the Euphrates [הנהר] to the Wadi of Egypt, and you will be gathered one by one, O people of Israel. And on that day a great trumpet will be blown, and those who were lost in the land of Assyria and those who were driven out to the land of Egypt will come and worship the Lord on the holy mountain at Jerusalem.

In the Baal Epic, Baal wins victory over both Yamm and Nahar. Similarly, Yʜwʜ will champion over the channels of Ephrates/River (Nahar) and Egypt (Yamm). The mythological forces are demythologized in the Isaianic text. Here, the combined bookends of Isa 27:1 and 27:12–13 signify an intertextual allusion to Isa 11:15–16, with regard to the comparable motif between the Baal Epic (destruction of the "seven heads") and Isa 11:15: "And the Lord will utterly destroy the tongue of the sea [ים] of Egypt; and will wave his hand over the River [הנהר] with his scorching wind; and will split it into *seven channels*, and make a way to cross on foot."[19] Thus, these recapitulations accentuate not only the demise of the two superpower empires, Assyria and Egypt, but also the joyous return of the exiles scattered across the extreme ends of the diasporic regions.

To summarize, key parts of Isa 24–27 in its present form betray the ancient Near Eastern mythological *Chaoskampf* motifs, especially from *Enuma Elish* and Baal Epic. Comparable adaptations indicate the widespread popularity and influence of these religiopolitical worldviews and at the same time the intentional inversion in Isaiah's resolute polemics. The

---

19. See Marvin A. Sweeney, "Textual Citations in Isaiah 24–27: Toward an Understanding of the Redactional Function of Chapters 24–27 in the Book of Isaiah," *JBL* 107 (1988): 39–52 (50).

polemics are not only against the daunting religious idols but also against the menacing empires.[20] Ideological subversions of Marduk signify Marduk's incapacity and the ensuing downfall of Babylon, even though the exact *Sitz im Leben* of each adaptation remains uncertain.[21] What seems certain may be the unadulterated denial of the chaotic and imperial forces and the accompanied emphasis on YHWH as the sole powerful God. On this aspect too those chaotic forces can function both as the mythological gods and as the metaphorical symbols of empires. Furthermore, other than 25:6-8, the rest of the examples assessed above (24:1, 21-23; 27:1, 12-13) may have been later editorial glosses, functioning to frame the brackets of the texts. All these issues are intricately related to how those motifs and polemics function in the place of Isa 24-27 within its larger literary context, the subject to which we now turn.

2. INTERTEXTUALITY: ISAIAH 24-27 AND ITS SURROUNDING TEXTS

It is an emerging scholarly consensus that Isa 24-27, despite its formal distinctness, picks up and continues the themes of Isa 13-23, whereas it appears to be more dissimilar to Isa 28-33.[22] In this study, I will argue that Isa 24-27 do share notable commonalities with both the preceding and, equally significantly, the following texts. Our primary focus will be on the select catchwords or catchphrases that uniquely occur in these sections. But thematic similarities, such as the double/multiple meanings of the city

---

20. Concerning chapter 26, which is not included in the discussion above, note Johnson, *From Chaos to Restoration*, 99-100: "Our investigation of the communal lament in 26.7-19 has revealed no evidence of an inner-community struggle such as O. Plöger and P. Hanson are inclined to imagine in this literature. The people are united in their desire for deliverance from the oppressor."

21. In tune with this polemical subversion against Babylon in Isa 24-27, it is my contention that Isa 44-45 should be also read as a polemic *against* Persia. Accordingly, YHWH's anointing and commissioning Cyrus to rebuild Jerusalem and to release her captives was intended to abjectly deny Marduk's authority described in the Cyrus Cylinder and thereby to downplay Cyrus as no more than a mere instrument of YHWH's divine purpose (see 10:5). See Amélie Kuhrt, "Ancient Near Eastern History: The Case of Cyrus the Great of Persia," in *Understanding the History of Ancient Israel* (ed. Hugh G. M. Williamson; Oxford: Oxford University Press, 2007), 107-27.

22. Christopher R. Seitz, *Isaiah 1-39* (Louisville: John Knox, 1993), 115-27, 172-79; Blenkinsopp, *Isaiah 1-39*, 346-48; Patricia K. Tull, *Isaiah 1-39* (Macon, Ga.: Smyth & Helwys, 2010), 258-60, 367-70.

and land/earth, will be assessed as well. These analyses reveal the double function of Isa 24–27: on the one hand, with regard to Isa 13–23, this section picks up the themes of judgment against the nations and employs the polemics against empires through the mythological motifs; on the other hand, with regard to Isa 28–33, this section intensifies the anonymity of the city and earth, thereby paving the smooth transition for the theme of the righteous versus the wicked within the internal religiopolitical struggles for the following section.

2.1. Isaiah 24–27 in Relation to Isaiah 13–23

First let us examine the linguistic and thematic correlations between Isa 13–23 and Isa 24–27. In spite of evident shifts between the two sections, there are certain words and phrases that uniquely recur in both. For example, the following repetitive phrase occurs in both chapter 21 and chapter 24:

> 21:2: A stern vision is told to me; the betrayer betrays, and the destroyer destroys [הבוגד בוגד והשודד שודד]. Go up, O Elam, lay siege, O Media; all the sighing she has caused I bring to an end;

> 24:16: From the ends of the earth we hear songs of praise, of glory to the Righteous One. But I say, I pine away, I pine away. Woe is me! For the treacherous deal treacherously, the treacherous deal very treacherously [בגדים בגדו ובגד בוגדים בגדו].[23]

In Isa 21, concerning the nebulous "wilderness of the sea," the prophet pronounces the upcoming coup and upheaval that will result in the downfall of the oppressor. Now, the setting of Isa 24 is different but its nuance seems similar. Here, in the context of the cosmic debacle, over against the momentary rejoicing of the survivors, the prophet cries out concerning the impending attack. Thus, this phrase (בגד + בגד), which uniquely occurs in these two passages in the book of Isaiah (cf. 33:1; 48:8), bridges Isa 21 and Isa 24 by means of a linguistic correlation.

---

23. Note Wildberger, *Isaiah 13–27*, 499. For another phraseological correlation between 17:6 and 24:13, see ibid., 488; Sweeney, "Textual Citations in Isaiah 24–27," 42–43.

Strikingly, these two texts share further similarity. The identity of the oppressor in Isa 21 and that of the "earth" in Isa 24 are ambiguous.[24] Both cases in turn exhibit a double meaning. In Isa 21, the oppressor may be Assyria or Babylon. If it is the former case, Elam and Media are spurred to overthrow the Assyrian hegemony. But in the latter case, it would be Persia, along with Elam and Media, that would upend the Babylonian empire (cf. Jer 50:1; 51:48, 53, 56).[25] Such anonymity and double meaning seem strange within Isa 13–23. However, in anticipation of Isa 24–27, this subtle feature flows rather smoothly.

Likewise, in Isa 24, the identity of "the city of chaos" (literally, "the city of formlessness"; cf. Gen 1:2) is ambivalent. Some interpreters propose that it refers to Jerusalem, whereas others read it as Babylon.[26] Again, in the former case, the repeatedly occurring word ארץ may have meant the "land" of Judah.[27] Once we designate this word as the "land" of Judah, the echoes of certain key words cohere well. Note the intertextual allusion of Isa 1 in 24:20:

1:2, 8: I reared children and brought them up, but they have rebelled [פשע] against me.... And daughter Zion is left like a booth in a vineyard, like a [hut] [כמלונה] in a cucumber field, like a besieged city.

24:20: It sways like a hut [כמלונה]; its transgression [פשעה] lies heavy upon it, and it falls, and will not rise again.[28]

---

24. On another, yet related, intertextual reuse of Isa 17:6 in Isa 24:13, J. Todd Hibbard offers an insightful analysis: "Our author has evidently picked up an oracle originally aimed at the wayward Northern Kingdom and reapplied it in part to his portrayal of the judgment and devastation of *the earth*" (*Intertextuality in Isaiah 24–27*, 49; emphasis added).

25. Sweeney, "Textual Citations in Isaiah 24–27," 44.

26. On Jerusalem as the city of chaos, see Johnson, *From Chaos to Restoration*, 19–47. On Babylon as the city of chaos, see Seitz, *Isaiah 1–39*, 178; Sweeney, *Isaiah 1–39*, 318–19, 336.

27. Tull, *Isaiah 1–39*, 368–69: "By far the most frequently recurring word in Isaiah 24, found sixteen times in twenty-three verses, is [ארץ]."

28. Note also the verbatim allusion of Amos 5:2 ("fallen, no more to rise, is maiden Israel" [נפלה לא־תוסיף קום]) in Isa 24:20 ("it falls, and will not rise again" [ונפלה ולא־תסיף קום]).

Strikingly, the word "hut" (מלונה) occurs only in these two verses in the entire Hebrew Bible.[29] Read this way, the "chaotic city" connotes Jerusalem whose people have broken the "eternal covenant" (24:5) and thus the land of Judah is pronounced of its devastating fall.

Alternatively, in the latter case, rendering the word ארץ as the "earth" fits more suitably with Babylon as the soon-to-be demolished empire. This option also runs coherently with the mythological undercurrents in 24:1, 21-23.[30] We should note that the similar phrase can be employed in two different contexts. For example, a unique phrase in Jeremiah's oracle originally denounces Judah: "I will utterly destroy them, and make them an object of horror [שמה] and of hissing [שרקה] and an everlasting disgrace" (Jer 25:9; see also 25:18; 29:18). Later, in the oracle against Babylon, the author employs the same phrase to condemn Babylon: "Babylon shall become a heap of ruins, a den of jackals, an object of horror [שמה] and of hissing [שרקה], without inhabitant" (Jer 51:37; see also 49:13; 51:43).[31] If we follow the same tendency of innerbiblical exegesis, it is likely that the author of Isa 24 employed the language of Isa 1 and shifted the guilt and doom from daughter Zion to daughter Babylon. Thus, in light of the present form, the motif of YHWH's punishment of the heavenly hosts and the return of YHWH's reign on Mount Zion reads more properly with the prerequisite of the conquest of Babylon.

Another example pertains to the expression of the pangs of a birthing mother in Isa 21 and Isa 26:

---

29. I am indebted to Professor Noah Hacham, the Hebrew University of Jerusalem, for informing this observation.

30. See Berges, *Book of Isaiah*, 164: "For one thing, the previous oracles of judgment against individual nations are brought into focus on a 'world plane'. The sixteenfold הארץ/ארץ in the 23 verses of Isaiah 24 speaks clearly."

31. Martin Kessler argues that chapter 25 and chapters 50–51 of Jeremiah are keys to the entire book of Jeremiah: "Babylon had been appointed (by YHWH!) to its role as punitive instrument (25:9) and this role is narrated and described until 49:39.... After such a 'mild' conclusion, the Babylon oracles open with a harsh thunderbolt, as the one who had fulfilled her earlier role of 'club' or 'hammer,' as YHWH's punitive instrument, so effectively, is now placed on the rubbish heap; she is receiving the most violent punishment of all, while Israel/Judah are promised liberation.... Indeed, Jeremiah 50–51 affirms the nexus between Babylon's doom and Israel's redemption" (*Battle of the Gods*, 182).

21:3: Therefore my loins are filled with anguish; pangs have seized me, like the pangs of a woman in labor [צירים אחזוני כצירי יולדה]; I am bowed down so that I cannot hear, I am dismayed so that I cannot see;

26:17: Like a woman with child, who writhes and cries out in her pangs when she is near her time [כמו הרה תקריב ללדת תחיל תזעק בחבליה], so were we because of you, O Lord (see also 13:8; 66:7–9).

Interestingly, this feminine imagery of 21:3 follows the treachery of the treacherous in 21:2. Thus, in the case of intertextual allusion, we have a case of a split-up pattern: from 21:2–3 to 24:16 and to 26:17.[32] There is a conceptual development. In 21:2–3, the prophet in the first person singular form reacts to the harsh vision and is appalled at the ravaging of the destroyers (cf. Jer 50:43). Now, in 26:17, it is the collective group in the first person plural form, presumably the righteous ones, who complain over the inefficacy of their uprightness but nevertheless hold fast to YHWH's restoration.[33] The conceptual correlation and progress from 21:3 to 26:17 seem to resemble the linkage or transition from 13:8 (and 66:7–9) to 26:17, which Marvin A. Sweeney succinctly delineates:

By using the vocabulary and imagery of childbirth, which appear in 13:8 and 66:7–9, Isa 26:17–18 aids in linking the major themes of Isaiah 13 and 66—judgment against Babylon and rebirth for Israel at Zion—to those of Isaiah 24–27, that is, universal judgment followed by universal rebirth centered at Zion.[34]

In addition to these phraseological and thematic correlations, other features make the transition from Isa 13–23 to Isa 24–27 notably smooth. Although Isa 13–23 congeal together with the subheading משא (meaning "burden" or "oracle"), only the first half of this section has specific designees, such as Babylon (13:1), Moab (15:1), Damascus (17:1), and Egypt (19:1). In the latter half, the designees are abstract or cryptic—e.g., "wilderness of the

---

32. Benjamin D. Sommer, *A Prophet Reads Scripture: Allusion in Isaiah 40–66* (Stanford, Calif.: Stanford University Press, 1998), 68–69.

33. Seitz, *Isaiah 1–39*, 195.

34. Sweeney, "Textual Citations in Isaiah 24–27," 49. See also Hibbard, *Intertextuality in Isaiah 24–27*, 150–59.

sea" (21:1), Dumah (21:11), "desert plain" (21:13), "valley of vision" (22:1)—with the exception of Tyre (23:1).[35]

Precisely, this abstractness or anonymity of the latter part of Isa 13–23 fits perfectly well with the ambiguous addressees in Isa 24–27, such as the city, land/earth, and empire. We may thus posit an intentional editorial arrangement of the non-specific designees: from Isa 21 ("wilderness of the sea" presumably Babylon) to Isa 22 ("valley of vision" presumably Jerusalem) and to Isa 24–27 ("the city of chaos," 24:10; the "strong city," 26:1; the "lofty city," 26:5). Subsequently, by this logic, it is no coincidence that the subsequent—and seemingly discordant—section starts with key cities, whether specific or not: "Ephraim" (28:1), "Ariel" (29:1), and so on.

What would this rather mutual and congenial feature between Isa 13–23 and 24–27 signify? As noted by many commentators, there is a progressive expansion in that, beyond any specific nation (Isa 13–23), the target of the divine chastisement covers the cosmic forces of mythological and/or political powers (Isa 24–27). At a certain level, Babylon may have been intended as the target of the harsh demolition announced in Isa 24–27.[36] However, it is significant that Babylon's doom is pronounced in 21:9, "Fallen, fallen is Babylon" (cf. Jer 51:8), and nowhere do we find the word "Babylon" in Isa 24–27. Such an anonymity of the target in Isa 24–27 can present an open-endedness when it comes to the possible double or triple identities and meanings of the city, land/earth, and empire. This open-endedness, whether chronologically or geographically, can invite the readers to readily identify with any pertinent targets of Yнwн's judgment or redemption. This aspect is also closely associated with the relationship between Isa 24–27 and 28–33, which is the subject of our next discussion.

---

35. See Hyun Chul Paul Kim, "Isaiah 22: A Crux or a Clue in Isaiah 13–23?" in *Declare Ye among the Nations: Oracles against the Nations in Isaiah, Jeremiah, and Ezekiel* (ed. Else K. Holt et al.; London: T&T Clark, forthcoming).

36. Unlike Assyria or Egypt, whose drastically positive future is hinted in some texts (Isa 19:16–25), Babylon is hardly depicted of anything positive at all. This is understandable if we read Isaiah from the standpoint of the Judeans/Jerusalemites. For them, Babylon was the word so heinous that even to utter that word would have caused enormous pain. Consider Johnson, *From Chaos to Restoration*, 99: "In the aftermath of 587, it would have been evident to any survivor that the hated city was Babylon, and not some supra-historical entity."

2.2. Isaiah 24–27 in Relation to Isaiah 28–33

We also find linguistic and thematic correlations between Isa 24–27 and 28–33. Admittedly, Isa 28–33 is a composite whole, glued together by the six "woe" phrases (28:1; 29:1, 15; 30:1; 31:1; 33:1). However, there are discernible intertextual clues which link Isa 28–33 to Isa 24–27.[37] For example, the imagery of the intoxicated "city of formlessness" in chapter 24 coincides with the similar words and phrases in chapter 28, accusing the indulgent leaders of Ephraim:

> 24:9, 20: No longer do they drink wine [יין] with singing; strong drink [שכר] is bitter to those who drink it…. The earth staggers like a drunkard [שכור], it sways like a hut; its transgression lies heavy upon it, and it falls, and will not rise again;

> 28:1, 3, 7: Ah, the proud garland of the drunkards of Ephraim [שכרי אפרים], and the fading flower of its glorious beauty, which is on the head of those bloated with rich food, of those overcome with wine!… Trampled under foot will be the proud garland of the drunkards of Ephraim [שכורי אפרים]…. These also reel with wine [יין] and stagger with strong drink [שכר]; the priest and the prophet reel with strong drink [שכר], they are confused with wine, they stagger with strong drink [שכר]; they err in vision, they stumble in giving judgment (cf. 19:14; 25:6; 29:9).

The language of "strong drink" or "beer" (שכר) occurs infrequently in the book of Isaiah. In particular, the pursuers of strong drink in 5:11, 22 display comparable motifs with those in Isa 28.[38] Thematically, the devastation is in a larger scale in Isa 24, as if the earth or land itself is intoxicated

---

37. For a meticulous analysis on the semantic comparisons between chapters 24–27 and chapters 28–33, see Willem A. M. Beuken, "Woe to Powers in Israel That Vie to Replace Yʜwʜ's Rule on Mount Zion! Isaiah Chapters 28–31 from the Perspective of Isaiah Chapters 24–27," in *Isaiah in Context: Studies in Honour of Arie van der Kooij on the Occasion of His Sixth-Fifth Birthday* (ed. Michaël N. van der Meer et al.; Leiden: Brill, 2010), 25–43 (25): "Since the preceding chapters 13–23 and 24–27 appear to form a coherent bipartite entity … the subsequent chapters 28–39 can be studied from the point of view of how they pursue the basic events of chapters 24–27: the break-through of Yʜwʜ's kingship on Mount Zion (24:21–23) and its inauguration by the returning exiles at that very place (27:13)."

38. It is intriguing that just as the (six) woe-oracles follow the song of the vineyard in chapter 5, the (six) woe-oracles of chapters 28–33 follow another song of the

on the verge of being swept away. In Isa 28, the expression narrowly aims to condemn the leaders, including the priests and the prophets.

Another example concerns the themes of covenant and death, embedded with the mythological notion:

> 24:5; 25:8: The earth lies polluted under its inhabitants; for they have transgressed laws, violated the statutes, broken the everlasting covenant [ברית עולם].... he will swallow up death [המות] forever. Then the Lord God will wipe away the tears from all faces, and the disgrace of his people he will take away from all the earth, for the Lord has spoken;

> 28:15, 18: Because you have said, "We have made a covenant with death [ברית את־מות], and with Sheol we have an agreement; when the overwhelming scourge passes through it will not come to us; for we have made lies our refuge, and in falsehood we have taken shelter'... Then your covenant with death [בריתכם את־מות] will be annulled, and your agreement with Sheol will not stand; when the overwhelming scourge passes through you will be beaten down by it.

Direct citations are not apparent. Yet, the language of the (eternal) "covenant" is unique (see also 55:3). If the intertextual correlations are intact, we can read that contrary to YHWH's victory over Mot, the hallucinated leaders of Israel have succumbed in their pact with Mot. Such opposite situations vividly highlight the society contaminated by the rebelliousness of those vassals of Mot. The mythological concept thus not only connects these two distant texts but also underscores the graveness of human sinfulness.

The aforementioned example has close affinity with the following example, which utilizes the language of "earth" and "dust" for the highs and lows of humanity:

> 26:5, 19: For he has brought low the inhabitants of the height; the lofty city he lays low. He lays it low to the ground [עד־ארץ], casts it to the dust [עד־עפר].... Your dead shall live, their corpses shall rise. O dwellers in the dust [עפר], awake and sing for joy! For your dew is a radiant dew, and the earth [ארץ] will give birth to those long dead;

---

vineyard in chapter 27. Now we add that both texts share the common language and metaphor of intoxication.

29:4: Then deep from the earth [מארץ] you shall speak, from low in the dust [מעפר] your words shall come; your voice shall come from the ground [מארץ] like the voice of a ghost, and your speech shall whisper out of the dust [מעפר].

In Isa 26, the "strong city" (26:1) of the righteous nation is said to be exalted, whereas the "lofty city" (26:5) of the wicked will be cast to the dust.[39] As if the wicked are those who sold their souls to Mot, they are like the dead who do not live (26:14).[40] But the righteous shall rise and awake from the dust (26:19). Here, in addition to the apparent dichotomy between the "fortified"/"lofty" city of the wicked (i.e., 25:2 [קריה בצורה]; 26:5 [קריה נשגבה]; 27:10 [עיר בצורה]) and the "strong" city of the righteous (26:1 [עיר עז]), there is a distinction between the pious "we" group and the wicked rulers. In a judicious analysis on Isa 26, Hans Snoek expounds the tension extant in the depictions between the "we/they group," the pious believers (26:7–12, 16–20), and the "other lords," the wrongdoers (26:13–14; see also 24:10–16).[41]

This sociopolitical and cosmic dichotomy of Isa 26 recurs in Isa 29. Narrowing the focus onto Jerusalem, Isa 29 describes the shocking downfall of Ariel. The motif and implication are different from those of Isa 26; yet, the linguistic expression and thematic nuance are reminiscent of Isa 26. Read together, the usage of the prepositions is intriguing. Just as the haughty ones are condemned to be brought down "to" (עד) the ground and the dust (Isa 26), in a similar way, the massacred Ariel is to howl "from" (מן) the ground and the dust (Isa 29). The wicked in Isa 26 may point to the empires ensconced in the chaotic forces. However, in this intertextual correlation, Jerusalem labeled as Ariel may not have been thoroughly

---

39. Concerning the linguistic overlap between 25:11b–12 and 26:5–6, as well as their intertextual relationship to 2:9–17, see Hibbard, *Intertextuality in Isaiah 24–27*, 131–34. See also Hyun Chul Paul Kim, "Little Highs, Little Lows: Tracing Key Themes in Isaiah," in *"A Light to the Nations": Essays Honoring Joseph Blenkinsopp and His Contribution to the Study of Isaiah* (ed. Richard Bautch and J. Todd Hibbard; Grand Rapids: Eerdmans, forthcoming).

40. Berges, *Book of Isaiah*, 168: "They are numerically far superior to the righteous, which may indicate that the position of an eschatological separation of righteous and sinners was represented only by a minority group."

41. Hans Snoek, "(Dis)Continuity between Present and Future in Isaiah 26:7–21," in *The New Things: Eschatology in Old Testament Prophecy: Festschrift for Henk Leene* (ed. Ferenc Postma et al.; Maastricht: Uitgeverij Shaker, 2002), 211–18.

excluded (Isa 29), much the same way Jerusalem, disguised as the "valley of vision" in Isa 22, makes a part of the oracles against the nations section (Isa 13–23).

The next example has unique language that connects 21:2 and 24:16 (discussed above) concerning "the destroyer/ravager/treacherous one." This expression also recurs in Isa 33:

> 33:1: Ah, you destroyer [שׁוֹדֵד], who yourself have not been destroyed [שָׁדוּד]; you treacherous one, with whom no one has dealt treacherously [וּבוֹגֵד וְלֹא־בָגְדוּ]! When you have ceased to destroy, you will be destroyed [שׁוֹדֵד תּוּשַׁד]; and when you have stopped dealing treacherously, you will be dealt with treacherously [לַבְגֹּד יִבְגְּדוּ־בָךְ]."

Beyond the observation that via this intertextual connection chapter 33 correlates with chapters 21 and 24, the immediate question concerns who this treacherous one is. Various candidates are proposed, such as the empires of Assyria, Babylon, and the like. At the least, the anonymity of this target picks up the pattern of the unknown identity in Isa 24–27. In a larger flow, the treacherous one should denote the superpower tyrants of Assyria or Babylon disclosed in Isa 13–14. In the immediate section, however, this destroyer can depict the wicked as opposed to the righteous, again the theme adumbrated in Isa 26 (see also Isa 1–2). Willem A. M. Beuken trenchantly surmises this intertextual flow: "Against this background, Isaiah 28–31 applies the judgment on the earth as it has been announced in Isaiah 24–27 to the concrete situation of Jerusalem. Rulers and people in this city do not hold out against the kingship which YHWH has founded on Mount Zion."[42]

To summarize, despite apparent discrepancies, Isa 24–27 comprises key linguistic expressions and thematic clues that can be also found in Isa 13–23 and 28–33. These intertextual correlations seem unique and notable enough to consider intentional editorial arrangement of Isa 13–33 in its present form. Undeniably, the linguistic and thematic interrelationship should not be taken by a rigidly linear reading. Its redactional complexity ought not be dismissed. Nevertheless, in light of the analyses above, a rough conceptual progress and mutuality might be discernible: Isa 13–23 addresses the foreign nations, and yet the tendency shifts from specific names to abstract code-words; Isa 24–27 expands the dimension from

---

42. Beuken, "Woe to Powers in Israel," 43.

nations to cosmic and mythological forces, while picking up this anonymizing tendency, leading to various double meanings of the designations
(such as the city, land/earth, and empire); and, equally significantly, Isa
28–33 builds up on the motif of the cosmic upheaval, together with the
open-endedness of the anonymity, which concretely links to the possible
setting back to the land of Israel and Judah (against Assyria and Babylon
respectively) and at the same time implicates the religiopolitical internal
conflict between the righteous and the wicked within the community (in
the postexilic Yehud province).

3. FORMATION OF ISAIAH 24–27:
SOCIOHISTORICAL SETTINGS AND OPEN-ENDEDNESS

In light of the observations made above, mostly done synchronically, a
diachronic investigation may be in order, not necessarily for the redactional reconstruction but rather for the sociohistorical settings and pertinent implications from their open-endedness vis-à-vis anonymity and
multivalence. About a century earlier, Franz Delitzsch had already made
a penetrating observation: "All attempts to historicize [Isa 24–27] will fail,
since everything which seems to be set within a historical context serves
only as an eschatological emblem … its base of operations in on the other
side of all the history which has happened until now."[43] Hence, instead of
conjecturing the specific redactional layers of each passage, we will posit
the possible compositional processes and their implications.

Concerning the redactional sequences, first of all, no matter how
conjectural it may be, Isa 24–27 betrays the preexilic "Assyria" redaction.
Admittedly, the word "Assyria" only occurs in 27:13 (cf. 27:12), and even
this seems to be a later editorial insertion as one of the "on that day" passages. However, select words and motifs still signify the ravaging threat
Assyria posed to northern Israel and subsequently in the siege of Jerusalem. Jerusalem survived the ordeal but the involved horrors and after-
maths tend to linger in the texts. In the end, the collapse of this seemingly
inviolable city is eerily depicted (e.g., chapter 24).

---

43. Quoted from Wildberger, *Isaiah 13–27*, 462. Note also Johnson, *From Chaos
to Restoration*, 97: "The proposals for the date have ranged from the eighth to the
second century. To be sure, most recent scholars have rejected the extreme ends of
this continuum and have come to view the sixth-fourth centuries as the most likely
provenance. But one would hope for greater precision in the dating of a composition."

Second, more notable evidence points to the exilic "Babylon" redaction. Jerusalem fell, and how she was accused, destroyed, and taunted by the enemy Babylonian empire can be more tangibly observed in the texts. Various signifiers present the pain and anguish Babylon inflicted on Zion, expressed in the impassioned polemics against the mythological symbols, such as Baal, Mot, Nahar, and, above all, Marduk. Here, the typical prophetic warning on the sins of the "land" (of Judah) is transfigured into the cosmic havoc wrought on the "earth" (including Babylon). It is not Baal but YHWH who vanquishes the chaotic forces, slaying Leviathan and any sea monsters. The dreadful Mot, who easily overpowers Baal, will be swallowed by YHWH, and YHWH will punish the faithless and treacherous rulers of heaven and earth, denying any authority Marduk may have claimed and reestablishing the divine reign on Mount Zion.

Third, Isa 24–27 in the present form unmistakably betrays the postexilic "anonymizing" redaction, or "universalization," which comprises double/multiple meanings and open-ended designees.[44] The texts are rooted in the anticipation of the historical future first and foremost, as opposed to the apocalyptic future per se.[45] However, certain elements do reveal what may be called eschatological or even "protoapocalyptic" in the later literature of the Second Temple period. For instance, beyond the realm of cosmic upheaval with the mythological motifs, many key characters are made anonymous. The city is labeled, but in cryptic ways. Babylon is never mentioned, leading to double or triple meanings: Is the "city of formlessness" Jerusalem, Babylon, or even Susa? If Babylon is the hated destroyer par excellence, why is it not named at all in Isa 24–27? Is it because Babylon is presumed to have fallen in Isa 21, if read sequentially? Or, more likely, was it anonymized to make the designees open-ended

---

44. On "universalization," see Hibbard, *Intertextuality in Isaiah 24–27*, 49: "Here we see what will continue to emerge throughout these chapters as the 'universalization' of prophetic material originally directed toward an individual state (most often Israel). In this way the tradition records continuity in God's action and its effect, but enlarges the object of God's judgment (and blessing) to include the entire earth" (see also 216).

45. Brian Doyle, "Fertility and Infertility in Isaiah 24–27," in *The New Things: Eschatology in Old Testament Prophecy: Festschrift Henk Leene* (ed. Ferenc Postma et al., 2002), 88: "The text as such does not appear to reflect a past event nor to propose an event in the distant eschatological future. The metaphors speak of immanence, of a belief that YHWH is going to transform things now, that he has punished but now he will deliver."

with various identities? The anonymity of the city enables the readers to posit the tension of two cities beyond Jerusalem and Babylon. In a way, it leads from "the tale of two cities" to "the tales [plural!] of two cities."[46]

Similarly, that both *Enuma Elish* and *Baal Epic* are juxtaposed in the final form of the texts shows the redactional anachronism through which Yhwh's power can be read against the ensuing empires in the open-ended readings and rereadings, from Assyria (and Egypt[47]), to Babylon to Persia, and even to Greece. It is for this rationale that most of the passages dealing with the ancient Near Eastern mythological motifs in Isa 24–27—"on that day" passages (24:1–3, 21–23; 27:1, 12–13; see also 25:9; 26:1; 27:2, 6)—seem to be later editorial editions, rather than earlier prophetic speeches.

Last, but not least, the anonymization functions well as a transition into Isa 28–33, where the cases of internal class struggle and oppression in Israel and Judah resurface.[48] In addition to the apparent tension between the righteous and the wicked in Isa 26, the rivalry between two cities in Isa 25–26 underscore the portrayal of dichotomous sociopolitical groups. Christopher R. Seitz cogently describes such a contrast:

> In the central panel of this four-chapter presentation (chaps. 25:1–26:6), a clear contrast is set up between the destruction of "the fortified city" (25:2) and the worthy establishment of "a strong city" whose gates open to "the righteous nation that keeps faith" (26:1–2). A further contrast exists between the mountain where God prepares a feast for all peoples (25:6–9) and the high fortifications that are Moab's pride (25:12).... This contrast ... is the central theme of chapters 24–27.[49]

---

46. Seitz, *Isaiah 1–39*, 179.

47. John Day considers that Leviathan and the dragon in Isa 27:1, which he takes as one monster, refers to Egypt: "In my view Leviathan in Is. 27:1 most probably denotes Egypt but it could be Babylon or Persia (*God's Conflict with the Dragon and the Sea*, 112, see also 144–45).

48. Arguing for a case of rewriting (*relecture*) of Isa 1–12 within Isa 28–31, Reinhard G. Kratz trenchantly delineates two innerbiblical exegetical modifications, (1) Zionization and (2) the separation of the good and evil in the people: "The change of perspective represents a new theological orientation on the Zion tradition and prepares for the separation of the good and evil in the people, which is brought about in the salvation oracles (cf. 30:19) and the later interpretations" ("Rewriting Isaiah: The Case of Isaiah 28–31," in *Prophecy and Prophets in Ancient Israel: Proceedings of the Oxford Old Testament Seminar* [ed. John Day; New York: T&T Clark, 2010], 260).

49. Seitz, *Isaiah 1–39*, 179. Concerning various theories on the divergent groups

Here the double meanings of the chasm between the righteous and the wicked are possible again. On the one hand, the tension may signal to the recalcitrant rulers over the poor and needy, tracing as far back as the eighth century Judah. On the other hand, the tension may reveal the struggle within the community, between the *golah* returnees and the people of the land/earth (הארץ), implied in the conflict between the righteous and the wicked.

In conclusion, Isa 24–27 contains notable phrases and motifs that hold this seemingly disjointed literary material together in thematic associations with the empire, earth, and city. First and foremost, key subunits display relevant and resolute polemics against the cosmic forces of the ancient Near Eastern mythological traditions, *Enuma Elish* and Baal Epic in particular. Although the original intention of such demythologizing efforts may have targeted foreign idols and religious symbols, such parallel expressions occurring consistently at the key places of these chapters (esp. "on that day" passages) signify polemical intentions against the dominant "empires."

Moreover, analyzing key intertextual correlations between Isa 24–27 and the surrounding sections (Isa 13–23 and 28–33), we have observed that Isa 24–27 functions as a hinge and builds close affinity with both the preceding and the following sections. On the one hand, these correlations demonstrate its literary interdependence with continuous polemics against enemy nations and oppressing powers. Yet, on the other hand, there is a thematic development in which the notions of judgment or salvation against one specific target were reapplied to other broader targets via the processes of *relecture* or *Fortschreibung*, such as Babylonization (of Assyria), anonymization (of Babylon), or universalization (including all nations and peoples beyond Israel and Judah). Such a development is well illustrated especially in the double meaning and shift, from the "land" (of a specific nation) to the "earth" (in a larger, cosmic scale).

Last, but not least, in terms of both intertextual correlations and redactional procedures, we can further detect the literary functions of these chapters vis-à-vis religious and sociopolitical struggles. This is best exemplified in the implied contests between the "city of chaos" (24:10), or "fortified city" of the wicked (25:2; 26:5; 27:10), and the "strong city"

---

in Isa 24–27, especially during the early restoration period of the Yehud, see Donald C. Polaski, *Authorizing an End: The Isaiah Apocalypse and Intertextuality* (BibInt 50; Leiden: Brill, 2001), 51–70.

of the righteous (26:1). Despite the recurring pronouncements of YHWH's impending defeat of the chaotic forces, those who wait for God (25:9; 26:8) seem outnumbered and threatened. In fact, the threefold menacing forces in 27:1 heighten the insurmountable adversity—"Leviathan the fleeing serpent," "Leviathan the twisting serpent," and "the dragon." Nevertheless, the "righteous nation" (26:2) can join the songs of salvation invoked and sung in key recurring subunits (e.g., 25:1–5; 26:1–6; 27:2–5).[50] Over against the "cities" of the ruthless (25:3–5), therefore, the "poor" and "needy" (25:4; 26:6) clearly hear and sing aloud the dawn of YHWH's righteous reign in the "city" of Zion (24:23; 27:12–13).

---

50. For the identification of these subunits as songs or hymns, see John D. W. Watts, *Isaiah 1–33* (rev. ed.; WBC 24; Nashville: Thomas Nelson, 2005), 370–71. In addition to these subunits, Wildberger labels 25:9–10a as "an eschatological song of thanksgiving" (*Isaiah 13–27*, 459).

CITY OF PRIDE, CITY OF GLORY:
THE OPPOSITION OF TWO CITIES IN ISAIAH 24–27

Micaël Bürki

The name of Yahweh is a strong tower: the righteous run to him, and are safe. The rich man's wealth is his strong city, like an unscalable wall in his own imagination. (Prov 18:10–11)

1. INTRODUCTION

Recent research on chapters 24–27 of the book of Isaiah highlight the numerous intertextual links of these texts with other oracles inside the book of Isaiah, other prophets, the book of Daniel, Psalms, and the myths of origin in Genesis.[1] These studies show that these chapters are the result of a literary work and that they constitute a kind of conclusion to the oracles against the nations (chs. 13–23). However, the internal structure of these chapters and their logic, as well as the history of their redaction, remains to be discussed.

---

1. J. Todd Hibbard, *Intertextuality in Isaiah 24–27: The Reuse and Evocation of Earlier Texts and Traditions* (FAT 2/16; Tübingen: Mohr Siebeck, 2006); Erich Bosshard-Nepustil, *Vor uns die Sintflut: Studien zu Text, Kontexten und Rezeption der Fluterzählung Genesis 6–9* (BWA[N]T 5; Stuttgart: Kohlhammer, 2005); Donald C. Polaski, *Authorising an End: The Isaiah Apocalypse and Intertextuality* (BibInt 50; Leiden: Brill, 2000); Dominic Rudman, "Midrash in the Isaiah Apocalypse," *ZAW* 112 (2000): 404–8; John Day, "The Dependence of Isaiah 26.13–27.11 on Hosea 13.4–14.10 and Its Relevance to Some Theories of the Redaction of the 'Isaiah Apocalypse,'" in *Writing and Reading the Scroll of Isaiah: Studies of an Interpretive Tradition* (Craig C. Broyles and Craig A. Evans; VTSup 70; Leiden: Brill, 1997), 357–68; Marvin A. Sweeney, "Textual Citations in Isaiah 24–27: Toward an Understanding of the Redactional Function of Chapters 24–27 in the Book of Isaiah," *JBL* 107 (1988): 39–52.

The motif of the cities, the anonymous one, and Zion occupies a central place within these chapters. There have been many attempts to reveal the identity of the anonymous city and to propose a sociohistorical context to these texts. Babylon, Jerusalem, a city of Moab, Nineveh, Carthage, Tyre, Samaria, and even Rome were potential candidates.[2] It appears, however, that the different occurrences of the city refer to different oracles concerning different cities. However, their identity is deliberately kept quiet, and this feature is generally considered as part of the desire to give a more universal significance to its message.[3]

In this essay I want to highlight the opposition between the description of the anonymous city and the description of Zion. While one is elevated, the other is abased. This pattern refers directly to the same movement described in Isa 2 depicting the elevation of Zion and the abasement of human beings into dust. The description of those cities draws its inspiration also from wisdom literature, metaphorically representing Yahweh as the fortress of the righteous one, while the city in ruins symbolizes false securities. In this view, the political identity of the city is no more of interest. This kind of representation should be viewed as a common feature of ancient Near East imagery as it is illustrated by the study of Marti Nissinen about Assyrian prophecy:

> the cities are not mentioned merely as geographical locations of prophetic performances, and this is what makes it relevant to study of the cities in Assyrian prophecy. In the sources pertinent to prophecy, cities are, in fact, meaningful as ideological rather than spatial entities. Cities represent something that concerns and embraces the whole empire: they are embodiments of the divine presence and the king's reign, manifestations of the fundamental unity of god, king, and people... by the same token, in the framework of imperial ideology, the cities are representations of the royal power.[4]

------

2. See a summary of these different propositions in Brian Doyle, *The Apocalypse of Isaiah Metaphorically Speaking: A Study of the Use, Function and Significance of Metaphors in Isaiah 24–27* (BETL 151; Leuven: Leuven University Press, 2000), 37–45.

3. Ulrich F. Berges, *The Book of Isaiah: Its Composition and Final Form* (trans. Millard C. Lind; Sheffield: Sheffield Phoenix, 2012), 161–80.

4. Marti Nissinen, "City as Lofty as Heaven: Arbela and Other Cities in Neo-Assyrian Prophecy," in '*Every City Shall Be Forsaken': Urbanism and Prophecy in Ancient Israel and the Near East* (ed. Lester L. Grabbe and Robert D. Haak; JSOTSup 330; Sheffield: Sheffield Academic Press, 2001), 174–239 (208).

Biblical authors seem to take over these representations to attribute the power of the human kings to Yahweh and to his city, Zion.

2. Description of the City in Isaiah 24–27

2.1. The Town of Chaos (Isa 24:10–12)

> The town of chaos is broken down; every house is shut up, that no man may come in. There is a crying in the streets because of the wine; all joy is darkened, the mirth of the land is gone. In the city is left desolation, and the gate is struck with destruction. (Isa 24:10–12)

The anonymous city is first mentioned by the expression "town of chaos" (קִרְיַת־תֹּהוּ, Isa 24:10) and then simply by "city" (עִיר, v. 12). As many commentators have already observed, קִרְיַת־תֹּהוּ should refer to the chaos mentioned earlier at creation described in the primeval history (Gen 1:2).[5] In Second Isaiah, the word תֹּהוּ (Isa 41:29; 44:9; 45:18) describes idols as human work in opposition to God's creation.[6] In the same way, the city as cluster of civilization and culture is in opposition to nature, God's creation. The expression "city of chaos" does not simply refer to the complete devastation of the city. Rather, it sets in contrast human deeds and divine creation stressing the triviality of human creations. As Brevard Childs states it: " 'city of chaos' is an attack against 'earthly human power.' "[7]

2.2. Glorification of Yahweh (Isa 24:14–16)

> Lift their voices and shout joyfully; they praise the pride of Yahweh in the lights. In the east extol Yahweh, along the seacoasts extol the fame of Yahweh, God of Israel. From the ends of the earth we hear songs: majesty to the just one. (Isa 24:14–16)

---

5. Joseph Blenkinsopp, *Isaiah 1–39: A New Translation with Introduction and Commentary* (AB 19; New York: Doubleday, 2000), 351–52.

6. Jacques Vermeylen, *Du prophète Isaïe à l'Apocalyptique Isaïe, I–XXXV, miroir d'un demi millénaire d'expérience religieuse en Israël* (2 vols.; Paris: Gabalda, 1977–1978), 1:354 n. 2.

7. Brevard S. Childs, *Isaiah* (OTL; Louisville: Knox, 2001), 179.

The description of the desolation is immediately followed by a psalm celebrating the glory of Yahweh (14–16a). This section uses the terms גאון ("pride," v. 14) and צבי לצדיק ("majesty to the just one," v. 16). These words used to describe Yahweh are closely linked with the theme of excessiveness. The word גאון ("pride") rarely refers to Yahweh. The word appears essentially in the oracles against the nations (OAN) with a negative sense used to describe the tyrants (Isa 13:11, 19; 14:11; 16:6; 23:9). However, it occurs also in only three cases to describe Yahweh in a positive sense, which is also assigned to the English word "pride" to depict honor (Isa 2:10, 19, 21; 60:15). In these occurrences, the word גאון is systematically used to describe Yahweh in contrast to the tyrant, who is abased while Yahweh is lifted up. In the same way the word צבי ("splendour") describes the vainglory of the tyrants (Babylon [13:19], Tyre [23:9], and Ephraim [28:1–4]) and occurs only with a positive meaning to make a contrast (Isa 4:2; 24:16; 28:1, 5). While this psalm is a very different piece than the first verses of the chapter, their juxtaposition establishes a contrast: on one hand, the city's abasement and on the other, the elevation of Yahweh. The banished joy of the anonymous city (v. 11) now resonates in the songs rising in honor of Yahweh (v. 14); the darkness covers the city of chaos (v. 11), while lights are shinning in the presence of Yahweh (v. 15).[8]

2.3. The Reign of Yahweh in Jerusalem (Isa 24:23b)

> Then the moon shall be confounded, and the sun ashamed; for Yahweh of Hosts will reign on Mount Zion, and in Jerusalem; and before his elders shall be glory. (Isa 24:23)

Chapter 24 closes with a reference to Jerusalem. This verse is clearly an interpolation distinct from the preceding verses on death (24:16b–22) and the following psalm (25:1–9). It introduces the motif of the city of Yahweh to offer a contrast with the desolation of the anonymous city. Here again, the contrast is made between the darkness symbolized by the shame of the moon and of the sun closing the section on death (24:16b–23a) with the glory of Yahweh on the top of Mount Zion. The reference to the glory of

---

8. On the translation of ארים by "light" and not "east," see Otto Kaiser, *Isaiah 1–39* (trans. R. A. Wilson OTL; Louisville: Knox, 1974), 186 n. a.

Zion also introduces the following psalm of chapter 25, which mentions both cities.[9]

2.4. The Palace of the Arrogant and Yahweh's Fortress for the Needy (Isa 25:2–4)

> Indeed, you have made the city into a heap of rubble, the fortified town into a heap of ruins; the palace of strangers is no longer a city; it will never be rebuilt. So a strong nation will extol you; the town of wicked nations will fear you. For you are a fortress for the poor, a fortress for the needy in their distress, a shelter from the rainstorm, a shade from the heat. (Isa 25:2–4)

Chapter 25 opens with a psalm opposing the "fortified town," the "palace of the arrogant," and the "town of wicked nations" to Yahweh, who is presented as a "fortress" for the poor and the needy against the "blast of tyrants" (v. 4). The adjective בצורה ("fortified") used to describe the city designates cities with a fortification (e.g., Deut 3:5; 2 Kgs 18:13). Prophets use it, however, as a symbol of vain assurance (e.g., Zeph 1:16; Zech 11:2). It appears with the same sense in chapter 2 of Isaiah as one of the four metaphors of excessiveness: ועל כל־מגדל גבה ועל כל־חומה בצורה ("against every high tower, for every fortified wall," Isa 2:15). The expression ארמון זרים ("palace of the strangers") appears in the Septuagint as ἀσεβῶν πόλις ("palace of the arrogant") reading זדים ("arrogant") instead of זרים ("strangers") (25:2).[10] Commentators are divided about which reading to keep.[11] The Masoretic Text seems to refer to a foreign invader. However, the "strangers" could also refer not to one invader, but to many foreign nations. The following expression to describe the city, "town of wicked nations" (קרית גוים עריצים, v. 3), indicates that the town represents many nations. The word עריצים designates in Isaiah the wicked one in a general sense (Isa 13:11; 29:20; 49:25). The expression גוים עריצים could therefore designate the foreign nations enumerated in the OAN. They also are all accused of being arrogant, proud, and wicked. In this manner, the reading

---

9. On the structural and unifying function of the motif of the city in chapters 24–27, see Richard J. Coggins, "The Problem of Isaiah 24–27," *ExpTim* 90 (1978–1979): 328–33.

10. See also Isa 29:5.

11. Vermeylen, *Du prophète Isaïe*, 264 n. 2; Willem A. M. Beuken, *Jesaja 13–27* (HTKAT; Freiburg: Herder, 2007), 341–42.

of the Masoretic Text and the Septuagint would point to the same referent: the foreign nations of the OAN. Therefore, all the expressions of this psalm ("the fortified town," "the palace of the strangers," "a strong nation," and "a town of wicked nations") designate the same anonymous city.

Its description is opposed to the presentation of Yahweh as a fortress for the needy. The word מָעוֹז ("fortress") is used in Isaiah to describe the cities of the northern kingdom (Isa 17:9), Tyre, the "fortress of the sea" (Isa 23:4, 14), and Egypt (30:2, 3). But the real fortress is Yahweh (17:10; 27:5). These occurrences point to the metaphoric usage made of this term in Isaiah and other prophets (e.g., 2 Sam 22:33; Jer 16:19; Joel 3:16 [4:16]; Nah 1:7). This is also a feature of lyrical literature (e.g., Pss 27:1; 28:8; 30:2, 3).

In this psalm Yahweh is glorified for two different reasons linked to the motif of the city. He is praised because he destroyed the strong city, and he is worshipped because he is the real city in which the poor find security. This psalm takes over the typical pattern of the OAN and of Isa 2: the inhabitants of heights are abased and the poor are lifted up with the city of Yahweh (Isa 2:9, 11; 5:15–16).

2.5. The Anonymous City Identified with Moab (Isa 25:10b–12)

> Moab shall be trodden down in his place, even as straw is trodden down in the water of the dung-hill. He shall spread forth his hands in the midst of it, as he who swims spreads forth his hands to swim; but Yahweh will lay low his pride together with the craft of his hands. The high fortress of your walls has he brought down, laid low, and brought to the ground, even to the dust. (Isa 25:10b–12)

Verses 10b–12 close the chapter with a new reference to the city. In this way, it creates a frame with verses 2–4.[12] Here again the city is characterized by its high walls: מִבְצַר מִשְׂגַּב חוֹמֹתֶיךָ ("the high fortress of your walls," v. 12). The word מִבְצָר ("fortress") is commonly used to describe fortified cities (e.g., Num 13:19; Josh 10:20), but it appears also, mainly in the Psalms, to describe Yahweh as a fortress (e.g., Pss 9:10; 18:3; 46:8). The last word of the expression, חוֹמָה, describes explicitly the "high wall." In Isaiah this word is also used with a metaphorical sense: "the wall" represents the salvation offered by Yahweh (26:1; 60:18). However, there is in this verse a strong intertextual connection with Isa 2 and the high wall as

---

12. See Doyle, *Apocalypse of Isaiah*, 237–40.

pride's metaphor (v. 15). In this verse, the expression חומה בצורה ("forti-fied wall") is in parallel with מגדל גבה ("lofty tower") insisting on the height of these constructions. The intertextuality appears through the common use of two verbs שחח and שפל, describing the abasement of the walls in 25:12 and human pride in 2:10, 11, 17.[13] The mention of the transformation of the wall into dust (25:12) is also parallel with the return of human beings to the dust (Isa 2:10, 19).[14] Therefore this intertextual-ity with chapter 2, where high walls and fortifications are a metaphor for human pride, suggests reading the mention of the city in the same way.

There is, however, a major objection to this reading: in verse 10, the city is explicitly identified with Moab. Since the other references to the city remain quiet about its identity, this mention of Moab is quite strange. For this reason, this mention of Moab is generally understood as evidence of late editing. A scribe would exclude Moab from the universal invitation to the festival banquet mentioned in preceding verses in accordance with the negative vision of Moab reflected in different texts of the Persian Period (Deut 23:4; Neh 13:1). At this time, Moab would not have been any longer a real enemy of Israel, for it disappeared in the beginning of Persian peri-od.[15] This mention of Moab would then be a codename for the enemies of Israel.[16]

There is, however, another possible explanation for the identification of the anonymous city with the land of Moab in the context of the Apoca-lypse of Isaiah. The mention of Moab's pride refers to the oracle against Moab of Isaiah (16:6) and also of Jeremiah (48:29–30). In the OAN of Isaiah, the accusation against the nation aims most of the time at a well-known feature of the nation. For example, the oracle against Tyre is aimed at its merchants and their commercial activities through the sea (Isa 23:8); the oracle against Assur is aimed at its extreme violence, which is also a well-known characteristic of this nation (Isa 10:7);[17] . The object of the

---

13. See also Isa 5:15 for human pride and Isa 26:5 for high walls.

14. Sweeney, "Textual Citations in Isaiah 24–27," 46–7.

15. Josephus (A.J. 10.181–182) indicates that Moab disappeared during the campaign of Nebuchadnezzar in 582 B.C.E., but this disappearance could also be the consequence of pressure by Arabian tribes mentioned in Ezek 25:4, 5, 10. See André Lemaire, "Amon, Moab, Edom, à l'âge du Fer en Jordanie," in La Jordanie de l'âge de la pierre à l'époque Byzantine (Paris: Ecole du Louvre, 1987), 60–65 (63).

16. Ronald E. Clements, Isaiah 1–39 (NCB; Grand Rapids: Eerdmans, 1980), 210.

17. On the images of the enemies in the oracles against the nations, see Goran

accusation of pride in the oracle against Moab of Isaiah is far less clear. This oracle is a lamentation over the ruins of Moab into which the accusation was inserted (Isa 16:5). The only remembrance of this nation is the numerous names of cities mentioned in the oracle (twelve in Isa 15 and seven in Isa 16). This feature appears also in the oracle against Moab in Jer 48. This oracle insistently designates the numerous cities as the targets of the destruction.

> The destroyer will come against every town. Not one town will escape. The towns in the valley will be destroyed. The cities on the high plain will be laid waste. (v. 8)

> Its cities will be laid waste and become uninhabited. (v. 9)

> Moab will be destroyed. Its towns will be invaded. (v. 15)

> Come down from your place of honor; sit on the dry ground, you who live in Dibon. For the one who will destroy Moab will attack you; he will destroy your fortifications. (v. 18)

> Judgment will come on the cities on the high plain on Holon, Jahzah, and Mephaath, on Dibon, Nebo, and Beth Diblathaim, on Kiriathaim, Beth Gamul, and Beth Meon, on Kerioth and Bozrah. It will come on all the towns of Moab, both far and near. (vv. 21–24)

This feature seems to be insignificant in the frame of the oracle against the nations, but it does not occur concerning the other nations. Finally, the oracle against Moab in Ezekiel confirms this view. The oracle is concise, but it designates the cities of Moab as "the splendor of the land."

> So look, I am about to open up Moab's flank, eliminating the cities, including its frontier cities, the splendor of the land—Beth Jeshimoth, Baal Meon, and Kiriathaim. (Ezek 25:9)

These oracles agree in presenting Moab as composed of many cities, which seems to have been the pride of the nation. Archaeology shows that the kingdom of Moab arose as a unified kingdom during the ninth

Eidevall, *Prophecy and Propaganda: Images of Enemies in the Book of Isaiah* (ConBOT 56; Winona Lake, Ind.: Eisenbrauns, 2009).

century B.C.E.[18] At that time, it was essentially composed of farmsteads. During the seventh and sixth century B.C.E., the number of sites increased quickly, they became larger, and public buildings are attested. They disappeared, however, some decades later at the beginning of the Persian period, leaving behind them only ruins and forsaken places. In view of this, biblical oracles against Moab have kept the memory of these ephemeral cities.[19] Rereading these oracles, the author of the Apocalypse of Isaiah made of Moab and its numerous cities a paradigm of the proud city. That is the reason for the reference to Moab as a synonym of the anonymous city.

2.6. The Strong City (Isa 26:1–4)

> In that day this song shall be sung in the land of Judah: we have a strong city; salvation will he appoint for walls and bulwarks. Open the gates, that the righteous nation which keeps faith may enter in. You will keep him in perfect peace, whose mind is stayed on you; because he trusts in you. Trust in Yahweh forever; for in Yah, Yahweh, is an everlasting rock. For he has brought down those who dwell on high, the lofty city: he lays it low, he lays it low even to the ground; he brings it even to the dust. The foot shall tread it down; even the feet of the poor, and the steps of the needy. (Isa 26:1–6)

While chapter 25 closes with the mention of the abasement of the anonymous city, chapter 26 moves on with the glorification of Zion, the strong city (עִיר עָז), reproducing the opposition. Here again, the city is not depicted in a concrete way: "its walls and bulwarks" symbolize salvation for the righteous nation. This metaphorical description of the city and of

---

18. Bruce Routledge, *Moab in the Iron Age, Hegemony, Polity, Archaeology* (Philadelphia: University of Pennsylvania Press, 2004); E. Gaß, *Die Moabiter: Geschichte und Kultur eines ostjordanischen Volkes im 1. Jahrtausend* (ADPV 38; Wiesbaden: Harrassowitz, 2009).

19. Moab was a very short-lived nation whose identity was closely linked with the erection of its cities; on this see Bruce Routledge, "Learning to Love the King: Urbanism and the State in Iron Age Moab," in *Urbanism in Antiquity, From Mesopotamia to Crete* (ed. Walter E. Aufrecht, Neil A. Mirau, and Steven W. Gauley; JSOTSup 244; Sheffield: Sheffield Academic Press, 1997), 130–44. On buildings as support of cultural memory, see an overview in John Ma, "City as Memory," in *The Oxford Handbook of Hellenic Studies* (ed. George Boys-Stones, Barbara Graziosi, and Phiroze Vasunia; Oxford: Oxford University Press, 2009), 248–59.

its different components (walls, bulwarks, or gates) occurs also in the glorious description of Zion in Isa 60:18. It is a recurrent theme of lyrical and wisdom literature (Pss 24; 46:2–6; 48:14–15; Prov 18:10–12; 25:28). However, the mention of the land of Judah (v. 1) seems to suggest a geographical and political reading of this image.

From verse 5, attention turns again to the "lofty city" (קריה נשגבה). These verses draw abundantly on Isa 2 in the same way as Isa 25:11b–12. The main difference between these texts is the mention of the poor and the needy, who will put their feet on the city's debris. This detail expresses the reversal between those who lived in high places and the poor who will now dwell in Zion.[20] The anonymous city stands obviously in contrast with Zion.

2.7. YAHWEH AS FORTRESS (ISA 27:5)

> I am not angry. I wish I could confront some thorns and briers! Then I would march against them for battle; I would set them all on fire, unless they take me as fortress and make peace with me; let them make peace with me. (Isa 27:4–5)

The last chapter opens a perspective on the future. Yahweh will go on in confronting "thorns and briers" until people take him as a "fortress" (מעוז). This word was already used to describe Yahweh as a "fortress for the needy and for the poor" (Isa 25:4).

2.8. THE FORTIFIED CITY IS FORSAKEN (ISA 27:10)

> For the fortified city is solitary, a habitation deserted and forsaken, like the wilderness. (Isa 27:10)

The last occurrence of the anonymous city describes it as a ruin. The destruction took place. The expression עיר בצורה ("fortified city") was also used in chapter 25. Verse 9 refers to Jacob and its idolatry, the Asherim, and the sun images. It seems to be a clear attempt to relate the anonymous city with Samaria.[21] While its anonymity is preserved in accordance with

---

20. See also Isa 14:32; 23:17–18; 60:16; 61:6.
21. See Isa 17:8; Hos 14:9; See Berges, *The Book of Isaiah*, 177–78.

all of chapters 24–27 and their metaphorical understanding of the city, these verses could reflect a political reading of these texts.

2.9. THE LAST VISION OF JERUSALEM (ISA 27:13)

> It shall happen in that day, that a great trumpet shall be blown; and they shall come who were ready to perish in the land of Assyria, and those who were outcasts in the land of Egypt; and they shall worship Yahweh in the holy mountain at Jerusalem. (Isa 27:13)

The last words of the Apocalypse of Isaiah finish off the description of Zion elaborated through these chapters. They announce the coming of the Diaspora to Jerusalem.

3. CONCLUSION

At the end of this itinerary on the path of the two cities in Isa 24–27, we observed that the anonymous city and Zion appear alternately. This succession forms the structure of these chapters and binds the different sections together. Both cities are presented in opposition one to the other: Jerusalem is elevated on Mount Zion, while the lofty city is abased and turned into dust. However, the opposition is not between God and the empire of evil, as it is often stated, nor do these texts offer an eschatological perspective. The intertextual linkages with Isa 2 and also with wisdom literature reveal that the elevated city embodies all that is high, every kind of false security that could take the place of Yahweh. This is an anthropological statement, but not one that necessarily concerns only foreign nations. This opposition could also define the righteous one in opposition to the wicked one inside the border of Israel.

In Isa 2, the opposition is clearly made between the elevation of Yahweh on Mount Zion (vv. 2–5) and the abasement of human beings into dust (vv. 21–22).[22] Chapters 24–27 get back to this structure, but they replace human beings with the anonymous city. This difference could be an indication of a double entendre in these texts. The opposition of the

---

22. On the concentric structure of Isaiah 2, see Berges, *The Book of Isaiah*, 63–66; Hugh G. M. Williamson, "The Formation of Isaiah 2.6–22," in *Biblical and Near Eastern Essays: Studies in Honour of Kevin J. Cathcart* (ed. Carmel McCarthy and John F. Healey; JSOTSup 375; London: T&T Clark, 2004), 57–67.

two cities could also reflect the political, social, and ideological tensions between Jerusalem and Samaria during the Persian period. This is suggested by the implicit reference in the last description of the anonymous city (Isa 27:9–10) as well as by the oracle against Samaria (Isa 28), the location of which just after chapters 24–27 needs to be clarified.

"Kingship" and "Kingdom":
A Discussion of Isaiah 24:21–23; 27:12–13

Wilson de A. Cunha

1. Introduction

Isaiah 24–27 remains as one of the most difficult parts of Isaiah and has spurred a substantial number of academic dissertations up to the present day.[1] One of its most difficult problems concerns the issue of ideological coherence. Already in 1892, Bernhard Duhm denied any ideological coherence for the chapters concerned. He saw two types of genres in Isa 24–27: (1) songs, which comprise Isa 25:1–5, 9–11; 26:1–19; 27:2–5; (2) oracles, consisting of chapter 24; 25:6–8; 26:20–27:1, 12, 13. Duhm claimed the songs are responsible for breaking the ideological unit of Isa 24–27.[2] Contrarily, John Skinner argued for the unity of theme of Isa 24–27 by explaining the songs in Isa 25:1–5, 9–11; 26:1–19; 27:2–5 as "representing flights of the author's imagination, depicting the feelings of the redeemed community after the great judgment is past."[3] As such, the songs

---

1. Recently published monographs include Brian Doyle, *The Apocalypse of Isaiah Metaphorically Speaking: A Study of the Use, Function and Significance of Metaphors in Isaiah* 24–27 (BETL 151; Leuven: Leuven University Press, 2000); Reinhard Scholl, *Die Elenden in Gottes Thronrat: Stilistisch-kompositorische Untersuchungen zu Jesaja 24–27* (BZAW 274; Berlin: de Gruyter, 2000); J. Todd Hibbard, *Intertextuality in Isaiah 24–27: The Reuse and Evocation of Earlier Texts and Traditions* (FAT 2/16; Tübingen: Mohr Siebeck, 2006); Stefan A. Nitsche, *Jesaja 24–27: Ein dramatischer Text. Die Frage nach den Genres prophetischer Literatur des Alten Testaments und die Textgraphic der großen Jesajarolle aus Qumran* (BWA[N]T 166; Stuttgart: W. Kohlhammer, 2006).

2. Bernhard Duhm, *Das Buch Jesaia: Übersetzt und erklärt* (3rd ed.; HKAT 3.1; Göttingen: Vandenoeck & Ruprecht, 1914), 148–49.

3. John Skinner, *The Book of the Prophet Isaiah* (2 vols.; rev. ed.; CBSC; Cambridge: Cambridge University Press, 1897), 1:203.

were not to be seen as later insertions, as Duhm had argued, "but as the expression of the various moods of the prophet."[4] Since then, a number of monographs have argued for the thematic unity of Isa 24–27.[5] The present article must be seen as another attempt to argue for the unitary character of the Apocalypse of Isaiah.[6] From a synchronic point of view, it will argue that the theme of Yahweh's kingship and of his kingdom unites the chapters under study. Except for brief treatments of the "kingship" motif in Isa 24–27,[7] this important theme has not been applied thoroughly to the whole section. The first part of this paper will address Isa 24:21–23, where the kingship motif is explicitly introduced. Isaiah 27:12–13 will then be explored. A final section will deliberate on the relationship between the two passages above and will note their contribution to the overall theme of the Apocalypse, namely, that of kingship and kingdom.

2. Isaiah 24:21–23: Yahweh's Kingship

The clearest reference to Yahweh's kingship is found in Isa 24:23c: "because Yahweh of hosts has become king."[8] The use of מלך to qualify Yahweh as king occurs only a few times in the book of Isaiah (e.g., Isa 6:5; 33:22; 41:21; 43:15; 44:6; 52:7 [אלהים]). Despite the infrequency of these occurrences, the concept of Yahweh's kingship occupies a central role not only in the message of the prophet Isaiah (see Isa 6:5), but also in the book as a whole. This article will explore the significance of the theme of Yahweh's kingship insofar as it lends ideological coherence to Isa 24–27.

The interpretation of the construction כי מלך יהוה צבאות is debatable. Some modern Bible versions and commentators translate the *qatal* verb מלך with the future tense: "because Yahweh of hosts will reign" (e.g., NIV; NAB; RSV).[9] Others translate it with the present tense: "because

---

4. See John Gray, *The Biblical Doctrine of the Reign of God* (Edinburgh: T&T Clark, 1979), 198.

5. For a brief discussion of the unitary or fragmentary character of Isa 24–27 with reference to secondary literature, see Doyle, *Apocalypse of Isaiah*, 13–14.

6. I do not believe that Isa 24–27 belongs to the "apocalyptic" genre. I use the term here because it has become customary to label Isa 24–27 as such. Other scholars have adopted a similar procedure. See, e.g., Antoon Schoors, *Jesaja: uit de grondtekst vertaald en uitgelegd* (Bussum: Unieboek, 1972), 143.

7. See, e.g., Gray, *Biblical Doctrine of the Reign of God*, 195–224.

8. Unless otherwise noted, all translations of biblical texts are my own.

9. See, e.g., Duhm, *Buch Jesaia*, 153; Edward J. Kissane, *The Book of Isaiah: Trans-

Yahweh of hosts is king/reigns" (e.g., ESV; LEI; ELB).[10] A few interpret מלך as a past tense verb (e.g., ZUR: "denn König geworden ist der HERR der Heerscharen").[11] The question must be settled on the basis of the placement of the predicate in relation to the subject. In Isa 24:23c, the predicate precedes the subject. Syntactical construction of the type predicate/subject must be translated as "subject/has become king" (see 2 Sam 15:10; 2 Kgs 9:13; also Ps 47:9; Isa 52:7).[12] The meaning is that Yahweh "hat (im prägnanten Sinn) die Königsherrschaft angetreten."[13] In what sense can one speak of Yahweh as becoming king?

The concept must be understood within the framework of Yahweh's enthronement.[14] On the basis of his study of the so-called "enthronement psalms" (see, e.g., Pss 47:9; 93:1; 96:10; 99:1), Sigmund Mowinckel proposed that expressions such as יהוה מלך (subject/predicate; see Pss 93:1; 96:10; 99:1) or מלך יהוה (predicate/subject; see Ps 47:9; Isa 52:7) indicate the day of Yahweh's epiphany as king in Zion during the first day of the New Year festival.[15] During the first day of the festival, "the Lord, Yahweh,

---

lated from a Critically Revised Hebrew Text with Commentary (2 vols.; Dublin: Richview, 1960), 1:267; Hans Wildberger, *Jesaja 13–27* (BKAT 10; Neukirchen-Vluyn: Neukirchener, 1978), 888; Brevard S. Childs, *Isaiah* (OTL; Louisville: Westminster John Knox, 2001), 177.

10. See, e.g., Franz Delitzsch, *Commentar über das Buch Jesaja* (ed. Carl F. Keil and Franz Delitzsch; Biblischer Commentar; Leipzig: Dörffling & Franke, 1889), 291; John D. W. Watts, *Isaiah 1–33* (WBC 24; Waco: Word, 1985), 327.

11. Joseph Blenkinsopp, *Isaiah 1–39: A New Translation with Introduction and Commentary* (AB 19; New York: Doubleday, 2000), 357: "Yahweh has inaugurated his reign."

12. See discussion in Jan Ridderbos, "Jahwah Malak," *VT* 4 (1954): 88.

13. Ridderbos, "Jahwah Malak," 87–89 (88).

14. It is not possible to discuss here the evidence Sigmund Mowinckel adduced for the concept of the New Year festival and its relation to ancient Israelite cultus. For further information, see Sigmund Mowinckel, *The Psalms in Israel's Worship* (trans. D. R. Ap-Thomas; 2 vols.; The Biblical Resources Series; Grand Rapids: Eerdmans, 2004), 118–30.

15. In the light of Ridderbos's discussion of the expressions מלך יהוה/יהוה מלך (see "Jahwah Malak," 87–89), Mowinckel's interpretation of the construction subject/predicate (see Pss 93:1; 96:10; 99:1) as indicating that "Yahweh has become king" must be criticized. The fronting of the subject has the purpose of adding emphasis, namely, that is Yahweh and not Marduk or Baal who is king. The criticism, however, does not affect the current interpretation of Isa 24:23, because one finds there the construction predicate/subject (see also Ps 47:9; Isa 52:7).

becomes king, he shows himself as king, and performs kingly deeds, and in the graphic conception and presentation of the cult this is all gathered up in the definite picture of his royal entry and arrival, invisibly mounted on the cherub-borne throne."[16]

Mowinckel saw no contradiction between the concepts of Yahweh's enthronement as king during the festival and Yahweh as Israel's everlasting king. For him, such contradiction is "modern and rationalistic."[17] He argued that the concept of Yahweh's enthronement must be located in Israel's cult for the cult "re-experiences as a new reality the fundamental fact of salvation."[18] Thus, it is the day of Yahweh's epiphany in the cult during the festival that came to be seen as the "day of Yahweh."[19]

That כי מלך יהוה צבאות refers to Yahweh's enthronement is clear from several ideological links between Isa 24:21–23 and the so-called "enthronement psalms." The links are enumerated below as follows.

(1) Acclamation of Yahweh as king: see Pss 47:9; 93:1; 96:10; 97:1; 99:1; Isa 24:23
(2) Zion as the seat of Yahweh's kingship: see Ps 99:2; Isa 24:23
(3) Defeat of enemies: see Pss 47:7–10; 96:7–9; 97:7; 99:1–2; Isa 24:21. Among Yahweh's enemies in Isa 24–27, the following must be included: "the high ones of the earth" (Isa 24:4), "the inhabitants of the height" (Isa 26:5), "the fortified city" (Isa

---

16. Mowinckel, *Psalms in Israel's Worship*, 105. Mowinckel (*Psalms in Israel's Worship*, 120) equated the New Year festival with the "harvest festival" based on Exod 34:22; 23:16. A minor issue is his interpretation of the expression בצאת השנה as "in the beginning of the year." However, almost all translations agree in interpreting that phrase as "at the end of the year." More generally, it must be noted that the evidence for an "enthronement festival" in ancient Israel is sparse, a point for which Mowinckel has been criticized. Nonetheless, and despite being late, the present writer believes that Zech 14:16, an evidence Mowinckel himself adduced, provides substantial evidence for his theory. Even if one wishes to deny the existence of an "enthronement festival," the existence of an "enthronement tradition" in ancient Israel cannot be denied, because there is ample evidence for it (see, e.g., Pss 47; 93–99). For this point, see Hibbard, *Intertextuality in Isaiah 24–27*, 85.

17. See Mowinckel, *Psalms in Israel's Worship*, 115.

18. See Mowinckel, *Psalms in Israel's Worship*, 115. Further on the same page, Mowinckel claims that "in the cultic experience the whole attention is concentrated on that which is again witnessed as something actual; it is there conceived as something happening at that moment."

19. See Mowinckel, *Psalms in Israel's Worship*, 116.

25:1–5), "Moab" (Isa 25:10–12), Leviathan (Isa 27:1) and possibly "Death" (Isa 25:8)[20]

(4) Yahweh's glory: Ps 97:6; Isa 24:23

As for the last point mentioned above, the term "glory" in Isa 24:23 raises questions, because it is here used without the definite article or possessive pronoun (see Ps 29:3: "the God of *the* glory").[21] In the present context, it is most likely a reference to the glorious appearance of Yahweh as king.[22] Because of the reference to "elders" in the present context, commentators have rightly pointed to the revelation of the glory of Yahweh on Mount Sinai to Moses and the elders of the people as described in Exod 24:16–17.[23] But there may be more behind the mentioning of "glory" in Isa 24:23, especially if one links it with the concept of Yahweh as king. Two options of interpretation are possible, and they need not exclude each other. First, Ps 97:6 links the "glory of Yahweh" as king with the trembling of the earth (see 97:2–5). In the context of Isa 24:21–23, it is interesting to note that a similar description of the earth as "tottering" precedes the appearance of Yahweh as king. Second, the term "glory" appears in parallel with "marvelous deeds" in Ps 96:3. Because Isa 25:1 celebrates Yahweh's "marvelous deeds," it may be that "glory" in Isa 24:23 already points forward to a discussion of Yahweh's deeds as described in Isa 25:1–5. In any case, Yahweh's "glory" as king is the reason for the "outshining" of the moon and sun (see also Isa 60:19–20).[24] To continue the discussion, Isa 24:21–23 must be interpreted as the day of Yahweh's epiphany as king, much like in the "enthronement psalms." Intertextual contacts between Isa 13:10 and Isa 24:23a–b make this point clear. On the day of Yahweh's epiphany (see Isa 13:9), celestial bodies fail to give out their light (Isa 13:10). A minor difference exists between Isa 13:10 and 24:23a–b, as the latter portrays celestial bodies as being outshined by Yahweh's glory (Isa 24:23c), whereas in Isa

---

20. For other possible connections, see Hibbard, *Intertextuality in Isaiah 24–27*, 85. From several links between the "enthronement psalms" and Isa 24:21–23 + 25:6–8, Hibbard has concluded that the author of the Isaianic text under discussion read "several texts" and chose "to interact with many or all of them in the composition of his own material." In my view, however, the reason for the ideological similarities is Israel's cultus in which Yahweh's kingship was certainly celebrated.

21. See Beuken, *Jesaja 13–27* (HTKAT; Freiburg: Herder, 2007), 337.

22. See ibid.

23. See Blenkinsopp, *Isaiah 1–39*, 357.

24. See Gray, *Biblical Doctrine of the Reign of God*, 206.

13:10 the celestial bodies' failure to give light functions as a harbinger of Yahweh's dreadful day. Despite this minor difference, the picture in both texts is still close enough to be viewed as an intertextual connection that characterizes Isa 24:21–23 as the day of Yahweh's epiphany.

It is important to note that the day of Yahweh in Isa 13:9–11 is ultimately a day of judgment against the "violent" (עָרִיץ). Even though this term does not appear in Isa 24:21–23, it does occur three times in Isa 25:1–5 (see vv. 3–5). In terms of ideological similarity, Isa 25:5 is very close to Isa 13:11 as both texts speak of the humiliation of the "violent." And although Isa 24:21–23 continues in Isa 25:6–8 framing Isa 25:1–5, the connection between Isa 24:21–23 and 25:6–8 with Isa 25:1–5 must not be overlooked. The day of Yahweh as king (Isa 24:21–23) results in Yahweh's defeat of his enemies, which are symbolized in the "fortified" city of Isa 25:2 and in the "violent" of Isa 25:3–5. The celebration of Yahweh's victory over his enemies in Isa 25:6–8 finds its main cause in the events of Isa 25:1–5. As such, the judgment against the עָרִיץ in Isa 13:9–11 functions as another intertextual link with Isa 24:21–23 and lends support to taking Isa 24:23c as an indication to Yahweh's day.

If the analysis above stands, then Isa 24:21–23 will have to be viewed as not only the climax of Isa 24:1–20 but also as the climax of Isa 13–23. Whereas the oracles against the nations begin with a proclamation of Yahweh's coming day, Isa 24:23 declares that that day has now arrived. The declaration of the arrival of Yahweh's day initiates a series of divine judgment that will ultimately culminate in the concrete establishment of Yahweh's kingship in Zion, namely, his restored people (Isa 27:12–13). Before Isa 27:12–13 can be analyzed, the rest of this section will discuss the identity of Yahweh's enemies and the seat of Yahweh's kingship.

2.1. The Identity of Yahweh's Enemies

One of the most difficult issues in Isa 24:21–23 is the interpretation of the phrase "host of the height." A common interpretation takes this phrase as a reference to "celestial beings," namely, angels or simply "celestial powers."[25]

---

25. See Blenkinsopp, *Isaiah 1–39*, 356–57; J. Alec Motyer, *The Prophecy of Isaiah: An Introduction and Commentary* (Downers Grove, Ill.: InterVarsity Press, 1993), 206; Duhm, *Buch Jesaia*, 153; Delitzsch, *Commentar über das Buch Jesaja*, 292; Wilhelm Gesenius, *Philologisch-kritischer und historischer Commentar über den Jesaia* (2 vols; Leipzig: Vogel, 1821), 2:772.

In the light of Isa 24:21b's punitive tone, some have concluded that the celestial beings implied in "the host of the height" are rebellious fallen patron angels who are imprisoned until their final judgment (see Dan 10:13, 20; LXX/4QDeut[J] Deut 32:8; 2 Pet 2:4; Jude 6; Rev 20:1–3).[26] However, there is nothing in Isa 24–27 that would suggest that Isa 24:21b refers to angels.

It seems best to take the parallelism in אדמה/מרום as a case of *merism* indicating the *kosmos*. Willem Beuken has recently taken this position and has pointed to the *merism* ארץ/מרום in Isa 24:18 as further support.[27] The point is that Yahweh's kingship challenges any power in the world, a view that is consistent not only with Yahweh's destruction of the world (Isa 24:1–20) but also of the nations (see Isa 13–23). In the context of Isa 24–27, the punishment of Yahweh against the "host of the height" involves both divine—excluding angels—and human powers.

The noun מרום may be taken as "heavens" (see Isa 24:18: "windows of[28] the height [= 'heavens']"; see also LXX Isa 24:21: τὸν κόσμον τοῦ οὐρανοῦ).[29] Following this reading, צבא המרום signifies celestial bodies, such as the sun, moon, and stars (see Isa 24:23a–b; 40:26). If this is correct, then Isa 24:21b will likely reflect a criticism of worship of celestial bodies.[30] This practice is amply attested in Mesopotamia and ancient Israel, especially during the reign of Manasseh (687/6–642 B.C.E.).[31] In the enthronement psalms, "other gods" are defeated (see Pss 95:3; 96:4; 97:7) and are called

---

26. See, e.g., Geoffrey W. Grogan, "Isaiah," in *Isaiah–Ezekiel* (ed. Frank E. Gaebelein and Richard P Polcyn; EBC 6; Grand Rapids: Zondervan, 1986), 155.

27. See Beuken, *Jesaja 13–27*, 334, 335. This position, however, is older and can already be found in John Calvin, *Commentary on the Prophet Isaiah* (trans. William Pringle; Grand Rapids: Baker, 2003), 185.

28. Following the proposed emendation in Bruce K. Waltke and Michael O'Connor, *An Introduction to Biblical Hebrew Syntax* (Winona Lake, Indiana: Eisenbrauns, 1990), 160 §9.8c as ארבות ממרום. For further discussion, see 159 § 9.8a–c.

29. See also Vulg.: *militiam caeli*.

30. See Hibbard, *Intertextuality in Isaiah*, 76.

31. For a general discussion of the practice of astral worship in ancient Israel, see Fabrizio Lelli, "Stars," *DDD*, 809–15. For archaeological evidence for the practice of astral worship in the Levant and Mesopotamia, see Peter van der Veen, "'The Seven Dots' on Mesopotamian and Southern Levantine Seals: An Overview," in *Die Zahl Sieben im Alten Orient: The Number Seven in the Ancient Near East* (ed. Gotthard G. Reinhold; Frankfurt: Lang, 2008), 11–22. Most likely, Manasseh felt compelled to adopt religious practices from the Assyrians; see John Bright, *A History of Israel* (4th ed.; Louisville: Westminster John Knox, 2000), 312: "Like his grand-father before him, Manasseh apparently felt impelled to pay homage to his overlord's gods; altars

to tremble before Yahweh and worship him (see Ps 97:7) at his appearance as king over all the earth. Because of his kingship, Yahweh is proclaimed as "a great king over all gods" (see Ps 95:3). In the context of Isa 24–27, divine beings are punished, such as Leviathan (see Isa 27:1) and possibly Mot (see Isa 25:8).[32]

On the other hand, מרום can also refer to human power (see Tg. Isa. 24:21: "the Lord will visit the *forces* of the *stronghold, those who dwell in strength*").[33] In Isa 24–27, the noun מרום as an indication of human arrogance is found in Isa 24:4c (אמללו מרום עם הארץ, "the exalted of the people languish" [see NASB]) and 26:5a (כי השח ישבי מרום, "because he has brought the inhabitants of the height low"). In this sense, "the army of the height" may indicate human power. In this vein, it is important to note that the collapse of a "fortified city" in Isa 25:1–5 is bracketed by the announcement of Yahweh's punishment on the "high ones/kings" in Isa 24:21–23 and the celebration of his reign in Isa 25:6–8. Further support for this view can also be found in the parallel passage of Isa 13:9–11, which proclaims that the "day of Yahweh" comes to put an end to the "arrogance of the arrogant" and to humiliate "the haughtiness of the violent." As such, Isa 24:21 must be taken as indication of Yahweh's punishment of his divine and human enemies. This interpretation fits in well with the rest of Isa 24–27, where both divine (see Isa 27:1) and human powers (see Isa 24:4; 25:1–5; 26:5) are punished.

2.2. The Seat of Yahweh's Kingship: Zion

The theme of Yahweh's kingship in Zion in Isa 24:23 has strong connections with the ideology found in the "enthronement psalms." Psalm 99:2 declares, for instance, that "the Lord is great in Zion, and exalted is he above all peoples."[34] As it will be seen later, Zion is repeated again in Isa

---

to astral deities, probably of Mesopotamian origin, were erected within the Temple itself."

32. Although Isa 25:8 has been often taken as a declaration of Yahweh's defeat of Mot, the lack of a conjunction *waw* attached to the verb "to swallow" makes its subject ambiguous. As the text now stands in MT, "death" may be taken as the subject of the sentence. LXX Isaiah, for instance, has interpreted Isa 25:8a in this way.

33. Translation taken from Bruce D. Chilton, *The Isaiah Targum: Introduction, Translation, Apparatus, and Notes* (ArBib 11; Collegeville, Minn.: Liturgical Press, 1990), 49.

34. Or "above all gods" if one decides to follow LXX B and minuscules.

27:13, a repetition that rounds off Isa 24–27 and indicates a movement from Yahweh's kingship to his kingdom.

3. ISAIAH 27:12–13: YAHWEH'S KINGDOM

3.1. THE CLIMACTIC FUNCTION OF ISAIAH 27:12–13

Some scholars usually link Isa 27:12–13 with Isa 27:1 on account of the phrase "on that day." Duhm, for instance, viewed 27:1, 12–13 as the only passages belonging to the apocalyptic author in the text of Isa 27:1–13. For him, "that day" of Isa 27:12–13 is the same day of Isa 27:1 when God will afflict the Syrian, Egyptian, and Parthian in a historicized interpretation of Isa 27:1's triple reference to the "serpent."[35] As for the rest of Isa 27:1–13, Duhm judged the song of Yahweh's vineyard in Isa 27:2–5 as a strange composition situated in Isa 27:1–13. As a matter of fact, he conjectured that Isa 27:2–5 must have been written in the margins of the manuscript, because it does not fit in its present literary context.[36] He further argued that there is a "gap" between Isa 27:1, 7 caused by the introduction of Isa 27:2–6. He viewed Isa 27:8 as a gloss written next to Isa 27:10 and one which was introduced into the text in the wrong place. He also found a gap between Isa 27:11, 12. His overall judgment was that Isa 27:7, 9–11 constituted the remaining of a later exhortation.[37]

Others have argued that Isa 27:12–13 and Isa 27:2–11, for that matter, are later secondary compositions in relation to Isa 24:1–27:1. Wallace E. March, for instance, has championed the view that Isa 27:12–13 serves as a fitting conclusion to Isa 27:1–13. His more substantial arguments can be summarized as follows. First, Isa 27:12–13 speaks of a gathering of people

---

35. See Duhm, *Buch Jesaia*, 168. See also Otto Procksch, *Jesaia: Übersetzt und erklärt* (KAT 9.1; Leipzig: Deichertsche, 1930), 331, 334; Wilhelm Rudolph, *Jesaja 24–27* (BWA[N]T 62; Stuttgart: Kohlhammer, 1933), 50. For a very early historicization of the Leviathan and *tannin* imagery in Isa 27:1, see Tg. Isa.: "In that day the Lord, with his great, strong and powerful sword, will deal with the king that makes himself proud like Pharaoh, the former king, and with the king that exalts himself like Sennacherib, the second king, and he will kill the king who is strong as the sea serpent that is in the sea."

36. See Duhm, *Buch Jesaia*, 164: "das Lied c. 27:2–5, das ganz gewiss am Rande gestanden hat, weil es mit seiner Umgebung nichts zu tun hat."

37. See Duhm, *Buch Jesaia*, 166. Karl Marti (*Das Buch Jesaja: Erklärt* [KHC 10; Tübingen: Mohr Siebeck, 1900], 201–2) followed Duhm closely.

who are "scattered abroad." March points out that Isa 24:21–26:21 lacks any hint of people being scattered. Instead, people are portrayed as expecting the "triumph of Yahweh in Jerusalem" (see Isa 25:6–8; 26:1–6, 20–13). Second, Isa 27:13 used the expression "holy mountain" instead of the more usual "on this mountain" (see Isa 25:6, 7, 10), suggesting "later theologizing." Third, March argues that Isa 27:12–13 introduces "new language and imagery" that are not found in Isa 26 and that Isa 27:12–13 lacks any reference to "established motifs." He then concludes that Isa 27:12–13 "should not be considered as the conclusion of the unit beginning with 26:20."[38] March went on to argue that Isa 27:1 functions as the climactic conclusion to Isa 24:21–23: while the latter announces "the imminent triumph of Yahweh," the former declares "the finality of this victory."[39] For the reasons outlined above, March limited his study to Isa 24:1–27:1.

More recently, Marvin A. Sweeney has argued that Isa 27:12–13 and Isa 27:1–11 find their compositional date later in the seventh century B.C.E. His reasons are as follows. First, Isa 27:2–12 refers consistently to Jacob/Israel but not to Judah/Jerusalem, the only exception being Isa 27:13. Second, the references to Egypt/Assyria are striking if an exilic or postexilic setting is assumed for Isa 27:2–13 (however, see Zech 10:10). Third, Isa 27 cites passages that condemn the northern kingdom, such as Isa 27:2–6 (see Isa 5:1–7) and Isa 27:9 (see Isa 17).[40] Different from March, however, Sweeney clearly argued that "the intention of 27:2–13 is determined by its placement in the context of chs. 24–27."[41] Notwithstanding diachronic clues that Isa 27:1–13 may have been an earlier composition than Isa 24–26, the present article will turn to a synchronic analysis concerning the literary function of Isa 27:12–13 in relation to Isa 24:21–23.

In its present literary context, Isa 27:12–13 must be linked not with Isa 27:1, as some have done, but with Isa 24:21–23. First, the construction "and/but it will be on that day" + *yiqtol* + Yahweh as subject occurs only in

---

38. Wallace E. March, "A Study of Two Prophetic Compositions in Isaiah 24:1–27:1" (Ph.D. diss., Union Theological Seminary, 1966), 171–73.

39. March, "Study of Two Prophetic Compositions," 174.

40. Marvin A. Sweeney, *Isaiah 1–39 with an Introduction to Prophetic Literature* (FOTL 16; Grand Rapids: Eerdmans, 1996), 350–51.

41. Sweeney, *Isaiah 1–39*, 352. See also Ronald E. Clements, *Isaiah 1–39* (NCB; Grand Rapids: Eerdmans, 1982), 223: "we should not doubt that this short section [Isa 27:12–13] has been intended to round off the whole eschatological hope in chs. 24–27, and provides one of the important redactional touches which seek to give a unified message to the book as a whole."

24:21 and 27:12 in the whole of Isa 24–27 (in the rest of Isaiah, this same construction appears only in Isa 7:18; 11:11). Even though the expression "on that day" appears in 27:1, 12, a stronger connection between 24:21 and 27:12 exists based on the syntactic observation above. Second, both sections have conceptual similarities as the repetition of the following terms/phrases shows:

(1) it will be on that day that Yahweh will… (see Isa 24:21a; 27:12a)
(2) on Mount Zion/on the holy mountain (see Isa 24:23c; 27:13e)
(3) in Jerusalem (see Isa 24:23c; 27:13e)

Furthermore, Isa 27:12–13 continues the picture of Yahweh as king that had already appeared in Isa 24:21–23. The use of the lexeme פקד in Isa 24:21; 26:21; 27:1 carries that picture forward. As Isa 27:1–13 is seen as a unit (see discussion below), the theme of Yahweh's kingship climaxes in Isa 27:12–13. The following hopes to clarify the assertions just made.

Isaiah 26:21 and 27:1 clearly portray Yahweh as a divine warrior. The expression יהוה יצא in Isa 26:21 has the connotation of "marching out" to do battle (see Isa 42:13: "Yahweh goes out [יצא] as the warrior; as a man of war [מלחמה] he stirs up [his] anger").[42] Isaiah 27:1 continues to portray Yahweh as a divine warrior when it refers to his "heavy, great, and strong sword."[43] The verse depicts Yahweh's sword bringing judgment on Leviathan. The portrayal of Yahweh as a divine warrior further continues in the vineyard song of Isa 27:2–5[6] (see מלחמה in Isa 27:4). The defeat of Leviathan is not the climax to the theme of Yahweh's kingship (see Isa 24:21–23). Rather, Leviathan's defeat initiates the process of restoration of Yahweh's people (see Isa 27:2–11), culminating in their return to worship Yahweh as king on Mount Zion (see Isa 27:12–23).

---

42. See Patrick D. Miller, *The Divine Warrior in Early Israel* (Cambridge: Harvard University Press, 1973; repr., Atlanta: Society of Biblical Literature, 2006), 94–95.

43. For other references to Yahweh's sword in Isaiah, see 34:5 and 66:16. Outside Isaiah, see Deut 32:41; Ezek 21:8–10; 30:24–25; 32:10; Zeph 2:12; Pss 7:13; 17:13; 45:4; Job 40:19 (divine messengers are also portrayed as having swords: see Num 22:23, 31; Josh 5:13; 1 Chr 21:16; 21:27).

3.2. The Gathering of Yahweh's People (Isa 27:12-13)

There is disagreement about the relationship between verses 12 and 13 of Isa 27. This disagreement is reflected in the edition of Isaiah in 1QIsaᵃ and BHS. While a long empty space separates Isa 27:12-13 in 1QIsaᵃ, a *setumah* comes in between Isa 27:12, 13 in BHS. Briefly stated, the harvest imagery in Isa 27:12 seems to have a narrower scope as it takes place within the idealized borders of the land promised to Abraham ("from the stream of the river [Euphrates] to the brook of Egypt"; see Gen 15:18), whereas Isa 27:13 has a wider scope (see "in the land of Assyria/in the land of Egypt").[44] Be that as it may, the reference to the borders with Egypt and Assyria (Isa 27:12) parallels Assyria and Egypt in Isa 27:13. The harvest metaphor in Isa 27:12 is described in concrete terms in Isa 27:13. As Wilhelm Gesenius pointed out a long time ago, the meaning of Isa 27:12 is clear because this verse is clarified by Isa 27:13: what is said in metaphorical terms in Isa 27:12 is said in concrete terms in Isa 27:13.[45]

One of the most difficult issues in Isa 27:12-13 is the sentence יחבט יהוה משבלת הנהר. The term חבט can mean either "to beat off" olive trees (see Deut 24:20) or "to beat out" grain (see Judg 6:11; Ruth 2:17).[46] In Isa 28:27, it refers to the "beating out" of black cumin with a stick. Another difficulty is שבלת, which can denote an "ear of corn" (see Gen 41:5-7, 23-24, 26-27; Ruth 2:2; Job 24:24; Isa 17:5), a "branch of an olive tree" (see Zech 4:12), or a "body of water" (Ps 69:3, 16).[47] One of the problems with Isa 27:12b is that the direct object of the predicate is not explicitly stated. As a solution, some have proposed different emendations to the MT. One suggestion has been to place שבלת after נחל מצרים and to take it as the direct object of חבט. This proposal finds its basis on an attempt to achieve metrical balance for the following lines יחבט יהוה מהנהר//

---

44. See the discussion in Hugh G. M. Williamson, *The Book Called Isaiah: Deutero-Isaiah's Role in Composition and Redaction* (Oxford: Clarendon, 1994), 177-80.

45. Gesenius, *Jesaia*, 2:821: "Der Sinn dieses Verses kann nicht zweifelhaft sein, da er durch den folgenden erklärt wird, welcher das hier bildlich Gesagte in eigentlichen Ausdrücken wiederholt."

46. See George B. Gray, *A Critical and Exegetical Commentary on the Book of Isaiah, I–XXXIX* (ICC; Edinburgh: T&T Clark, 1912), 461.

47. See *HALOT*, 8369, II. The definition "ear of corn" is taken from BDB, 987. *HALOT*, 8369, defines שבלת as "an ear of grain."

עד נחל שבלת מצרים.[48] With this emendation, שבלת means "ear of corn" and not "stream" as it is no longer in a construct relationship with "river." A simpler emendation is to attach the preposition מן to הנהר so as to create שבלת מהנהר, in which case שבלת functions as the direct object of חבט.[49] Some have argued that שבלת as "stream" linked to "river" is superfluous, while שבלת in connection with חבט demands understanding it as an "ear of corn."[50] However, the problem with the emendations above is their lack of support in all of the extant textual witnesses.[51]

A preferable solution to emending the MT is to see the direct object as already implicit in חבט. Two options are available: to beat out "olive trees" (see Deut 24:20) or to beat off "grain" (see Judg 6:11; Ruth 2:17). Scholars are divided on this issue. Gray prefers "beating out olive trees," because the process of picking up (see לקט in Isa 27:12c) berries follows that of beating out olive trees.[52] Others prefer to see a double entendre in שבלת, thus preferring "to beat off grain" as the meaning for חבט.[53] However, links with Isa 24:13 strongly support the view that Isa 27:12 refers to the "beating out of olives trees" that are gathered one by one. It is to a discussion of Isa 24:13 in relation to Isa 27:12 that we now turn.

---

48. See Procksch, *Jesaja*, 335. Procksch counted seven beats for each one of the lines above, whereas the present writer counts eight.

49. See Procksch, *Jesaja*, 331; Otto Kaiser, *Der Prophet Jesaja: Kapitel 13–39* (ATD 18; Göttingen: Vandenhoeck & Ruprecht, 1973), 185 n. 1; Hans Wildberger, *Jesaia 13–27* (BKAT 10.2; Neukirchen-Vluyn: Neukirchener, 1978), 1022 n. 12a–a; Watts, *Isaiah 1–33*, 348 n. 12a; Blenkinsopp, *Isaiah 1–39*, 376 n. l. The emendation discussed above is already found in BHS's critical apparatus. Similarly, Johannes Lindblom (*Die Jesaja-Apokalypse: Jes. 24–27* [LUÅ 34.3; Lund: Gleerup, 1938], 60) has proposed to emend the preposition מן to הנהר. For him, a later scribe read שבלת as "stream" and attached it to "river." However, the original poet certainly had meant "ear of corn" and had placed it as the direct object of the verb "to beat out," so argued Lindblom.

50. See Rudolph, *Jesaja 24–27*, 27; Gray, *Critical and Exegetical Commentary*, 461. As for the suggestion that שבלת as "stream" seems superfluous, it is important to note that "stream" forms a smooth parallelism with נחל ("wadi").

51. See 1QIsa^a (משבל הנהר), LXX (ἀπὸ τῆς διώρυγος τοῦ ποταμοῦ), Tg. Isa. (מכיף נהרא), Syr. (ܡܢ ܐܬܠܒܐ ܕܢܗܪܐ), and Vulg. (*ab alveo Fluminis*).

52. See Gray, *Critical and Exegetical Commentary*, 461. For a similar position, see Gesenius, *Jesaia*, 2:821–22; Motyer, *Prophecy of Isaiah*, 225.

53. See Jimmy Jack McBee Roberts, "Double Entendre in First Isaiah," *CBQ* 54 (1992): 39–48 (40–41); Doyle, *Apocalypse of Isaiah 24–27*, 362 n. 99; Scholl, *Die Elenden in Gottes Thronrat*, 148 n. 3; Beuken, *Jesaja 13–27*, 409.

3.3. The Identity of the Returnees

Links between Isa 17:4–5 and Isa 27:12–13 have already been discussed in the scholarly literature.[54] Less discussed is the relationship between Isa 24:13 and 27:12–13. Both passages share the use of harvest imagery (see "like the beating of olive trees, like gleanings, when the harvest is done" in 24:13 with "the Lord will beat olive trees/grain" in Isa 27:12). The use of "gleanings" in Isa 24:13 "implies the sparing of a few from judgment."[55] The theme of "sparing a few" is also found in 24:6: "and a few will be left." Taken together with Isa 24:14–15, the picture of judgment in the "midst of the earth" in Isa 24:13 points to the salvation of a remnant, portrayed as "rejoicing" in Isa 24:14.[56] Similarly, the judgment implied in the harvest imagery in Isa 27:12 points to salvation for the "children of Israel" as the verse portrays them being picked up "one by one." The connection between Isa 24:13 and 27:12 thus characterizes the "children of Israel" (27:12) as those "who are spared from the judgment" announced in Isa 24:1–20; 26:20.

Some have argued that Isa 27:12–13 betrays Jewish particularism in contrast with Isa 25:6–8, which has a more universalistic tone.[57] However, Isa 27:12–13's shared ideology with Isa 24:13 precludes such a conclusion. The judgment upon the "world" (see Isa 24:4) must be seen as a means to forge a renewed community for Yahweh based on the "gleanings" that are left over after harvest. In the context of Isa 24–27, this new community must be identified with "the righteous nation" of Isa 26:2 that is allowed to enter the "fortified city" of Isa 26:1. Isaiah 27:13 further characterizes "the children of Israel" as those who come to "mount Zion" to worship Yahweh as king (see Isa 24:21–23).

It is important to note the reference to "a great trumpet [שׁופר]" in Isa 27:13. Mowinckel has linked the "blowing of the horns" (see Pss 47:6; 81:4; 98:6) with the celebration of the supposed "enthronement festival" in

---

54. See, e.g., Marvin A. Sweeney, "New Gleanings from an Old Vineyard: Isaiah 27 Reconsidered," in *Early Jewish and Christian Exegesis: Studies in Memory of William Hugh Brownlee* (ed. Craig A. Evans and William F. Stinespring; Atlanta: Scholars, 1987), 51–66 (55–56); Hibbard, *Intertextuality in Isaiah*, 195–99.

55. See Wilson de A. Cunha, "A Brief Discussion of MT Isaiah 24,14–16," *Bib* 90 (2009): 530–44 (540).

56. For a fuller discussion of this passage, see Cunha, "Isaiah 24,14–16," 540–41.

57. See, e.g., Marti, *Buch Jesaja*, 201.

ancient Israel.[58] Indeed, the "blowing of the trumpet" has in this context a religious connotation (see "they will worship" in Isa 27:13e). In the light of the discussion of Yahweh's kingship above, the "blowing of the trumpet" must be seen as a call to Yahweh's remnant to return to Zion to worship Yahweh as king.

3.4. The Place of Yahweh's Kingdom: Zion

The repetition of "Zion" in Isa 27:13 indicates that the theme of Yahweh's kingship, initiated in Isa 24:21–23, has now reached full circle. Whereas Yahweh appears as king on Zion in Isa 24:23, the concrete expression of his kingship is similarly located on Zion in Isa 27:13.

4. Conclusion

Because of the diversity of genres encountered in Isa 24–27, its ideological coherence has been contested in the scholarly literature. The present article has dealt with Isa 24:21–23 and 27:12–13 in an attempt to point to a way of seeing coherence in these important chapters. It has shown that Isa 24–27 coheres ideologically in that it starts with the proclamation of Yahweh's kingship and ends with the concrete demonstration of his rule, namely, his restored community. This community, however, is to be identified with the remnant motif found in Isa 24:13 and elsewhere in the book and points to a characterization of Yahweh's community as a "righteous nation" (see Isa 26:2). The article has argued against taking Isa 27:12–13 as a case of Jewish particularism and has shown that Isa 24–27 envisages a time when Yahweh's community will be identified as those who come to Zion to worship him as "king."

---

58. See Mowinckel, *Psalms in Israel's Worship*, 122.

Isaiah 24:21–25:12: A Communicative Analysis

Archibald L. H. M. van Wieringen

In my monograph on the unity of the Isaiah book and in my commentary on Isaiah, I speak about Isa 24–27 as a "coda."[1] Although this indication is not incorrect, beyond the chapters 13–23, which are characterized by explicit indications of topographical spatial decors, the word "coda" suggests that there is no *dramatic progress* in the text.[2] In this contribution, I would like to examine Isa 24:21–25:12 from a communication-oriented approach in order to shed light on the communicative developments that take place in this text and to make clear that the text-internal reader also takes part in this communication progress.

1. The Structure of Isaiah 24–27

Standardly, the structure of larger text units is characterized by the so-called elaboration formulas in the book of Isaiah. The common formula והיה ביום ההוא ("and upon that day it will come to pass") occurs in Isa 24–27 three times, namely, in 24:21; 27:12, 13. The prepositional phrase

---

1. Archibald L. H. M. van Wieringen, *The Reader-Oriented Unity of the Book Isaiah* (ACEBTSup 6; Vught: Skandalon, 2006), 44; idem, *Jesaja* (Belichting van het bijbelboek; Leuven: Vlaamse Bijbelstichting; 2009), 31–32. See also, for example, Peter R. Ackroyd, *Exile and Restoration: A Study of Hebrew Thought of the Sixth Century BC* (5th ed.; London: SCM, 1983), 221; Ulrich Berges, *Das Buch Jesaja: Komposition und Endgestalt* (HBS 16; Freiburg: Herder, 1998), 181.

2. The idea of a dramatic progress is typical for the Dutch *Jesaja Werkplaats* and was introduced by Willem A. M. Beuken in his Dutch commentary on Isaiah 40–55: *Jesaja* (3 vols; PredOT; Nijkerk: Callenbach, 1979–89). See for a different use also Klaus Baltzer, *Deutero-Isaiah: A Commentary on Isaiah 40–55* (trans. Margaret Kohl; Hermeneia; Augsburg: Fortress, 2001), 14.

ביום ההוא ("upon that day") in first position further occurs in Isa 26:1; 27:1; 27:2, that is, without the verb היה.[3]

In Isa 25:9, the phrase ביום ההוא occurs as well, however in second position and, moreover, constructed not with the verb היה, but with the verbal form ואמר ("and he will say"). Isaiah 25:9, therefore, cannot be considered as marking a caesura with the same weight as the elaboration-formulae do.

The use of the expression בהר הזה ("on this mountain"), which is similar to the expression ביום ההוא, does not function as a caesura formula. From a syntactical point of view, this expression has a different position in the clause, namely, not in first position, and from a semantic point of view, this expression is not about time, but about the spatial decor.

Schematically, the structure of Isa 24–27 is, therefore, as follows:

main text unit	first elaboration	second elaboration
24:1–20		
	24:21–25:12	
		26:1–21
		27:1
		27:2–11
	27:12	
	27:13	

This structure is important for the communication in Isa 24:21–25:12 as well: somehow this text passage must be a continuation of the communication in 24:1–20 and will be continued in the three elaborations in 26:1–21; 27:1; 27:2–11, whereas, from a communicative point of view, the text passage itself is on the same communicative level as 27:12, 13. In this contribution, I will focus on Isa 24:21–25:12 and its communicative relation with 24:1–20.

---

3. For the importance of the formula והיה ביום ההוא, see among others also Gerhard F. Hasel, *The Remnant: The History and Theology of the Remnant Idea from Genesis to Isaiah* (AUM 5; Berrien Springs, Mich.: Andrews University Press, 1974), 260; see also Joseph Blenkinsopp, *Isaiah 1–39: A New Translation with Introduction and Commentary* (AB 19; New York: Doubleday, 2000), 346.

2. The Structure of Isaiah 24:21–25:12

Firstly, I will give attention to the structure of Isa 24:21–25:12. This structure is characterized by the alternation of the various communicative participants.

In verses 21–23, the Lord is staged as a third person. The Lord is not addressed, but he is discoursed: the Lord acts against מלכי האדמה ("the kings of the earth," v. 21) and, therefore, מלך ("he is King") in a place, mentioned in the form of a hendiadys, בהר ציון ובירושלם ("on the mountain of Zion and in Jerusalem," v. 23).

The sender of this text passage does not manifest himself by using a first person, but remains anonymously in the background.

In Isa 24:21–23, therefore, there is no I-you communication. Because of this, the text must be considered as belonging to the so-called discourser, the text-internal figure which is responsible for staging the characters which perform in the text.

This situation changes in Isa 25:1. The Lord is mentioned by using a vocative. As a result of this, a "you" arises in the communication. Next, this "you" is expressed in the personal pronoun אתה ("you," v. 1). Not only is the addressed "you" visible from the beginning, namely, in the use of the first person singular, but the speaker is as well. The addressed יהוה is אלהי ("my God," v. 1).

Whereas the first person is only explicitly present in verse 1 in the phrase אלהי ("my God") and the verbal phrases ארוממך ("I exalt you") and אודה ("I praise"), the second person singular is continuously present: the vocative יהוה ("oh Lord"), the personal pronoun אתה ("you"), the suffixes in ארוממך ("I exalt you") and שמך ("your name"), the verbal forms עשית ("you made," v. 1) and שמת ("you put," v. 2), the suffix in יכבדוך ("they glorify you," v. 3), and the verbal forms היית ("you were," v. 4) and תכניע ("you brought down," v. 5).

In Isa 25:6, the situation changes again. The Lord is renominalized as יהוה צבאות ("the Lord of hosts"). This renominalization marks the point that the Lord no longer functions as a vocative, but that he is present in the text as a third person. The Lord is no longer addressed, but he is again discoursed. This implies that, as from verse 6, the discourser is again speaking.

From verse 9b onwards, this discourser delegates his voice to someone else, who is introduced in verse 9a using the formula ואמר ביום ההוא ("and he will say on that day"). As from verse 9b, the situation changes again: the speaker appears to be a first person plural. This first person plural is visible in the suffix in אלהינו ("our God"); the verbal form קוינו ("we hoped"); the suffix in ויושיענו ("and he saved us"); and the verbal forms קוינו ("we hoped"), נגילה ("let us shout with joy"), and ונשמחה ("and let us rejoice," v. 9).

The question arises as to where the direct speech, which begins in verse 9b, ends. The first person plural does not occur in verses 10–11. Moreover, the Lord is not addressed anywhere in the direct speech, but remains present as a third person. The mild form of renominalization of יהוה in the expression יד־יהוה ("the hand of the Lord," v. 10), instead of ידו ("his hand"), gives the impression that the text from verse 10a onwards belongs to the discourser once again. Verse 12, however, shows that this is not the case. The suffix second person singular in חומתיך ("your walls") indicates that there is someone addressed in the text, due to which the text has to be a direct speech. The one addressed must be identified with מואב ("Moab," v. 10b). Furthermore, verse 12 cannot be disconnected from verses 10–11, because verse 12 is a polysyndeton using the conjunction ו in first position and because verse 12 does not contain a renominalization of יהוה concerning the verbal form השח ("he will have brought down"); thus not: "the Lord will have brought down").

As a result, after the introductory formula in verse 9a by the discourser, verses 9b–12 in their entirety form a direct speech, and they are spoken by the we-figure.[4] Schematically, the structure of Isa 24:21–25:12 is as follows:

24:21–23	discourser		about the Lord
25:1–5		I-figure	to the Lord
25:6–9a	discourser		about the Lord
25:9b–12		we-figure	about the Lord

The discourser delegates his voice twice: first, to the I-figure without an introductory formula, and next, to the we-figure with an introductory formula in verse 9a. The discourser, characteristic for his function, only

---

4. *Pace* among others: Brian Doyle, "A Literary Analysis of Isaiah 24,10a," in *Studies in the Book of Isaiah: Festschrift Willem A.M. Beuken* (ed. Jacques van Ruiten and Marc Vervenne; BETL 132; Leuven: Leuven University Press, 1997), 177–80.

speaks *about* the Lord. The I-figure, conversely, speaks *to* the Lord, but the we-figure speaks only *about* the Lord as well.

3. The Semantic Theme "high/low" in Isaiah 24:21–25:12

The four subunits of Isa 24:21–25:12 are semantically characterized by the common theme "high/low." In all four subunits, this semantic theme is present, although in different forms.[5]

The discourser introduces the theme "high/low" concerning the spatial decor, as if the creation decor of heaven and earth were concerned. The Lord inspects both the high space and the low space. Concerning the high space, the word מרום ("high/height") is used twice; concerning the low space, twice the word is אדמה ("earth/ground") (v. 21). Next, the text zooms in on the low space, where God acts against the kings. They are transported to an even lower space: they disappear in a בור ("cistern"), a place which functions as a מסגר ("prison") (v. 22).

The discourser's text in verses 21–22 is characterized by semantic repetitions closely following upon each other, which indicate both the spatial decor of the theme "high/low" and the things which take place in this spatial decor: twice מרום and אדמה in verse 21 and the concatenation of the verb אסף ("to gather") and the noun אסיר ("prisoners," i.e., the "gathered ones") in verse 22. These three couples are included by the word repetition of the verb פקד ("to conduct a visitation") in verses 21 and 23.

In the concluding verse of this subunit, the special decors of high and low are mentioned once more. Now, the negative aspect is situated in the highest place, not mistakenly, but intentionally shaped as the moon and the sun which are ashamed and white-faced because of the acts of the Lord in an initially desperate situation.[6] On the ground, the Lord is King on

---

5. The theme of "high/low" is not very often mentioned explicitly in the exegetical analyses of Isa 24:12–25:12; see, however, Glenn Miller, "Isaiah 25:6–9: God's Banquet," *Int* 49 (1995): 175.

6. For the use of the word לבנה ("the white one") as a poetic indication of the moon, see Helmer Ringgren, "לבן *lnb*," in *Theologisches Wörterbuch zum Alten Testament* (ed. Gerhard J. Botterweck and Heinz-Josef Ringgren; Stuttgart: Kohlhammer, 1984), 451–54 (454). For the meaning of בוש (and of the parallel verb חפר) connected to the question of confidence as being ashamed after the disappearance of hope, see Fritz Stolz, "בוש *bōš* zuschanden werden," in *Theologisches Handwörterbuch zum Alten Testament* (ed. Ernst Jenni and Claus Westermann; 2 vols.; Zürich: Theologischer Verlag 1978), 1:269–72 (270–71).

Zion and in Jerusalem. As a result of this, a new and positive "high" is created by explicitly naming Zion a הר ("mountain").

The second subunit, in which the I-figure is speaking, opens with the element "high" in the clause ארוממך ("I exalt you," v. 1). The Lord, who makes "high" and "low," is made "high" by the I-figure. The reason for this exaltation is, according to the words of the I-figure, the fact that the Lord makes "low." This lowness is expressed by using the noun מפלה ("ruin," v. 2), something fallen down (the root נפל), and the verbs כנע ("to bring down") and ענה ("to become low," v. 5).

This lowness has the special feature in that it is represented as a גל ("heap of stones"), therefore as a heap of rubble (v. 2). In the view of the I-figure, that which is destroyed or ruined is a negative counterimage to the positive הר ("mountain"), which is Zion. Using this expression, the content of the direct speech of the I-figure has a connection to verses 21–23 of the discourser: Zion, made "high" by God within the special decor "low," contrasts with the fortress, a fake "height" made "low" by God.

The similarity in the use of the theme "high/low" between the discourser and the I-figure concerns mainly "lowness." Whereas the discourser removes the anonymity by using the proper names Zion and Jerusalem, the indication of the city remains anonymous in the direct speech of the I-figure.

The third subunit, verses 6–9a, belongs to the discourser again. The aspect "high" is present in the phrase בהר הזה ("on this mountain," vv. 6 and 7). Because the text concerned belongs to the discourser, the demonstrative function refers to בהר ציון ("on the mountain of Zion") in verse 23. The aspect "low" can be considered to be present in the verb בלע ("to swallow down," vv. 7 and 8). In this way, the objects לוט ("shroud," v. 7) and מות ("death," v. 8) belong to "low" as well.[7]

This discourser's text is a continuation of the first discourser's text. The "low" that became "high," namely, בהר ציון ("on the mountain of Zion," v. 23), is now openly represented as being "high," namely, בהר הזה ("on this mountain," vv. 6 and 7). This discourser's text has a direct connection with the text of the I-figure because of the repetition of the verb עשה ("to do") with the Lord as subject, at the beginning of both subunits in verses

---

7. The interpretation of מות with "low" is very obvious in view of the association of שאול "Sheol" with the word מות "death." See in particular Yitzhak Avishur, *Stylistic Studies of Word-Pairs in Biblical and Ancient Semitic Literatures* (AOAT 210; Kevelaer: Butzon & Bercker, 1984), 257–58.

2 and 6. Whereas, in the text of the I-figure, the Lord does things which belong to "low," in the discourser's text, the Lord does things which belong to "high."

The last subunit, verses 9b–12, forms the direct speech of a we-figure. Once again, the contrast "high/low" plays an important role in the text. The aspect "high" is expressed positively in the prepositional phrase בהר הזה ("on this mountain") in verse 10 and negatively in the words מדמנה ("dunghill") in verse 11 and מבצר ("fortification"), משׂגב ("stronghold"), and חומה ("[upright] wall") in verse 12. The aspect "low" is shaped in the verbs דושׁ ("to tremble [flat]," v. 10 twice), the first time strengthened by the preposition תחת ("under"), and שׁפל ("to bring low," v. 11), and in the noun עפר ("dust," v. 12).

The direct speech of the we-figure proves itself to be a continuation of the discourser's text in verses 6–9a because of the repetition of the phrase בהר הזה. However, whereas in the discourser's text, not the nations, but rather the shroud that covers the nations and death are destroyed, in the direct speech of the we-figure, one single nation is concretized and made "low," namely, Moab.

The characteristic word repetitions, closely following upon each other in the discourser's text, which were used in verses 21–22 to express the theme "high/low," occur in the discourser's text in verses 6–9a once again, although not within the theme "high/low." The nouns משׁתה ("banquet"), שׁמנים ("fat dishes"), and שׁמרים ("aged wines") are repeated closely following upon each other in verse 6 and are continued with the combination of לוט ("shroud") and לוט ("to shroud") in verse 7. These three couples are included by the word repetition of עמים ("nations") in verses 6 and 7. This style is more or less continued in the repetition of the verb בלע ("to swallow [down])" in first position in verses 7 and 8 and of the noun פנים ("face") in verses 7 and 8.

This style concerning the theme "high/low" is also present in the direct speech that the discourser lets the we-figure speak in verses 9b–12 in the repetition of the verbs קוה ("to hope," v. 9), דושׁ ("to tremble [flat]," v. 10), פרשׂ ("to spread," v.11), שׁחה ("to stretch out," v. 11), and שׁפל ("to make low," vv. 11 and 12) and of the noun יד ("hand," v. 11) and in the couple ישׁע ("to save") and ישׁועה ("salvation") (v. 9). The text of the I-figure, however, is different. It is true that word repetitions occur (עיר, "city," in v. 2; קריה, "fortress," in vv. 2 and 3; זרים, "strangers," in vv. 2 and 5; עריץ,"violent," in vv. 3 and 4; מעוז, "strong refuge," in v. 4; צל, "shade," in v. 4 and 5; and חרב, "heat," in the vv. 4 and 5), but these are used in various contexts and rarely follow upon each other. This difference in style, expressing the contrast "high/low," marks the different positions of speaking between the I-figure and the we-figure, also because the direct speech of the I-figure is not introduced by a formula, whereas the direct speech of the we-figure does have an introductory formula.

4. The Spatial Position of the Discourser, the I-Figure, and the We-Figure in Isaiah 24:21–25:12

The discourser, the I-figure, and the we-figure not only uses the spatial semantic theme "high/low," but they themselves are also related to it.

In verses 21–23, the discourser takes up the position of an outsider. He speaks in the third person about what the Lord does, while he is overlooking the entire spatial decor from the highest height (עַל] צְבָא הַמָּרוֹם], "[over] the hosts of the highest," in v. 21) to the lowest lowness (עַל] בּוֹר], "[in] a cistern," in v. 22).

This position of the discourser becomes less abstract, when he introduces the proper names צִיּוֹן ("Zion") and יְרוּשָׁלַם ("Jerusalem") at the end of the first subunit in verse 23. Here, there is a transition from the anonymity found in the broad spatial decor of "high" and "low" to a concrete and positive spot: a place on the earth which is made "high" by the Lord.

This transition is strengthened by the deictic demonstrative pronoun זֶה ("this") in the second text of the discourser in verses 6–9a. Now the proper names צִיּוֹן and יְרוּשָׁלַם are mentioned and the discourser situates himself as being on Mount Zion. The familiarity with this mountain spot, as indicated by the deictic demonstrative pronoun, is, however, not expressed by using the proper names again in verses 6–9a. The well-known place is anonymously present. Because of this, the movement of the discourser from outside Zion onto Zion seems to be a movement that is not completed.

What is the position of the I-figure? His direct speech is not introduced by the discourser. The text-internal reader, therefore, is plunged, as it were, into the middle of this direct speech. Is the I-figure located at the position of the discourser in verses 21–23, thus outside Zion, or is he way ahead of the discourser and is the I-figure already located on Zion?

The I-figure does not mention anywhere in his direct speech where he is located. Only indirectly does he give some hints. In verse 1, the I-figure praises the Lord. The traditional spot to praise and to exalt the Lord is the temple on Mount Zion. This praise of God (as well as the entire direct speech) directly addresses the Lord, as indicated by the abundant use of the second person singular masculine. This implies that the I-figure is not located in an outsider's position as the discourser is, at least at the beginning of his first text-unit. These observations seem to imply that the position of the I-figure is on Zion already.

On the other hand, the I-figure puts on stage an anonymous city, especially in verses 2–3. It is the only city that plays a role in his direct speech. In verses 21–23, just one single city is mentioned by the discourser as well, though without using the words עיר ("city") and קריה ("fortress"): Jerusalem. In the words of the I-figure, however, this city does not look very much like Zion made "high" by the Lord. The height of the גל ("heap of stones," v. 2) is not used without irony: the expression "high" describes something that is actually "low." The city is not inhabited by people who can be considered to be the people of God, but they are זרים ("strangers," vv. 2 and 5).

In this way, therefore, the anonymous city in verses 1–5 is both Zion and not Zion.[8] Because of the fact that the identification with Zion precedes the nonidentification with Zion, the position of the I-figure does not seem to be located on Zion.

Thus, the position of the I-figure is an expression of the transition that the discourser makes between the end of verse 23 and the beginning of verse 6: from outside Zion onto Zion. In this transition, the I-figure is a delaying factor, as a result of which there is room for the opinion that Zion could also be wrong.

Where is the we-figure located? It is obvious that the we-figure is situated on Zion. The we-figure uses the same phrase בהר הזה ("on this mountain") as the discourser did in verses 6 and 10. Nevertheless, the position of the we-figure is more complex. The discourser stages the we-figure by using an anonymous introductory formula in which an adjunct of location is missing. The we-figure is introduced without location, as if the we-figure could not be located on Zion.

For the location (ב)הר הזה ("[on] this mountain"), the we-figure uses the same anonymity as the discourser did in verses 6–9a, as a result of which it seems to the text-internal reader as if the we-figure is ignorant of the removal of the anonymity by the discourser in verse 23. Conversely, the

---

8. Cf. also Christopher R. Seitz, *Isaiah 1–39* (IBC; Louisville: Knox, 1996), 172–79, who interprets Isa 24–27 as "a tale of two cities." See also Benedikt Otzen, "Traditions and Structures of Isaiah XXIV–XXVII," *VT* 24 (1974): 196–206 (203).

we-figure frankly uses no anonymity as far as the counterpart of הזה (ב)ההר
is involved. Moab is mentioned explicitly and is even given more attention than the anonymous positive spot. In the text-internal reader's view,
the we-figure seems to remove the I-figure's ambiguous indication of the
anonymous city by creating a negative identification, namely, with Moab.
The we-figure goes so far as to directly address the negative Moab at the end
of his direct speech in verse 12.[9]

5. The "Nations" in Isaiah 24:21–25:12

The different positions of the discourser, the I-figure, and the "we"- figure,
become even more visible in their opinion concerning the nations. In the
first discourser's text, the acts performed by the Lord are not against the
nations but against מלכי האדמה ("the kings of the earth," v. 21).

The words עם ("people") and גוי ("nation") do not occur in the text
before the direct speech of the I-figure. In verse 3, the I-figure makes a
contrast between עם־עז ("the people of strength") and קרית גוים ("the fortress of the nations"). The intervention of the Lord, as described in verse 2,
causes fear among the nations, the זרים ("strangers"), but results in praise
by the people of God, עם־עז ("the people of strength"). For עם־עז, the Lord
is a מעוז ("strong refuge") and a צל ("shade").

In verse 6, the discourser connects his text to the direct speech of the
I-figure by using the verb עשׂה ("to do"). However, the marvelous things
the Lord does are not directed towards the nations. The identified mountain, where the discourser himself is now present, becomes the decor of a
banquet that the Lord prepares לכל־העמים ("for all nations," v. 6) and of
the removal of the shroud that is lying על־כל־העמים ("over all the peoples") and of the veil that is lying על־כל־הגוים ("over all the nations," v. 7).
Not before all the nations have been put in a positive light does the salvation of God's people occur in the text by removing the disgrace of עמו ("his
people," v. 8).

The words עם and גוי are not used in the direct speech of the we-
figure. In spite of all, in verses 9b–12 there is no allusion to the positive

---

9. The special function of Moab in the communication, which I will deal with
further on, is ignored by many exegetes, as a result of which the proposal arises (which
is untenable from a text-critical approach) to read the (Canaanite) deity מות ("Mot")
instead of מואב ("Moab"); therefore *pace*, for example, Peter-Ben Smit, "Appetite for
Destruction: A Note on Isa 25:8a," *BN* 111 (2002): 45–47.

banquet for everyone, which the discourser describes in verses 6–9a. On the contrary, the nations are concretized in just one single nation, namely, Moab, which is admitted to the banquet. Whereas the discourser makes the movement up to Zion and the I-figure marks the transition by using an ambiguous indication of location, also concerning the people and the nations, the we-figure, notwithstanding his position on Mount Zion, takes a step backwards.

6. The Position of the Text-Internal Reader in Isaiah 24:21–25:12

Isaiah 24:21–25:12 makes use of several reader-oriented techniques.[10] The most remarkable reader-oriented technique in Isa 24:21–25:12 is the use of anonymities. These challenge the text-internal reader to make an identification. This means that there is work in store for the text-internal reader.

Initially, the play with the anonymities seems to be solved by the discourser in verses 21–23: finally, in the entire spatial decor, just one single name is mentioned using the locative indication בהר ציון ובירושלם ("on the mountain of Zion and in Jerusalem"). However, in the direct speech of the I-figure in verses 1–5, it suddenly appears unclear whether the city mentioned is or is not Jerusalem. In verses 6–9a, the discourser uses an anonymous locative indication, however much Zion is meant by it. Apparently, the moment has not yet arrived to reveal the definite identification. This delay increases in the direct speech of the we-figure. It seems that the we-figure is written away out of Zion. The location where he speaks from is not mentioned by the discourser and the play of the anonymities is solved by the we-figure in the opposite direction by using the proper name מואב ("Moab").

On the one hand, the text-internal reader may experience the movement of the discourser up to Zion, while on the other hand, it becomes clear to him that the movement is not fully made by the characters in the text, namely, the I-figure and the we-figure. The text-internal reader, therefore, is, as it were, left halfway in the middle.

---

10. For a description of reader-oriented techniques, see van Wieringen, *Jesaja*, 135–37; idem, "Assur and Babel against Jerusalem: The Reader-Oriented Position of Babel and Assur within the Framework of Isaiah 1–39," in *'Enlarge the Site of Your Tent': The City as Unifying Theme in Isaiah: The Isaiah Workshop–De Jesaja Werkplaats* (ed. Archibald van Wieringen and Annemarieke van der Woude; OtSt 58; Leiden: Brill, 2011), 49–62 (49–50).

The anonymities occur not only concerning the spatial decor, but also concerning the characters themselves. The I-figure and the we-figure are not identified. Concerning the I-figure, this anonymity is not very complicated. The prophetic voice can be heard in the "I"-voice. He addresses the Lord, and only the Lord, in Isa 24:21–25:12.

The we-figure is much more complicated. The we-figure is introduced by the discourser using a third person masculine singular in the verbal form ואמר ("and he will say," v. 9a). This form may be interpreted as an anaphoric reference to עמו ("his people," v. 8). It is true that the following direct speech could be spoken by God's people, for God's people designates those who await the Lord (v. 9b–h) and God's people could take up a position opposite to the nation of Moab (vv. 10–12), which apparently is not located בהר הזה ("on this mountain"), but תחתיו ("on his own spot," v. 10). However, this representation does not fit the discourser's text, in which not only the people of God but all the nations are present בהר הזה, without any exception, thus including Moab as well.

The third person singular, therefore, may be interpreted as a *collectivum* for all the nations. In that case, the exceptional situation occurs in which the nations speak about the Lord as being אלהינו ("our God," v. 9) and in which they excommunicate one of their fellow nations, namely, Moab, which would be contrary to the discourser's text as well.

The best thing to do, therefore, is to interpret the third person singular in the verbal form ואמר as an indefinite expression: "they say [one says]."[11]

Usually, an indefinite expression is an invitation to the text-internal reader to participate in the textual progress, especially in the case that this indefinite expression is followed by a first person plural, which can be used inclusively, that is, inclusive of the text-internal reader.[12] In fact, however, verses 9b–12 form a delay and the identification between the text-internal reader and the first person plural should not take place immediately.[13]

---

11. See John D. W. Watts, *Isaiah 1–33* (WBC 24; Waco: Word, 1985), 335, who, because of the content, lets "*a* Yahwist" = "some Yahwist" speak this direct speech which in fact is spoken by the we-figure.

12. For the exclusive and inclusive use of a first person plural, see van Wieringen, *Reader-Oriented Unity of the Book Isaiah*, 126–27.

13. *Pace* David M. Carr, "Reading Isaiah from Beginning (Isaiah 1) to End (Isaiah 65–66): Multiple Modern Possibilities," in *New Visions of Isaiah* (ed. Roy F. Melugin and Marvin A. Sweeney; JSOTSup 214; Sheffield: Sheffield Acadamic Press, 1996), 188–218 (192), who sees the *implied audience* speaking here without delay; *pace* Seitz, *Isaiah 1–39*, 192, who situates the delay on the side of the nations instead of on the side

The direct speech of the we-figure itself gives an indication concerning this delay. It is true that the direct speech, which starts in verse 9b, goes on through verse 12, but the first person plural is present only in verses 9b–10a. Along with the introduction of the character Moab in verse 10b, the first person plural is missing in the text. The problem concerning the length of the direct speech of the we-figure, therefore, is connected to the identification of the text-internal reader with the we-figure. In this way, the text-internal reader becomes even more aware of the choice he has to make.

7. THE TEXT-INTERNAL READER AND THE SPEAKING LORD IN ISAIAH 24:21–25:12

The text-internal reader not only experiences that the discourser speaks about the Lord, that the I-figure speaks to the Lord, and that the we-figure speaks both about the Lord and to the negative Moab, but is also confronted with the statement of the discourser that the festive event בהר הזה ("on this mountain") takes place according to the word of the Lord: כי יהוה דבר ("for the Lord has spoken," v. 8).

This statement is in line with the many anonymities that occur in the text of Isa 24:21–25:12. To whom the Lord has spoken is not mentioned.[14] Moreover, this statement challenges the text-internal reader to give the moment of speaking by the Lord a place among the events in Isa 24:21–25:12, because nowhere in the text is the Lord staged as a speaking character.

Because of the fact that it is the discourser who mentions that the Lord has spoken, it is plausible to suppose that the Lord has addressed him. As a matter of course, this act of speaking must have taken place before the discourser's text in verses 6–9a. It is not obvious, however, to suppose that this act of speaking precedes the discourser's text in verses 21–23 as well. The first discourser's text pays detailed attention to "low," where the

---

of the text-internal reader. The delay also presupposes that there is a different communication here than in Isa 7:14 concerning the Immanu-El, also using "one" ("they") and "we," because in 7:14 there is no delay; therefore *pace* van Wieringen, *Jesaja*, 157.

14. See J. Todd Hibbard, *Intertextuality in Isaiah 24–27: The Reuse and Evocation of Earlier Texts and Traditions* (FAT 2/16; Tübingen: Mohr Siebeck, 2006), 72 who also finds it unclear whom the Lord addresses; cf. also Miller, "Isaiah 25:6–9," 176, who considers verses 1–5 as being a surprise in the text of Isa 24:21–25:12.

mountain of Zion has not been erected as "high" yet. Making Zion "high" results in making the nations "high," but not before the second discourser's text. The undiscoursed word of the Lord, therefore, must have taken place between the two texts by the discourser.

This conclusion implies that the word spoken by the Lord to the discourser about the festive event on Mount Zion coincides with the direct speech of the I-figure to the Lord. The confession of the prophetic I-figure and the unrendered address by the Lord to the discourser, therefore, form a diptych.[15]

Schematically, the communication is therefore as follows:

	rendered communication		implicit communication	
24:21–23	discourser	about the Lord		
25:1–5	I-figure	→ the Lord	the Lord	→ discourser
25:6–9a	discourser	about the Lord		
25:9b–12	we-figure	about the Lord	text-internal reader	identification with "we"
		→ Moab	text-internal reader	no identification with "we"

The text-internal reader cannot hear the promise made by the Lord, before he has experienced the direct speech of the I-figure and has sensed the ambiguity of the anonymous city, that is, before he has become aware of the fact that Jerusalem can also be turned into a ruin by the Lord. In this way, the text-internal reader can make the choice to which Jerusalem he belongs and, subsequently, understand that the double option expressed in

---

15. In the case of a displacement of Isa 25:1–5 after 25:6–8, this communicative coherence is lost; therefore, *pace* among others Blenkinsopp, *Isaiah 1–39*, 360, 362; see also Hibbard, *Isaiah 24–27*, 74, who deals with Isa 24:21–23; 25:6–8 together and, after that, separately, with 25:1–5 and 25:9–12.

the direct speech of the I-figure and the unrendered word of salvation by
the Lord to the discourser do not exclude each other.

8. The Direct Speeches of the
Communication Participants in Isaiah 24:1–20

The discourser and the characters—the I-figure and the we-figure—staged
by the discourser do not occur only in Isa 24:21–25:12 but already in 24:1–
20, the first unit of the chapters 24–27.

The first direct speech in Isa 24:1–20 is a direct speech of the Lord
in verses 3a–b. This direct speech is marked by an introductory formula,
which is given after the direct speech: כי יהוה דבר את־הדבר הזה ("for the
Lord has spoken this word"). The direct speech starts in verse 3a, because
of the fact that the Lord is present as a third person in verses 1–2 and
because of the fact that הארץ, already present in verse 1a, is renominalized
in verse 3a.

The second direct speech belongs to the we-figure. As a matter of
course, this direct speech is characterized by the verbal form first person
plural שמענו ("we hear," v. 16a). Because of the fact that the imperative
כבדו ("glorify") in verse 15a supposes a direct speech as well and the
construction על־כן ("therefore") connects verse 15 to verse 14, the direct
speech consists of verses 14–16b.

Within the direct speech of the we-figure, psalms resound, which are
rendered using the words: צבי לצדיק ("honor to the righteous one," v.
16b). Whereas the direct speech of the Lord is marked by an introductory
formula afterwards, the direct speech of the we-figure has no marking at
all. Even the standard verb אמר ("to say") is not used.[16]

The third and last direct speech belongs to the I-figure and consists of
the verses 16c–17.[17] This direct speech is explicitly introduced using the
verbal form ואמר ("and thereupon I said," v. 16c). From a syntactical point
of view, this direct speech is not a continuation of the direct speech of the
we-figure, for that speech has no introductory verbal form to which the
wayyiqtol form ואמר can be connected. From a semantic point of view,

---

16. See, in particular, Samuel A. Meier, *Speaking of Speaking: Marking Direct Discourse in the Hebrew Bible* (VTSup 46; Leiden: Brill, 1992), 59,130–31.

17. *Pace*, among others, Ronald E. Clements, *Isaiah 1–39* (NCB; Grand Rapids: Eerdmans, 1980), 204, who incorrectly merges the I-figure with the discourser.

using the preposition ל ("to"), a contrast is suggested between לצדיק ("to the righteous one") and לי ("to me").[18]

Furthermore, Isa 24:1–20 contains many semantic anonymities and ambiguities, just as 24:21–25:12 does.

In Isa 24:1–20, no topographic proper name is used, whereas many locative names are present in the preceding chapters 13–23. This anonymity increases the ambiguity, which already starts with the expression הארץ in verse 1a. The noun ארץ can indicate both "land," namely, the land of the people of God, and "the earth" in general. Whereas verses 1–3 keep the text-internal reader guessing, though words such as עם ("people") and כהן ("priest") in verse 2 seem to tend towards the land of the people of the Lord, verse 4 makes the ambiguity explicit: הארץ is parallel to the תבל ("world"), on the one hand, and parallel to עם־הארץ ("the people of the land"), on the other hand. The last mentioned reading becomes prominent in expressions such as ברית עולם ("the everlasting covenant," v. 5).[19]

In verse 10, a קריה ("fortress") and, parallel to this expression in verse 12, a עיר ("city") are introduced. Both are anonymous. Because of the focus on ארץ as the land of the people of the Lord, קריה and עיר take on the shape of Jerusalem. However, this reading is turned round by verse 13, for בקרב הארץ ("in the middle of the land/in the middle of the earth") is parallel to בתוך העמים ("in the middle of the nations").[20]

Apart from the character "the Lord," all the speakers are not further specified. Only indirectly is the position of the we-figure indicated. The we-figure is not located at the edge of the earth, but hears psalms sounding from this edge (v. 16, מכנף הארץ, "from the edge of the earth"). This implies that the we-figure is located somewhere in the middle of the earth. In verse 13, this spot is described as not very pleasant: there is a city which

---

18. This contrast is argued primarily from a syntactical point of view. For a detailed survey of interpretations of verse 16d, see Hugh G. M. Williamson, *The Book Called Isaiah: Deutero-Isaiah's Role in Composition and Redaction* (Oxford: Clarendon, 1994), 252–53.

19. For the interpretation of verse 2, see also Thomas Kelly Cheyne, *Prophecies of Isaiah* (London: Kegan Paul, 1886), 145.

20. It is true that Berges, *Buch Jesaja*, 152–53 also sees the anonymity of the city, but he tends towards an identification with Babel; Isa 24:1–20, however, does not want to exclude a possible identification with Jerusalem so quickly. See, conversely, already Bernhard Duhm, *Das Buch Jesaia: Übersetzt und erklärt* (Göttingen: Vandenhoeck & Ruprecht, 1892), 151.

has been destroyed and, after its destruction, it falls prey to destruction again.

In verse 15, the we-figure uses an imperative second person plural. These addressed ones remain anonymous as well. The locative expression באֻרִים ("in the lights," v. 15b) may be interpreted as the place of the rising of the sun and the moon (since the expression is plural), which implies that the edge of the earth is meant.

Although the I-figure is not further specified as well, his position does not seem to be different from the position of the we-figure. He is located on a spot full of the act of בגד ("to act deceitfully," used five times in v. 16g–h).[21] The exclamation אוֹי לִי ("woe to me"), comparable to Isa 6:5, makes the I-figure the prophetic voice in the text.

Based on the observations discussed above, the direct speeches are schematically as shown in the table on the following page:

The אֶרֶץ is the most prominent semantic theme in the text of the discourser, of the Lord, of the we-figure, and of the I-figure. It is true that the Lord explicitly plays a role only in the first three verses and in the direct speech of the we-figure, but he is thought to be involved in the destruction of the אֶרֶץ in the other verses as well.

9. The Communication in Isaiah 24:1–20 in the Perspective of the Text-internal Reader in Isaiah 24:21–25:12

In Isa 24:20–25:12, the first steps are taken by which the amorphous אֶרֶץ takes the shape of a mountain with a proper name: Mount Zion in Jerusalem. During this process, the other participants are subjected to changes as well.[22]

In verse 3, the text-internal reader cannot identify the direct speech as a direct speech of the Lord before its end. After verse 3, however, the explicit presence of the Lord is negligible. This difficult visibility of the Lord prepares the invisible unrendered direct speech of the Lord at the same time as the direct speech of the I-figure in Isa 25:1–5.

---

21. For the figure of speech used in verse 16, see Ethelbert William Bullinger, *Figures of Speech Used in the Bible* (London: Messrs. Eyre and Spottiswoode, 1898), 280.

22. For the idea that, in Isa 25, the characters "the prophet," "the Lord," "singers of praise," and "Moab" (instead of the communication participants "the discourser," "the Lord," "the I-figure," and, to a lesser degree, "the we-figure") take a step forward, see Willem A. M. Beuken, *Jesaja 13–27* (HTKAT; Freiburg: Herder, 2007), 343.

reference	speaker	the Lord	we-figure	I-figure	content	addressee
24:1–2	discourser				about the Lord / about the אָרֶץ	
24:3a–b	discourser	the Lord			about the אָרֶץ	
24:3c	discourser				formula for 3a–b	
24:4–13	discourser				about the אָרֶץ	
24:14–16b			we-figure		about the Lord	→ the אָרֶץ edge inhabitants
24:16c–17				I-figure	about himself	→ the אָרֶץ-inhabitants
24:18–20	discourser				about the אָרֶץ	

This hidden presence of the Lord gives room to the position of the discourser. The word that the Lord has spoken in verse 3 is situated in the past by the discourser because of the *qatal* form דבר, on the one hand, but functions in the now moment of the communication because of the deictic demonstrative pronoun הז, on the other hand. In this way, the movement by the discourser towards Mount Zion between Isa 24:21–23 and 25:6–9a is prepared.

This movement removes the discourser from the amorphous spot from which he is discoursing in Isa 24:1–20, marked by the ambiguity of the word ארץ. The discourser appears to overlook the entire spatial decor in Isa 24:21–23 and, from this broad point of view, to zoom in on the only place with a proper name: the mountain of Zion in Jerusalem. The I-figure is clearly marked in Isa 24:1–20. He, too, takes a step forward in Isa 24:21–25:12. Because of the fact that the I-figure is undoubtedly present, he needs no further introduction when his direct speech takes place in Isa 25:1–5, and he is still identifiable for the text-internal reader.

In both direct speeches of the I-figure, the prophetic voice is recognizable. But whom does the prophetic voice of the I-figure address? In Isa 24:16c–17, the I-figure addresses the ארץ-inhabitants, in view of the vocative יושב הארץ "inhabitant of the land/inhabitant of the earth" (v. 17) which is used as a *collectivum*. Because of the fact that the we-figure in his direct speech, which precedes the direct speech of the I-figure, is located in the middle of the land/in the middle of the earth, the I-figure's direct speech could possibly address the "we"-figure; however, the text does not offer explicit certainty to the text-internal reader.

With regard to this communication, the elaboration Isa 24:21–25:12 takes a step forward as well: it becomes clear that there is no communication between the I-figure and the we-figure (or at least not yet). It is true that the I-figure speaks to the Lord in Isa 25:1–5, but not to the we-figure. This communicative setting makes his prophetic voice stronger towards the text-internal reader, the only communication participant who is able to follow the development in the direct speeches of the I-figure.

From the perspective of the text-internal reader, the we-figure appears unexpectedly. The we-figure's direct speech has neither an introductory formula nor a verbal form of the *verbum dicendi* אמר. The we-figure is only identifiable because of the verbal form first person plural שמענו ("we hear"), almost at the end of the direct speech. The identity of the we-figure cannot be derived from the direct speech, but his position in the middle is clearly in focus for the text-internal reader. This position is elaborated in

Isa 24:21–25:12. The we-figure remains located in the middle and, in contrast to the discourser and the I-figure, makes no movement towards Zion.
Therefore, a locative phrase in Isa 25:9a, the introductory formula of the
direct speech of the we-figure in verses 9b–12, is, as it were, unnecessary.

The we-figure hears psalms from the edge of the earth and, in the
psalms, he recognizes the Lord, the God of Israel. To be perfectly clear,
the we-figure explains what the psalm is about: there is honor for the righteous one. Just as the we-figure does not make a spatial movement (and
does not need to make such a movement), the we-figure also does not
evolve concerning the content. In the first elaboration Isa 24:21–25:12, a
psalm can be heard in verses 1–5 about how the Lord acts in favor of the
righteous ones.[23] If the we-figure is able to hear a psalm sung even from
the edge of the earth, the we-figure must be able to understand the psalmic
prayer text of the I-figure in Isa 25:1–5. However, the we-figure shows no
interest in his direct speech in verses 9b–12.

The central location, that is, the location on Zion, therefore, remains
deprived of psalms, whereas it is exactly Zion that is the place where
psalms should normally resound. The we-figure, who calls for psalms in
honor of Israel's God in Isa 24:14–16b, does not answer his own call (or
at least not yet). Moreover, the call is distantly formulated. The psalms
should resound not for אלהינו ("our God"), but for אלהי ישראל ("the God
of Israel," Isa 24:15), who actually should be "our God" for the we-figure.
The only development perceptible for the text-internal reader, therefore, is
the transition from the expression אלהי ישראל to the expression אלהינו
in Isa 25:9b.

The righteous one in the psalm mentioned in Isa 24:16b is not further
specified, in line with all the anonymities in verses 1–20. In the elaboration Isa 24:21–25:12, only the we-figure does not continue the anonymity
of the righteous one. The direct speech of the Lord is invisibly present, so
no identification by the Lord can be known to the text-internal reader. It is
true that, in verse 23, the discourser concretizes one single topographical
spot, namely Zion/Jerusalem, but he does not speak about its inhabitants.
When the discourser describes those participating in the divine banquet
in verses 6–8, they appear to come from all the nations. The I-figure, in
his direct speech in verses 1–5, speaks about the threatened one and the

---

23. See also Duhm, *Buch Jesaia*, 156; Marvin A. Sweeney, *Isaiah 1–39 with an
Introduction to Prophetic Literature* (FOTL 16; Grand Rapids: Eerdmans, 1996), 335.

threatening one only in general terms, but avoids any direct identification, exactly by continuing the anonymity. The exception is the we-figure, who identifies the unrighteous one with Moab in verses 10b–12. By doing so, the "we"- figure indirectly identifies himself with the righteous one. The text-internal reader is challenged to doubt this.

The next elaboration in Isa 26 has to deal with this. The communication which the discourser will bring about between the I-figure and the we-figure, as I have explained in an earlier publication, has to be understood as an ongoing communicative process of Isa 24:1–20 and 24:20–25:12.[24]

10. Concluding Remarks

The communication in Isa 24:21–25:12 is complex and exciting. The text-internal reader is confronted with delaying elements, brought in by the we-figure, so that he himself, in contrast to the we-figure, will not make any rash identifications.

This communicative setting is prepared by Isa 24:1–20, in which the communication participants take up their first positions. All the participants, the discourser and the characters "the Lord" and the I-figure, start moving by taking a step forward in Isa 24:21–25:12 and by bringing the anonymities and ambiguities to a favorable conclusion, except for the we-figure. The next elaborations in Isa 26:1–21; 27:1, 2–11 should resolve this tension for the text-internal reader in order to come to a solution in the final elaborations in Isa 27:11, 12, 13, 26.

---

24. Archibald L. H. M. van Wieringen, "'I' and "We" before 'Your' Face: A Communication Analysis of Isaiah 26:7–21," in *Studies in Isaiah 24–27: The Isaiah Workshop: The Jesaja Werkplaats* (ed. Hendrick J. Bosman and Harm van Grol; *OtSt* 43; Leiden: Brill, 2000), 239–51 (250–51).

Food of the Gods: Canaanite Myths of Divine Banquets and Gardens in Connection with Isaiah 25:6

Beth Steiner

1. Introduction

The change in tone and content in Isa 25:1 from the verses that precede it has sometimes led to the conclusion that it should be seen as separate from chapter 24, and for a while it was the *communis opinio* that 25:1–5 was a secondary interpolation. Some scholars still argue that 25:6–8 should follow directly on from 24:21–23,[1] but 25:4 presupposes Yahweh reigning on Zion and so can be linked to 24:23, the unnamed city in verse 2 connects with 24:10, and the apparent use of Isa 4:5b–6 by 25:4–5 fits well with the way in which Isa 24–27 reworks Isaianic traditions.[2] These thematic connections suggest that 25:1–5 was composed for its current setting,[3] and

---

1. Mathias Delcor, *Études Bibliques et Orientales de Religions Comparées* (Leiden: Brill, 1979), 122; J. Todd Hibbard, *Intertextuality in Isaiah 24–27: The Reuse and Evocation of Earlier Texts and Traditions* (FAT 2/16; Tübingen: Mohr Siebeck, 2006), 72. Cf. also Otto Plöger, *Theocracy and Eschatology* (trans. Stanley Rudman; 2nd ed.; Richmond: Knox, 1968), 59–60.

2. Wilhelm Rudolph, *Jesaja 24–27* (BWA[N]T 62; Stuttgart: Kohlhammer, 1933), 34–35; Marvin A. Sweeney, "Textual Citations in Isaiah 24–27: Toward an Understanding of the Redactional Function of Chapters 24–27 in the Book of Isaiah," *JBL* 107 (1988): 39–52 (45–46).

3. William R. Millar, *Isaiah 24–27 and the Origin of Apocalyptic* (HSM 11; Missoula, Mont.: Scholars Press, 1976), 43; Willem A. M. Beuken, "The Prophet Leads the Readers into Praise: Isaiah 25:1–10 in Connection with Isaiah 24:14–23 Seen against the Background of Isaiah 12," in *Studies in Isaiah 24–27: The Isaiah Workshop* (ed. Hendrick J. Bosman and Harm van Grol; OtSt 43; Leiden: Brill, 2000), 121–56; Brevard S. Childs, *Isaiah* (OTL; Louisville: Westminster John Knox, 2001), 184.

it is clear that the themes of judgment and enthronement in 24:21–23 are connected to those of redemption and feasting in 25:6–8, whether or not they were joined by a redactor. This imagery shows an emphasis on God's actions on Mount Zion and provides a dramatic climax to Isa 24–27. The banquet of all nations on the mountain in 25:6 is perhaps the most beautiful depiction of universal joy in these chapters and, as will be demonstrated, owes much to the mythological depictions of feasts and gardens from the surrounding cultures.

2. MOUNTAINS AND GARDENS IN CANAANITE AND ISRAELITE MYTHOLOGY

2.1. A SHARED MOUNTAIN?

Building on the nineteenth century German scholarly designations *Weltberg* and *Länderberg*, Richard Clifford carefully examined the arguments for a "cosmic mountain" in Canaan and Israel and demonstrated that such mountains were seen as the dwelling or meeting place of gods (sometimes with human), the source of water and fertility, a divine battleground, the place where heaven and earth meet, and the place where decrees are issued: "in these senses, the mountains are cosmic, that is, involved in the government and stability of the cosmos."[4] In 1956, Edzard Rohland set out what are commonly accepted as the four motifs of the Zion tradition: that Zion is the peak of Zaphon, the highest mountain (see Ps 48:2–3 [MT 48:2–3]), that it was the setting for the defeat of both the chaos waters (see e.g., Ps 46:2–3 [MT 46:3–4]) and the kings and the nations (see Pss 46:7; 48:4–6 [MT 48:5–7]; 76:4–7), and that the river of paradise flows from it (see Ps 46:4 [MT 46:5]).[5] These motifs combine the celebration of Yahweh's kingship on his mountain with the people's rejoicing over the security of Zion under his protection (see also Isa 9:3; 24:8; Zeph 2:15). The association of Zion with Zaphon can be observed most clearly in the Hebrew Bible in Ps 48, which connects the "holy mountain" (v. 2 [MT v. 1]) with Zion, Zaphon, kingship (v. 3 [MT v. 2]), and the assembled kings of nations (v. 5

---

4. Richard J. Clifford, *The Cosmic Mountain in Canaan and the Old Testament* (HSM 4; Cambridge, Mass.: Harvard University Press, 1972), 2–3.

5. Edzard Rohland, "Die Bedeutung der Erwählungstraditionen Israels für die Eschatologie der alttestamentlichen Propheten" (Ph.D. diss., Heidelberg, 1956), 142.

[MT v. 4]) and demonstrates Israelite faith in the mountain's inviolability.[6] The equation of Zion with Zaphon in the Hebrew Bible means that the former is often the focus of Baal traditions, as Mount Zaphon is clearly the location of Baal's palace (*KTU* 1.4.v.54–55) and throne (*KTU* 1.3.iv.1–3), and Athtar's failed attempt to replace Baal causes him to cry out that he cannot be king on Zaphon (*KTU* 1.6.i.63).[7] It has also been noted that Zaphon is aligned with the Hittite Mount Ḫazzi in Ugaritic administrative tablets and that they are corresponding terms in the alphabetic divine list in *KTU* 1.118.4, and so it is unsurprising that we see the transfer of Baal's Zaphon traditions (and those from Ḫazzi) to Zion.[8]

2.2. A Mountain of Victory

During the construction of Baal's palace on Mount Zaphon in *KTU* 1.4.v.19, 35, the precious stone lapis lazuli is used in order to demonstrate the royal nature of the project, and an Akkadian inscription from the Boghazköi archives describes a slab of lapis lazuli, which apparently served as a footstool for the king. This is very reminiscent of the "pavement of sapphire stone" underneath Yahweh's feet in Exod 24:10, which is now generally considered to be lapis lazuli, and it has been suggested that "painted or glazed pavements may have been known in ancient Israel,

---

6. The Aramaic version of Ps 20, written in demotic on the Papyrus Amherst Egyptian 63.xi.11–19, has the term *ṣpn*, which suggests that the reference to Zion in verse 3 of the MT may have been to Zaphon in an older, and possibly northern, tradition. On this see Mark S. Smith, *The Early History of God: Yahweh and the Other Deities in Ancient Israel* (2nd ed.; Grand Rapids: Eerdmans, 2002), 89, and 70 nn. 22 and 23 and for a translation of the psalm see Richard C. Steiner, "The Aramaic Text in Demotic Script," in *Canonical Compositions from the Biblical World* (vol. 1 *The Context of Scripture*; ed. William W. Hallo and K. Lawson Younger; 3 vols.; Leiden: Brill, 1997), 309–27. See also Clifford, *Cosmic Mountain*, 142–43.

7. Nicholas Wyatt, "Killing and Cosmogony in Canaanite and Biblical Thought," *UF* 17 (1986): 375–81 (380–81), rejects the apparent identification of Mounts Zaphon and Zion in Ps 48:3 [ET v. 2] as an argument for Yahweh's borrowing from Baal on the basis that Mount Zaphon can be seen as a mountain for all the gods. This requires unnecessary emendation, however.

8. It was in Otto Eissfeldt, *Baal Zaphon, Zeus Kasios und der Durchzug der Israeliten durchs Meer* (BRGA 1; Halle: Niemeyer, 1932), 1–48, that it was originally argued that Zaphon should be seen as the classical Mount Casius and the modern Jebel el-Aqraʿ, a position now generally accepted.

especially as part of the ornamentation of sanctuaries."[9] That Yahweh kept his kingly home on his mountain[10] can also be seen in Exod 15:17, which shows God's eternal kingship and victory through the establishment of his temple on the mountain. Because מכון לשבתך ("a place where you may dwell") only elsewhere appears in 1 Kgs 8:13, Day suggests that this is Baal mountain language.[11] This expression is parallel to "mountain of inheritance," which is probably influenced by the language found in *KTU* 1.3.iii.29–32, in which we find "mountain of my heritage" in parallel with "throne on which he sits" and "mountain of victory." This shows that "*nḥlt* in the myths is a place where power is exercised," and the god's territory, "*ǵr nḥlty*, then, is a mountain possessed inalienably, a patrimony, with the possible overtone of possession by conquest."[12] The fact that Zaphon is often referred to as the "mountain of victory" (e.g., *KTU* 1.101.2; 1.10. iii.28, 31), in addition to Anat's mention of Zaphon in connection with the battle with Yam in *KTU* 1.3.iv.1 and Baal and Mot's conflict there in *KTU* 1.6.vi.12–34, shows that the mountain is the setting for the deity's kingship, as a result of the divine combat which took place there. This reminds us that it was Baal's defeat of Yam that secured this as his home,[13] a tradition also seen throughout the Hebrew Bible, most notably for our purposes in Yahweh's defeat of Leviathan in Isa 27:1 and his reign on Zion in 24:23. Psalms such as 48:1–2 [MT 48:1–3] show that both the city and the temple are indicated by the name Zion, and temple and mountain are combined in mythology in Zech 14:6–8, where the divine warrior and living waters go forth from Jerusalem on the day of victory, and Joel 3:16–18 [MT 4:16–18], in which the divine warrior roars from Zion while the mountains and val-

---

9. Ernest W. Nicholson, "The Interpretation of Exodus XXIV 9–11," *VT* 24 (1974): 77–97 (92); Clifford, *Cosmic Mountain*, 112.

10. While the traditions in Exod 24 concern Mount Sinai, it is clear that such ideas were reused, especially as part of the Israelite cult, and adapted to Mount Zion, see Clifford, *Cosmic Mountain*, 154; John Day, *God's Conflict with the Dragon and the Sea: Echoes of a Canaanite Myth in the Old Testament* (UCOP 35; Cambridge: Cambridge University Press, 1985), 99.

11. Day, *God's Conflict with the Dragon and the Sea*, 98–99.

12. Clifford, *Cosmic Mountain*, 71–72.

13. The heights of Lebanon also seem to have adopted this combat in *KTU* 1.83. Day, *God's Conflict with the Dragon and the Sea*, 107, suggests that Baal traditions lie behind Zeus's battle with Typhon on Mount Casius as related in Apollodorus (*The Library* 1.6.3), Strabo (*Georg.* 16.2.7) and Herodotus (*Hist.* 3.5).

leys flow with wine, milk, and water from the temple.[14] The latter may have been influenced by the link between Baal's sacred mountain and temple, as shown when he opens the window in his house/temple to shout/thunder from his mountain (*KTU* 1.4.vii.26–30).

2.3. The Mountain as the Paradisiacal Garden

Psalm 24 tells us that those who wish to ascend Yahweh's hill must have moral integrity to do so (vv. 3–4), which shows that he is judge as well as creator (vv. 1–2), that is, he has sovereign rule over both nature and the moral realm.[15] This may well be connected with the way in which God's mountain became the place from which the rivers of paradise flowed (Rohland's second motif of Zion).[16] The only place in the Hebrew Bible in which the "garden of God" and the "holy mountain of God" are unmistakably associated is Ezek 28:13–14, and as it is possible that the passage was not composed by a single author we should naturally be cautious when making this connection. Nevertheless, the passage poetically combines the garden, the mountain, and the sanctuary:

> You were in Eden, the garden of God; every precious stone was your covering, carnelian, chrysolite, and moonstone, beryl, onyx, and jasper, sapphire, turquoise, and emerald; and worked in gold were your settings and your engravings. On the day that you were created they were prepared. With an anointed cherub as guardian I placed you[17]; you were on the holy mountain of God; you walked among the stones of fire (NRSV).

---

14. Howard N. Wallace, *The Eden Narrative* (HSM 32; Atlanta: Scholars Press, 1985), 77–78.

15. Aubrey R. Johnson, *Sacral Kingship in Ancient Israel* (2nd ed.; Cardiff: University of Wales Press, 1967), 73. Verses 7 and 9 also tell the gates to open for the king, similar to Isa 26:2.

16. For an attempt to give specific geographic locations for the rivers of paradise, see Ephraim A. Speiser, *Genesis: Introduction, Translation and Notes* (AB 1; New York: Doubleday, 1964), 17, and David Neiman, "Gihon and Pishon: Mythological Antecedents of the Two Enigmatic Rivers of Eden," in *Proceedings of the Sixth World Congress of Jewish Studies, Held at the Hebrew University of Jerusalem, 13–19 August, 1973, under the Auspices of the Israel Academy of Sciences and Humanities* (vol. 1; ed. Avigdor Shinan; Jerusalem: World Union of Jewish Studies, 1977), 321–28.

17. While this translation can be disputed, it is not necessary for our purposes to do so here.

It is especially notable that the landscape here is one of precious stones, and that a cherub is present as they are in both the sanctuary (2 Kgs 19:15) and the garden of Eden (Gen 3:24). Ezekiel 28 can also be linked with Gen 2, as both are texts which describe paradise and the dwelling place of God in the garden/on the mountain which is the source of life-giving waters, and it can be argued that Zaphon in Isa 14:13 is parallel to both the mount of assembly and the "high clouds." Clifford relates the latter to Job 26:7, suggesting that Zaphon should be understood as "heavens," which would surely imply that the mountain was understood as truly God's abode and paradise.[18] It is also possible to see a link between sacred mountains and gardens in the similar (inappropriate) religious activities that take place there in Isa 57:1–10 and 65:1–12, and all the trees in Eden (Gen 2:9), in contrast to outside the garden (Gen 3:18), have been compared to the luxuriant cedars on the mountain abode of the gods in the Assyrian Gilgamesh tablet 5.i.6–7 (see also the garden in 9.v.47–vi.35).[19] In the light of these associations between the Israelite mountain of God and paradise, it is interesting that Baal's mountain is also referred to as "pleasant place" (n'm)[20] in KTU 1.3.iii.29. This can be connected with Isa 17:10–11, in which the expression נטעי נעמנים, often translated as "pleasant plants," could be understood as "plants for the pleasant one," as a reference to the gardens of Adonis (see Isa 1:29–30; 65:3; and 66:17 for other possible references to the gardens of Adonis).[21] We do not, however, know whether Adonis was ever referred to as the "pleasant one,"[22] and it may be that "although you plant a planting of pleasantness" refers to the following "strange" gods in connection with Baal's "pleasant place."

Terje Stordalen raises the question of whether garden imagery came from the Ugaritic texts, as KTU 1.23.66–76 may assume an enclosed garden complete with a "watchman,"[23] an idea we can see in the vineyard

18. Clifford, *Cosmic Mountain*, 161–62 n. 85.

19. Wallace, *Eden Narrative*, 70.

20. Nicholas Wyatt, *Religious Texts from Ugarit: The Words of Ilimilku and His Colleagues* (2nd ed.; The Biblical Seminar 53; London: Sheffield Academic Press, 2002), 78, translates this "Paradise."

21. See Sergio Ribichini, "Adonis," in *Dictionary of Deities and Demons in the Bible* (ed. Karel van der Toorn, Bob Becking, and Pieter W. van der Horst; 2nd ed.; Leiden: Brill, 1999), 7–10 (9).

22. Edward J. Kissane, *The Book of Isaiah: Translated from a Critically Revised Hebrew Text with Commentary* (2 vols.; rev. ed.; Dublin: Richview, 1960), 1:192.

23. Terje Stordalen, *Echoes of Eden: Genesis 2–3 and Symbolism of the Eden Garden*

allegory in the verses immediately following Isa 27:1. Perhaps then what we have here is the idea that the elect will dwell in a holy mountain garden following the defeat of chaos, received from Canaanite traditions, which can be supported by Clifford's point that "unlike Baal, [Yahweh] is not a seasonal deity who suffers periodic defeat by Mot. His mountain is therefore impregnable and becomes a symbol of the secure place."[24] However, he does not consider the "pleasant place" to be the paradisiacal garden, but thinks that *n'm* here refers to a sacred place, parallel with *qdš*, and that in "designating a place [the term] is perhaps related to the use of the word in the *Krt* epic and in proper names. The god has shown favour to a particular place and has set it apart for himself."[25] Even if this is the case, the concept of a place chosen by the deity, when transposed to the Hebrew Bible in Isa 24–27, must surely designate a paradise of sorts, especially in conjunction with the divine kingship (24:23), an eschatological victory (27:1), and the defeat of death (25:8). We also find the continuation of the mountain and paradisiacal garden ideology seen behind Isa 25:6 in *1 En.* 25.4–7; 90.24–42, where it seems that Zion came to be seen as the abode of the just, in the same way that gehenna/the valley of Hinnom was the place of the punishment of the unjust.[26]

2.4. The Garden as the Center of the World

The geographical and meteorological phenomena of Mount Zaphon, in combination with the literary evidence, suggest that the mountain would have been the center of the Ugaritic cult, especially with regard to Baal's status as the storm-god.[27] In addition to being the cultic focal point, the mythological texts show that the mountain was seen as the center point of

---

in *Biblical Hebrew Literature* (CBET 25; Leuven: Peeters, 2000), 30–31, 156–58). See also Mark S. Smith, *The Rituals and Myths of the Feast of the Goodly Gods of KTU/ CAT 1.23: Royal Constructions of Opposition, Intersection, Integration, and Domination* (SBLRBS 51; Atlanta: Society of Biblical Literature, 2006), 122.

24. Clifford, *Cosmic Mountain*, 153.

25. Ibid., 70–71.

26. Ibid., 186.

27. Patrick N. Hunt, "Mount Saphon in Myth and Fact," in *Phoenicia and the Bible: Proceedings of the Conference held at the University of Leuven on the 15th and 16th of March 1990* (ed. Edward Lipiński; Studia Phoenicia XI; Leuven: Uitgeverij Peeters, 1991), 103–15.

human and divine order in the Ugaritic texts,[28] and Mark Smith posits that Baal's "pleasant place" in *KTU* 1.3.iii.29 is "perhaps garden language that, in biblical texts, is a recurring motif for the center point of the cosmos."[29] He uses as his basis the spatial distinctions in the Ugaritic myths and rituals between the "sown" (*mdr'*) and the "outback" (*mdbr*), noting that there is a "center" and a "periphery," as well as a "beyond" (not only in the environment but also in the nature of the deities), and that "within the center or area of human cultivation and civilization, deities are accorded sacred mountains or cult sites, but cosmic enemies are not"[30] (see the desert places as the domain of demons in Isa 13:21, 34:11–14).

In the Hebrew Bible, too, the garden can be seen as the center of the universe. The tree of life in Eden (Gen 2:9), and the garden itself, gained a cosmic significance, particularly in later apocalyptic and rabbinic writings. Often fed by the waters of paradise and symbolizing the *omphalos*, the navel of the world, Eden and Zion were placed at the center of the cosmos (see Ezek 47, wherein the prophet's vision depicts the temple as the center of a microcosmos, issuing fertilizing waters of life).[31] It was there in the symbolic middle of the earth, notes Edwin James,

> be it in a garden, city, temple or on a mountain or hill, that the gods descended to earth to hold converse with their appointed agents and embodiments, and to bestow their gifts often by means of the life-giving

---

28. Mark S. Smith, *The Origins of Biblical Monotheism: Israel's Polytheistic Background and the Ugaritic Texts* (New York: Oxford University Press, 2001), 29; Clifford, *Cosmic Mountain*, 2–3.

29. Smith, *Origins of Biblical Monotheism*, 29.

30. Smith, *Origins of Biblical Monotheism*, 27–28. Interestingly, he also points out that, although gods, Mot and Yamm are "beyond the periphery" by location— the underworld and the "waters beyond"—and do not have holy mountains like the beneficent gods (29). See also idem, *Rituals and Myths of the Feast of the Goodly Gods*, xiv–xv, 107; Paolo Xella, *Il mito di Šḥr e Šlm: Saggio sulla mitologia ugaritica* (Studi Semitici 44; Rome: Istituto di Studi del vicino oriente, Università di Roma, 1973).

31. Arent J. Wensinck, *The Ideas of the Western Semites Concerning the Navel of the Earth* (Verhandelingen der Koninklijke Akademie van Wetenschappen te Amsterdam 17; Amsterdam: Müller, 1916), 11–36; Edwin O. James, *The Tree of Life: An Archaeological Study* (SHR 11; Leiden: Brill, 1966), 143–44. The latter notes also the water and tree of life imagery in the book of Enoch and the Johannine new Jerusalem symbolism in the New Testament Apocalypse (1 En. 24:4; 25:4, 5; 26:1–6; 2 En. 8:2; Rev 22:1–2; T. Levi 18:11). See also Baruch Margulis, "Weltbaum and Weltberg in Ugaritic Literature: Notes and Observations on RŠ 24.245," *ZAW* 86 (2009): 1–23.

trees that sprang forth from the sacred waters "for the healing of the nations," for reinvigoration, and the boon of immortality.[32]

That Eden is the abode of Yahweh is insinuated by Gen 3:8; Ezek 28:13; 31:8–9; and the four rivers of Eden in Gen 2:10–14 associated with the holy mountain in Ezek 28:14, 16. The fertilizing waters that flow from the temple on Zion in Ezek 47:1–12; Zech 14:8; and Joel 3:18 (MT 4:18) are likely a reflection of El's dwelling at the source of the cosmic waters (e.g., *KTU* 1.3.v.6–8, see also the Hittite version in *KUB* 12.61.5), which may well have been in the mountains of Armenia.[33] Nicholas Wyatt feels that the position of El's home is representative of his all-encompassing author-ity: "This is the omphalos, the place of true reality, the still centre of the turning world. El, the absolute deity, is immovable, and all the other deities revolve around him,"[34] a powerful image reminiscent of Yahweh's seat in both the temple and the divine council.

3. Feasting in Canaanite and Israelite Tradition

With its connotations of an earthly paradise at the center of the earth inhabited by Yahweh, Mount. Zion becomes the perfect setting for an eschatological, universal banquet. A major banquet of the time would have been characterized by the consumption of wine and rich foods, and the repetition of these items in verse 6 confirms the generous and bountiful nature of the meal. It is perhaps also significant that wine is mentioned in this verse as a contrast to the earth's desolation in 24:4–13 depicted by the absence or bitterness of new wine. The food and drink in 25:6 is more than sustenance, however, as it represents life in contrast to the veil and cover-ing in verse 7, which represent sterility and death. While these symbols are usually understood to be a universal vision of hope, André Caquot put forward an alternative view. He proposed that ממחים in verse 6 comes

---

32. James, *Tree of Life*, 144. He also points out that in rabbinic literature (Tg. Ps.-J. Exod 28:30) the temple is said to be placed directly above תהום, the primeval deep. This may well be another reminder that it is Yahweh's victory over the powers of chaos (symbolized by the waters), which ensures his eternal kingship.

33. See John Day, *Yahweh and the Gods and Goddesses of Canaan* (JSOTSup 265; London: Sheffield Academic Press, 2000), 30–31 and n. 51 for this view and a discus-sion of others.

34. Wyatt, *Religious Texts from Ugarit*, 52 n. 64.

from מחה meaning "to efface," because the standard philological deriva-
tion from מֹחַ ("marrow") cannot be justified, and asserted that שׁמרים
מזקקים should not be seen as dregs purified, but the "pure dregs," and
therefore something disgusting.[35] While this argument is sound, Caquot
does not account for the rich food offered, which is clearly not a disgusting punishment, or for the universal and positive outlook which Isa 24–27
offers for all nations in the time after the final judgment.

3.1. VICTORY BANQUETS

There is little evidence in the Hebrew Bible of royal feasting in connection
with military victory, but we do have a Megiddo ivory from 1350–1150
B.C.E. which depicts the king feasting while music is played and prisoners are brought before him, suggesting a celebratory banquet following a
victory,[36] and the concept of a victory feast may well be present in our text.
Concerning the theme in Isa 25:6, Jeffery Lloyd asserts that "it is more
likely that the theme of the divine banquet was part of the cultural continuum of the ancient West Semitic peoples, rather than occurring inde-
pendently in each one of them."[37] Nevertheless, Isa 25:6–8 contains many
striking similarities to the Baal Cycle, which implies that the Canaanite
traditions had an effect on those of the Israelites. Victory feasts following
divine combats which lead to the enthronement of Marduk and Baal occur
in *Enuma Elish* 3.129–4.2 and *KTU* 1.4.vi.44–59 respectively, and the Hittite storm-god has his own banquet as part of his conflict with Illuyanka
in *KBo* 3.715–20. It is commonly believed that the banquet on Zion in Isa
25:6 drew on imagery from Baal's feast on Zaphon in particular. Not only
was victory—enthronement—feast a common pattern in the ancient Near
East, but it is apparent that it was applicable to various eras: in *Enuma
Elish*, it was set in primordial time; in the Ugaritic texts it is ambiguous
and possibly cyclical; and here in Isaiah we have an eschatological setting.
The finality of the Israelite passage is emphasized by Yahweh's swallowing of death in verse 8, and John Day points out that the fact that Baal's

---

35. André Caquot, "Remarques sur le 'Banquet des Nations' en Esaïe 25,6–8,"
RHPR (1989): 111–13, 115–18.

36. James B. Pritchard, *The Ancient Near East in Pictures Relating to the Old Testament* (3rd ed.; Princeton: Princeton University Press, 1969), no. 332.

37. Jeffery B. Lloyd, "The Banquet Theme in Ugaritic Narrative," *UF* 22 (1990):
169–93 (186).

kingship was associated with his victory over Mot and followed his feast on Zaphon shows that this verse is appropriately positioned after verse 6.[38]

3.2. Banquets in Connection with the Fertility Cult

Lloyd maintains that the important aspect of a banquet myth is not the eating or drinking but the events which occur while the meal is taking place.[39] This can be seen in the fact that "in celebration of the victory and in acknowledgment of the universal sovereignty of the Divine Warrior and King, a bloody sacrifice-banquet is held. This is an essential element in the mythic pattern with which we are dealing, and betrays the original fertility function of the ancient cult."[40] In other words, victory alone will not restore fertility; a sacrifice of the enemy warriors is required to release the earth's fecundity. The idea that a sacred offering as part of a meal had its background in the eating and drinking among gods supports the proposal that Isa 25:6 can be seen as having aspects of a sacrifice. Ernest W. Nicholson points out that in Exod 24 "there is no mention of any part of the meal being offered up sacrificially to God after the manner, for example, of the so-called communion sacrifice, which would have been a means of God's 'partaking' of the meal,"[41] and the same could be said of Isa 25. In fact Deut 32:38 seems to mock the pagan gods who were seen to eat and drink their offerings. On the other hand, all animals that were slain by the Israelites for food were seen as sacrifices to God, and surely any eating and drinking before God was seen as providing a sense of communion, especially if covenantal rites were understood as taking place.

The gathering of the nations and the idea of a victory banquet has also led some to link Isa 25 with the sacrificial feast of enemies in Ezek 39:17–20. Although the sacrifice is eaten by the birds and beasts, the feast can be seen as an inversion of the eschatological, joyous meal, and Clifford agreed that "possibly, the banquet for the victorious on the mountain and the slaughter-sacrifice of the enemies are one and the same—the celebration of the life and the kingship of the deity on the mountain site of his

---

38. Day, *God's Conflict with the Dragon and the Sea*, 150.

39. Lloyd, "Banquet Theme in Ugaritic Narrative," 171.

40. Paul D. Hanson, *The Dawn of Apocalyptic: The Historical and Sociological Roots of Jewish Apocalyptic Eschatology* (rev. ed.; Philadelphia: Fortress, 1979), 322.

41. Nicholson, "Interpretation of Exodus," 86.

temple."[42] The emphasis in this passage in Ezekiel may be on the slaughter, not the communion of people and their participation in the meal, but we can see in passages such as Zech 9:9–17 the combination of the judgment of enemies, their slaughter, and the feast of the redeemed,[43] so it is possible these ideas were linked in the Israelite mind and cult.

The great banquet of verse 6 in conjunction with the defeat of enemies and the commencement of God's rule on Zion has led many scholars to state that there is here a clear link between the rejoicing over the reign of Yahweh and the celebration of the festival cult in this text.[44] It is possible to see here an annual celebration of the kingship of Yahweh which demonstrates his choice and protection of Zion (see Isa 9:3 [MT 9:2]; Zeph 2:15), and it may be that Isa 24–27 has a relationship with the enthronement psalms or that the banquet for all the peoples was derived from them.[45] Whether or not there was an enthronement festival of Yahweh in Israel is still debated, but it is clear that we have enthronement traditions in the Hebrew Bible, especially in Pss 47, 93, and 96–99, which some feel represent a cultic day of God at which he ascended his throne to bring about the salvation of the people. In place of an annual feast, Isa 25:6 can be seen as a coronation banquet at which Yahweh is crowned at the end of time, perhaps as the event towards which the festival looked. Fieldhouse asserts that festivals often "occur at vital points in the human and cosmic lifecycle and themselves incorporate a cycle of events which represent or reflect the society's philosophy of history,"[46] and it is clear that a key feature of Yahweh's kingship, and the proposed enthronement festival, was the defeat of the chaos waters used to show his power and supremacy and the following celebration.

Because of Baal's status as god of rain and fertility, it is common to see the banquets following his victories over Mot and Yam as part of the cult associated with his enthronement and also with the New Year festival.[47] In *KTU*

---

42. Clifford, *Cosmic Mountain*, 177.

43. Hanson, *Dawn of Apocalyptic*, 316.

44. Day, *God's Conflict with the Dragon and the Sea*, 148; Hibbard, *Intertextuality in Isaiah 24–27*, 83. See also Smith, *Rituals and Myths of the Feast of the Goodly Gods*, for the importance of feasting in both myth and ritual settings.

45. Contra Hibbard, *Intertextuality in Isaiah 24–27*, 85.

46. Paul Fieldhouse, *Food and Nutrition: Customs and Culture* (London: Croom Helm, 1986), 92.

47. The two Hittite versions of the conflict between the weather-god and the dragon Illuyanka (*KUB* 17:5 and 3:7:20–24) seem to serve as aetiologies of the Hattian

1.4.vi.47–54, we have a list of gods who attended the banquet, and Theodor H. Gaster says the lines "define the guests as the deities who preside over the livestock, the civil authority, and the vintage—the three aspects of topocosmic life and activity upon which attention is especially concentrated at the autumn festival, when the god of the rains (Baal) resumes dominion over the earth."[48] The temporary death of Baal signifies a loss of fertility and life of the community, and his life marks the restoration of vitality,[49] as demonstrated by the symbolism of flowing oil and honey marking his return to life (*KTU* 1.6.iii.5–13), and we see similar beliefs in the Hittite myth of the disappearance of the storm-god when all the gods at the feast ate and drank but stayed hungry and thirsty on account of his absence (*CTH* 325). A comparable fertility banquet is found in Zech 14:16–19, a text which many compare with Isa 25:6–8 and which contains the compulsory pilgrimage of the nations to Jerusalem for the Feast of Tabernacles. The nations are told that if they do not go to Jerusalem to worship Yahweh as king they will get no rain, and "it seems reasonable to infer that such an eschatological picture … is based upon what was already the established complex of ideas associated with this festival in the form which had been current in Jerusalem," that is, that Tabernacles was connected with the gift of rain and the worship of Yahweh as universal king.[50] The celebration of the Feast of Tabernacles can be understood, then, as a modification of the pilgrimage to Zion and the great banquet, with the eschatologizing aspects as either a late development or an older tradition connected with the ancient practice of water drawing and God's gift of rain.[51] Häkan Ulfgard suggests that Zech 14:16–19 and Isa 25:6 may be the basis for such an eschatological understanding and that John 7:37–38, in which the water of life is connected with the festival, can be seen as early evidence of it.[52]

Purulli festival with regard to the restoration of order and fertility and were probably told during the course of the festival.

48. Theodor H. Gaster, *Thespis: Ritual, Myth, and Drama in the Ancient Near East* (rev ed.; New York: Harper & Row, 1961), 178.

49. Smith, *Origins of Biblical Monotheism*, 100.

50. Johnson, *Sacral Kingship in Ancient Israel*, 59.

51. Rain was considered to be released from the cosmic sea at Yahweh's discretion for the help or destruction of humankind, and the "bronze sea" in the Solomonic temple may have been a replica of this and played a part in the cultic ritual (1 Kgs 7:23–26; 2 Kgs 25:13), Johnson, *Sacral Kingship in Ancient Israel*, 59–60.

52. Häkan Ulfgard, *The Story of Sukkot: The Setting, Shaping, and Sequel of the Biblical Feast of Tabernacles* (BGBE34; Tübingen: Mohr Siebeck, 1998), 274.

3.3. The Universal Banquet

The feast in Isa 25:6 is particularly remarkable in the Hebrew Bible as a result of those who have been invited to it. Day first noted that the seventy sons of Asherah invited to the feast in *KTU* 1.4.iv.46 signify "the totality of the divine pantheon, [and] account for the universality of the banquet in Isa 25:6, where 'all peoples' come" and the seventy members of the host of heaven (see Deut 32:8; *1 En.* 89.59-60; 90.22) correspond to the supposed seventy nations (Gen 10) and are the same as those referred to in Isa 24:21-22.[53] The divine assembly and its members in the Hebrew Bible is perhaps best shown by Ps 89:5-8 [MT 89:6-9], in which the קהל קדשים ("assembly of the holy") and the סוד־קדשים ("council of the holy") are linked with the בני אלים ("sons of Gods") and the צבאות ("hosts"). We find similarities to this in the tablets from Ugarit, as we can see such terms as בני אלים and קדשים paralleled in the Ugaritic bn 'il/bn 'ilm (e.g., *KTU* 1.4.iii.14) and bn qdš (e.g., *KTU* 1.2.iii.20). El's gods congregated on a mountain (*KTU* 1.2.i.19-20, where the gods are also eating at table), which can be compared to the בהר־מועד ("mountain of assembly") of Isa 14:13. It is likely that the divine recipients of portioned lands convened on this mountain, seen in the "original" text of Deut 32:8, which is now mostly considered to be that of the LXX and 4QDeutʲ.

On the basis that the number seventy was symbolic in the ancient Near East for "totality" or "completeness," its presence could represent the collective entity Israel in Exod 24,[54] but Lloyd argues that we may have here the remnants of an older tradition in which seventy gods feasted on the mountain.[55] The translation of אצילי ("chieftains," v. 11) in the LXX— ἐπιλέχτων ("chosen ones")—may support this idea,[56] but many contend that the passages in Exod 24 and Isa 25 differ from the Ugaritic texts, because those invited to the banquets are people, not gods, on account of

---

53. Day, *God's Conflict with the Dragon and the Sea*, 149, 174-75. That the seventy members of the heavenly host may have had a link to the Ugaritic traditions was first suggested by Raymond J. Tournay, "Les Psaumes complexes: Les Psaumes 7 et 82: Structure et attaches littéraires," *RB* 56 (1949): 37-60 (53), and followed by William F. Albright, "Some Remarks on the Song of Moses in Deuteronomy XXXII," *VT* 9 (1959): 339-46 (343-44).

54. Ernest W. Nicholson, "The Antiquity of the Tradition in Exodus XXIV 9-11," *VT* 25 (1975): 69-79 (78).

55. Lloyd, "Banquet Theme in Ugaritic Narrative," 188.

56. Nicholson, "Interpretation of Exodus," 83.

Yahwistic monotheism. The main roles of the members of Yahweh's assembly in the Hebrew Bible are as rulers of nations (e.g., Deut 32:8–9), protectors of humanity (e.g., Zech 1:10–12), heralds of Yahweh's kingship (e.g., Ps 29), and judges (Ps 82), and it may be that there was no need for deities to attend the banquet in Isa 25:6, because these functions had all been performed by Yahweh within 24:21–25:5. On the other hand, perhaps verse 6 simply shows that it was all the faithful people who were invited to participate in the cultic meal.

Todd Hibbard sees a connection between Isa 25 and Isa 52:7–10, on the grounds that both show salvation through the deliverance of Zion (25:9; 52:7, 10; also God reigns in 24:23 and 52:7), which will affect all people (25:6–10; 52:10), and both refer to singing (25:1–5; 52:8) and rest (25:10; 52:9). The difference between the passages, he notes, is that while the nations are observers in Isa 52, they participate in the meal in 25:6.[57] The participation in the banquet is a seminal part of Isa 24–27, as supported by Donald C. Polaski, who affirms that the sequence in 24:21–25:12 has a chiastic structure that focuses on the feast.[58] Discrepancies in tense and person might argue against this, as does the fact that while 25:1–5 may be a hymn of praise, verses 9–10a do not seem to be, and the judgment of Moab in 25:10b–12 is surely not comparable to the punishment of the earthly kings and heavenly host in 24:21–23. Nevertheless, there is certainly a clear pattern of punishment, praise, and protection surrounding verse 6. Hibbard also disagrees with the opinion that there is a chiasm here, but he does consider the banquet to be the emphasis, because even though it "is not the only positive note sounded in this sequence, the additional acts of salvation on behalf of the people are presented in the context of the banquet,"[59] and it certainly seems that we can expect no further development after the climax of the meal.

That the festal banquet is the high point of the text and the fulfilment of a promise is supported by the common view that we have a covenant meal in Isa 25:6, and there is no doubt that the sharing of a meal is an effective way of celebrating a reconciliation and general bonding. However, 25:9–10a looks to the future still, and these verses may be part of an Isaian exegetical tradition concerning waiting and salvation, even though they

---

57. Hibbard, *Intertextuality in Isaiah 24–27*, 88–89.

58. Donald C. Polaski, *Authorizing an End: The Isaiah Apocalypse and Intertextuality* (BibInt 50; Leiden: Brill, 2001), 162.

59. Hibbard, *Intertextuality in Isaiah 24–27*, 75.

are the only example in which the nations have a positive and active role, not merely a subservient one.[60] This latter point is probably connected to the fact that, if a covenant is being made here, it is made with all peoples, which Polaski claims (on the basis of Gen 29; Judg 14; and 2 Sam 3) is linked to "the occasional use of מִשְׁתֶּה in the Hebrew Bible to signal an ethnic meeting-ground."[61] The inclusion of all the nations here marks an eschatological change in attitude, and it is notable that a feast would also have been used to mark an important development or change in the cult, as we can see from Melchizedek's instatement in Gen 14:18.

4. Conclusion

Yahweh's abode on Zion clearly combines the cosmic features of El's mountain—the divine assembly, the source of water, the issue of decrees—and those of Baal's: divine combat, victory, and enthronement. Hittite traditions are also clearly connected, as we often see gods standing on mountains in Hittite art,[62] and it is from Mount Ḫazzi that Ullikummi is seen rising out of the sea in *KUB* 33.87, supporting its link with Zaphon as the location of the theomachy.[63] In addition, a cylinder seal found at Ras Shamra depicts the Hittite storm-god atop a mountain, which is very reminiscent of both Israelite and Canaanite imagery. Ezekiel 28:13–16 is the first direct instance of combining the garden of Eden with the mountain motif, followed by 31:8–9, 47:1–12, and Zech 14:1–21 (see also Isa 33:20–24; 51:3), leading some to assert that the association must be a late one.[64] However, I agree with Day's assertion that there is strong evidence that Canaanite traditions of El's abode lie behind the garden[65] and with those who feel that the Eden narrative would have been naturally associated with local traditions of sacred mountains, especially in Israel where the Gihon served

---

60. This tradition includes passages from Isa 33; 49; 51; 59; 50; and 64, Hibbard, *Intertextuality in Isaiah 24–27*, 109–10.

61. Polaski, *Authorizing an End*, 166.

62. Clifford, *Cosmic Mountain*, 32.

63. It seems likely that this story lies behind the Greek Typhon myth, see Hesiod, *Theog.* 820–870.

64. Clifford, *Cosmic Mountain*, 159.

65. Day, *Yahweh and the Gods*, 26–29.

as a link between Jerusalem-Zion and the garden of Eden, as they would have been linked by their nature as a divine dwelling place.[66] Many traditions have all contributed to the picture of the banquet in Isa 25:6: "the meal on Zion, the banquet of Yнwн which is an imperial fete, a coronation ritual, a covenant meal and sacrifice, is the future of all Yнwн's people, indeed all the people on the earth."[67] Nevertheless, it seems most clear that this verse would suggest to its audience a sacrificial feast in connection with the enthronement of Yahweh, which had great significance for the people due to its background in the Canaanite celebratory feasts and sacrifices following cosmic victory. We see the luxury and fertility of Eden with the feasting in the temple in Ps 36:9 (see also Jer 51:34; Neh 9:25), and this tradition appears in the Baal Cycle in connection with the storm god describing his fertilizing rains (*KTU* 1.4.v.6–7), so Eden can be seen as "the terrestrial sacred mountain fertilized by the storm-god and in this sense a 'garden.'"[68] It has been suggested that Isa 14:13–14, in which we find both Yahweh dwelling on Zaphon and a use of the epithet Elyon, may show the transfer of mountain terminology through the Jerusalem Jebusite cult,[69] and certainly the Israelite cult passed down the traditions of mountain and garden to the later prophets. Combining its characteristics as holy sanctuary, divine abode, and source of fertility, the paradisiacal mountain becomes the perfect symbol for hope and life for the whole land in the context of the return from exile (e.g., Ezek 36:33–36), and the banquet of all nations demonstrates that vitality and communion with the victorious God will be available to all in the eschaton.

---

66. Wallace, *Eden Narrative*, 86.

67. Polaski, *Authorizing an End*, 191–92.

68. Mark S. Smith, "Mythology and Myth-Making in Ugaritic and Israelite Literatures," in *Ugarit and the Bible: Proceedings of the International Symposium on Ugarit and the Bible, Manchester, September 1992* (ed. George J. Brooke, Adrian H. W. Curtis, and John F. Healey; UBL 11; Münster: Ugarit-Verlag, 1994), 293–341 (324 n. 125); see also Wallace, *Eden Narrative*, 84.

69. John Day, "Ugarit and the Bible: Do They Presuppose the Same Canaanite Mythology and Religion?" in *Ugarit and the Bible: Proceedings of the International Symposium on Ugarit and the Bible, Manchester, September 1992* (ed. George J. Brooke, Adrian H. W. Curtis, and John F. Healey; UBL 11; Münster: Ugarit-Verlag, 1994), 35–52 (44).

Death and Feasting in the Isaiah Apocalypse (Isaiah 25:6–8)

Paul Kang-Kul Cho and Janling Fu

1. Text

⁶ ועשה יהוה צבאות
לכל־העמים בהר הזה
משתה שמנים
משתה שמרים
שמנים ממחים
שמרים מזקקים
⁷ ובלע בהר הזה
פני־הלוט הלוט
על־כל־העמים
והמסכה הנסוכה
על־כל־הגוים
⁸ בלע המות לנצח
ומחה אדני יהוה דמעה
מעל כל־פנים
וחרפת עמו יסיר
מעל כל־הארץ
כי יהוה דבר

⁶ Yhwh of Hosts will prepare,
For all peoples, on this mountain,
A feast of rich foods,
A feast of aged wine,
Of rich foods filled with marrow,
Of aged wine well refined.
⁷ He will swallow on this mountain
The cover that covers
All the peoples

And the veil cast
Over all the nations.
[8] He will swallow death in perpetuity.
The Lord YHWH will wipe away the tears
from all faces
And the reproach of his people, he will remove
from all the earth.
For YHWH has spoken.[1] (Isa 25:6–8)

Isaiah 25:6–8 describes an extraordinary event, even for the body of writings that is the Isaiah Apocalypse. "YHWH of Hosts," it proclaims, "will prepare, for all peoples, on this mountain, a feast of rich foods, a feast of aged wine" (v. 6a).[2] To boot, it declares—according to most modern translations—that YHWH "will swallow death in perpetuity" (v. 8aα). The climactic event of this extravagant feast YHWH prepares for all peoples is YHWH feasting on death, God swallowing the swallower. This shocking image has troubled ancient and modern exegetes alike, and they have proposed a number of translations and textual emendations in order to temper the shock. In this paper, however, we defend the MT and argue that v. 8aα is integral to the literary design and theological message of Isa 25:6–8. We pay particular attention to the multifaceted identity of death and the ways in which the theme of feasting both underlines the extraordinariness of, and, at the same time, provides the apt condition for, YHWH's swallowing of death.

2. GREEK TRANSLATIONS OF ISAIAH 25:8Aα

We turn first to the issue of translating verse 8aα: בלע המות לנצח. If we take verse 8aα as an independent clause, the logical and grammatical subject could be "the death" (המות). In fact, this is the judgment of the Septuagint, Theodotion, and the Greek tradition behind 1 Corinthians (15:54).[3] While these traditions agree that death is the subject, however, their opinions diverge concerning the verb (בלע). The Septuagint translates the verb (בלע) as an aorist active indicative. This results in the translation: "Death

---

1. Unless otherwise noted, all translations of biblical texts are our own.
2. See Jer 51:39; Ps 23:5.
3. LXX: "Death swallowed [them]" (κατέπιεν ὁ θάνατος); Theodotion: "Death was swallowed up" (κατεπόθη ὁ θάνατος); 1 Cor 15:54: "Death was swallowed up" (κατεπόθη ὁ θάνατος).

swallowed" (κατέπιεν ὁ θάνατος), which makes death appear at the feast, threatening to devour the food and drink God has prepared, the guests, or even God himself. The appearance of death at the feast, no doubt, was theologically problematic to the translators. The Septuagint resolves the problem by making death's destructive activity penultimate to the ultimate graciousness of God. The Septuagint of verse 8a reads: "Death, having prevailed, swallowed them up, but God has again taken away every tear from every face" (κατέπιεν ὁ θάνατος ἰσχύσας, καὶ πάλιν ἀφεῖλεν ὁ θεὸς πᾶν δάκρυον ἀπὸ παντὸς προσώπου; 25:8a NETS).[4] That God's grace trumps death's momentary threat is the point.

Theodotion had a more elegant solution. Objecting to the possibility that death should take part in the feast God prepares, Theodotion reads the verb (בלע) as passive, probably as a *pual*. This produces a more palatable depiction of the events at YHWH's table: "Death was swallowed up" (κατεπόθη ὁ θάνατος). Better still is Symmachus who makes God the (implied) subject of a future and active verb: "He [God] will make death to be swallowed up" (καταποθῆναι ποιήσει τὸν θάνατον). Both translations avoid depicting God swallowing death, although in doing so, they correctly recognize that the eschatological feast might be a dangerous occasion for death.

Returning to the MT, God alone is the active subject throughout the pericope (Isa 25:6–8). He takes the uncommon step of preparing the feast himself (25:6; cf. Jer 51:39; Ps 23:5).[5] He also is the one who will swallow the covering and the veil, the accoutrements of mourning (v. 7), and the one who wipes away the tears and removes the reproach of his people, the experience of death (v. 8). This implies that, as Symmachus correctly translates, we should understand God as the subject in Isa 25:8aα. As for the tense of the verb, we should understand it as future, since all the other verbs in the pericope are future, including the same verb (בלע) in

---

4. The word ἰσχύσας translates לנצח, which the Septuagint took verbally to mean "to be preeminent, victorious."

5. In Jer 51:31, the feast YHWH prepares is a means for punishing and judging Babylon. In Ps 23:5, YHWH prepares a feast as an award for his flock in the presence of the flock's enemies. Isaiah 25:6–8, without speculating on the history of tradition, may be understood as combining the two related motifs found in Jer 51 and Ps 23: The feast God prepares for all peoples is the locus of both judgment for the enemy of his flock and for rewarding his flock. We argue this point in greater detail below.

verse 7.[6] The resulting translation reads, "He [YHWH] will swallow death in perpetuity."

3. Death the Swallower, Swallowed

If we are correct in understanding Isa 25:8aα in this way, then the Septuagint translation, "death swallowed," conveys a meaning nearly diametrically opposed to the one intended by the Hebrew prophet. However, we should note that, if the Vorlage of the Septuagint was the MT, the Septuagint translation is grammatically possible. In fact, it may be argued that the prophet intended the phrase to be misread in precisely the way the Septuagint translates it. The ambiguity of Hebrew grammar and the strong traditional connection between death and swallowing, as we will discuss below, encourages the reader to construe the exact reading the Septuagint preserves. That is to say, the eschatological prophet may have intended the reader to first misread the ambiguous phrase בלע המות as "death swallowed" before deciphering its proper meaning: "God will swallow death."

Nicholas J. Tromp writes, "blʻ 'to swallow,' is a favourite word for characterizing the way Sheol receives the dead. The term evokes the unquenchable appetite and voracious muzzle of Sir Death."[7] In other words, the use of the verb בלע to characterize the descent into the netherworld in the Hebrew Bible alludes to a personified, and possibly deified, death comparable to the Ugaritic god of death, Mot. We turn first to the Ugaritic evidence.

Mot, in the final two tablets of the Baal Cycle (KTU 1.5–6), is understood as voracious and insatiable. When sending his messengers to Mot, Baal warns them to beware of Mot's mouth. He says:

> But take care, divine servants:
> Do not get too close to Divine Mot,
> Do not let him take you like a lamb in his mouth,
> Like a kid crushed in the chasm of his throat. (KTU 1.4.viii.14–20)[8]

---

6. Joseph Blenkinsopp (*Isaiah 1–39: A New Translation with Introduction and Commentary* [AB 19; New York: Doubleday, 2000], 358) proposes that a *waw* originally preceded the בלע.

7. Nicholas J. Tromp, *Primitive Conceptions of Death and the Nether World in the Old Testament* (Rome: Pontifical Biblical Institute, 1969), 172.

8. All translations of the Baal Cycle are taken from Mark S. Smith, trans., "The Baal Cycle," in *Ugaritic Narrative Poetry* (ed. Simon B. Parker; SBLWAW 9; Atlanta:

Mot was aware of his reputation as an indiscriminate and beastly devourer and protests to Baal:

> Is my appetite the appetite of the lion in the wild
> Or the desire of the dolphin in the sea?
> Or does it go to a pool like a buffalo,
> Or travel to a spring like a hind,
> Or, truly, does my appetite devour like an ass? (*KTU* 1.5.i.14–19)

He ends his protest with a reference to a feast where he threatens to kill Baal (*KTU* 1.5.i.22–27). In any case, if this protest was meant to disarm Baal, to cloud his judgment, it seems to have worked. Baal, who had warned his messengers to beware of Mot's mouth, himself falls victim to Mot's appetite. The actual scene of Baal's death and entrance into Mot's belly, the netherworld, is not preserved in the extant tablets, but his demise is foretold twice (probably by Mot himself). Mot says to Baal:

> Surely you will descend into Divine Mot's throat
> Into the gullet of El's Beloved, the Hero. (*KTU* 1.5.i.6–8)

Elsewhere, it reads:

> [One lip to He]ll, one lip to Heaven,
> [a to]ngue to the Stars.
> [Ba]al will enter his innards,
> Into his mouth he will descend like a dried olive,
> Produce of the earth, and fruit of the trees. (*KTU* 1.5.ii.2–6)

We note that a similar image is used to depict the appetite of the goodly gods in *KTU* 1.23, a text we will discuss in greater detail below:

> They set a lip to earth
> A lip to heaven.
> Then enter their mouths
> Fowl of the sky,
> And fish from the sea. (*KTU* 1.23.61–63)[9]

Scholars Press, 1997), 81–180. Smith also includes a transcription of the original texts, for those who want to consult them.

9. All translations of *KTU* 1.23 are taken from Mark S. Smith, trans., *The Rituals*

We also find similar language used as a metaphor to describe the prideful and the wicked in Ps 73: "They set their mouths against heaven, and their tongues range over the earth" (Ps 73:9 NRSV). These passages clearly indicate that Mot was thought to have an insatiable appetite. He opens his mouth, his upper lip to heaven and the lower to the netherworld, and swallows all that enters without discrimination. To enter his mouth, to be swallowed, and to pass through his throat and gullet is to enter the realm of death. Mot's mouth, throat, and gullet are the passageway to the netherworld, Mot's belly.[10] It is important to note that, in the Baal Cycle, Baal himself enters Mot's throat and dies, if only temporarily.

In the Hebrew Bible, death is not often depicted as a deity (see Isa 28:15, 18), though it is less infrequently personified (Hos 13:14; Hab 2:5).[11] Nevertheless, the biblical writers did use language that echoes and alludes to the personified conception of the chthonic powers and the realm of death we see more clearly in the Ugaritic literature just surveyed. In short, the Hebrew Bible conceives of death and the netherworld, in part, as a voracious and insatiable swallower.

This becomes evident in several metaphors used to describe a variety of negative, human characteristics. We saw already that the wicked are described as Mot-like in Ps 73. Habakkuk also compares greed and arrogance to personified death:

> Moreover, wealth is treacherous;
> the arrogant do not endure.
> They open their throats wide as Sheol;
> like Death they never have enough.
> They gather all nations for themselves,
> and collect all peoples as their own. (Hab 2:5 NRSV)

Proverbs compares violence to death:

> Like Sheol let us swallow (בלע) them alive
> and whole, like those who go down to the Pit. (Prov 1:12 NRSV)

---

and Myths of the Feast of the Goodly Gods of KTU/CAT 1.23: Royal Constructions of Opposition, Intersection, Integration, and Domination (SBLRBS 51; Atlanta: SBL, 2006).

10. Paul Layton Watson, "Mot, the God of Death, at Ugarit and in the Old Testament" (Ph.D. diss., Yale University, 1971), 145.

11. John F. Healey, "MOT מות," DDD, 598–603 (598).

It is interesting to note that Death, Sheol, and the Pit are used as the vehicle, as opposed to the tenor, in the metaphor. That is to say, the characteristics of personified death as a swallower are, to a certain extent, assumed to be more common and more familiar than greed, arrogance, and violence!

Death, however, does not only swallow figuratively. It also swallows its victims literally. In several passages, the netherworld (ארץ), much like the personified death, is imagined to have a mouth, which it opens to swallow its victims. We see this in the following passages: the Song at the Sea (Exod 15:12), in the judgment scene of Korah (Dothan and Abiram; Num 16:30, 32), and in Isaiah's oracle against the Jerusalem elite (Isa 5:14).

> The netherworld (ארץ) swallowed (בלע) them up. (Exod 15:12)

> But if YHWH creates something new, and the ground (אדמה) opens its mouth and swallows (בלע) them up, with all that belongs to them, and they go down alive into Sheol, then you shall know that these men have despised YHWH….The [netherworld] (ארץ) opened its mouth and swallowed (בלע) them up, along with their households—everyone who belonged to Korah and all their goods. (Num 16:30, 32, adapted from NRSV; see also 26:10; Deut 11:6; Ps 106:17)

> Therefore Sheol has enlarged its appetite
> and opened its mouth beyond measure;
> the nobility of Jerusalem and her multitude go down,
> her throng and all who exult in her. (Isa 5:14 NRSV)

In these passages, the netherworld acts at YHWH's command. Death is YHWH's instrument of punishment. That is to say, death and the netherworld are not self-determinative agents who can choose to swallow the living at their will. Those who go down to Sheol do so at the pleasure of YHWH, not for the pleasure of hungry death. While YHWH does not reside in the netherworld, he nevertheless rules over it. Overall, there is little, if any, hint of dualism in the Hebrew Bible when it comes to YHWH and death, in contrast to what we find in the Baal Cycle.

Returning to our discussion of the characteristics of death, Tromp demonstrates that the biblical authors used a number of words and phrases to talk about entering the realm of death.[12] The dead also "return"

---

12. Tromp, *Primitive Conceptions of Death*, 167–75.

(שוב) or "descend" (ירד) to Sheol, are "gathered" (אסף) to their peoples or "sleep" (ישׁי) with their fathers (אבותיו), and so on. But Tromp is right to characterize בלע as a common word for characterizing the way Sheol receives the dead. He is also right to note that בלע evokes personified death, since swallowing is a metaphor taken from the realm of human and animal behavior. Traditio-historically, there is an intimate connection between death and swallowing, a connection that was so familiar to the biblical writers that it could be used to illustrate the common vices of greed, arrogance, and violence.

Given this connection between death and swallowing, we can say that, when the prophet of Isa 25:8aα juxtaposes the figure of death and the verb בלע, he invites his reader to mishear and to mistake death as the swallowing agent at the feast. That is the dictate of tradition. This invitation to failure was not without purpose, however. The ambiguity sets up the reader not only for failure but also for an epiphanic awakening. By virtue of the misread phrase: בלע המות, death appears uninvited at the feast and threatens not only to devour the rich foods and the aged wines but also the guests and, if we are right to hear an echo of the Baal Cycle in which Mot swallows Baal, YHWH himself. The celebratory feast of YHWH's kingship is at the brink, so it would seem, of turning into a funerary feast. However, the would-be usurper is swallowed as soon as he appears on the scene. The emphatic identification of God, "The Lord YHWH," in the next phrase puts the lie to the fear that he might have been swallowed. And the tender, confident image of him wiping away human tears and removing the reproach of his people forces the reader to reread the ambiguous words: בלע המות לנצח, and discover in them a still more shocking meaning: Death will consume nothing. Rather, YHWH will swallow death in perpetuity. With this realization, the momentary pall is removed from the face of the reader—as perhaps the covering and the veil will be removed from all the peoples gathered at the feast. If we imagine the feast as an actual event, we can imagine the initial shock and fear of the people at seeing death. We can also imagine their relief and joy at its immediate destruction. Through misrecognition, the reader's experience of the text is made to mirror the experience of the eschatological celebrants at YHWH's table—the transformation of fear into joy and mourning into dancing.

In this light, the Septuagint translation redeems itself as a strong misreading that preserves a hidden meaning of the Hebrew. It preserves and makes explicit an intended misreading, thereby reminding us of the real threat of imminent death and the enduring comfort of God's ultimate victory over death: "Death, having prevailed, swallowed them up, but God has again taken away every tear from every face" (LXX Isa 25:8a NETS).

4. INTEGRITY OF ISA 25:6–8

Many past exegetes, as we discuss below, have judged that Isa 25:8aα was secondarily added to verses 6–8 either as a gloss or as an intensification of YHWH's activities, thus assigning the rhetorical artistry of the quarter verse to a later redactor. However, we agree with those who argue for the original integrity of verses 6–8. While the two common reasons given against the integrity of verses 8aα are not devoid of merit, the counter arguments are in sum stronger.

One reason cited to argue that verse 8aα is secondary is that the phrase disrupts the flow of imagery in verses 7–8. The appearance of death as an abstract personality does not belong to the sequence of concrete images (covering, veil, and tears) and, moreover, interrupts the narrative sequence. Otto Kaiser writes, the phrase "interrupts the direct continuity of thought between v. 7 and v. 8a; the covering which a mourner has over his face is removed, and then his tears are wiped away."[13]

We are sympathetic to this line of argumentation because we think that a narrative logic does bind Isa 25:6–8 together. In principle, however, we object to performing redactional surgery on the text to conform to a particular reading when other reasons, in this case structural and thematic, may speak better to the text's integrity.

In this regard, Hans Wildberger asks a simple but perceptive question: "Why was the verb בלע (lit.: swallow up) used?"[14] On the one hand, as we already discussed above, the complex of death, the netherworld, and the verb בלע is traditio-historically connected. Thus, the use of the verb בלע in verse 8 makes good sense. The inversion of the expected image of the swallowing death is an imaginative but recognizable transformation of a traditional motif. It presents the familiar and then defamiliarizes it in order to articulate a novel and profound theological insight: God abolishes death, the source of sorrow and shame, to inaugurate the eschatological kingdom of God. But, on the other hand, why does the prophet say that YHWH swallows up the cover and the veil in verse 7? The use of בלע in verse 7, taken

---

13. Otto Kaiser, *Isaiah 13–39* (Louisville: Westminster John, 1974), 199.

14. Hans Wildberger, *Isaiah 13–27* (trans. Thomas H. Trapp; CC; Minneapolis: Fortress, 1991), 532.

by itself, is awkward and, as a metaphor, adds no new insight. However, the use becomes more understandable when it is read as anticipatory of its (im)proper use in verse 8aα. The odd combination of subject (Yhwh), verb (בלע), and object (covering and veil) in verse 7 encourages the reader to search for the proper combination of subject, verb, and object. He finds it, so he thinks, in verse 8aα: Death will swallow. We discussed above how this baited misreading leads to the radical theological insight that God, not death, will do the swallowing. So to answer Wildberger's questions: The prophet used the verb בלע in verse 7 in anticipation of its use in verse 8. If we take away verse 8aα as secondary, it becomes difficult to explain the use of בלע in verse 7.

More than rhetoric connects the two uses of the verb בלע. They are also connected structurally and thematically. Structurally, it has been noted that verse 7aα and verse 8aα form an *inclusio*: "And he will swallow on this mountain.… he will swallow death in perpetuity." This is related to the thematic connection. We know that heads and faces were covered as a sign of mourning in ancient Israel (2 Sam 15:30; 19:5; Jer 14:13–14; Esth 6:12). The references to the cover and the veil should be interpreted in this light. The *inclusio*, then, both frames and connects the destruction of the cause of mourning, death (v. 8aα), and the expressions of mourning, covering and veil (v. 7). Furthermore, the motifs of tears and reproach, as instantiations of death-like experiences (v. 8), are extensions of the same moribund theme.[15] Therefore, the destruction of death is the middle term among the five actions God takes against death and its accessories (the covering, the veil, death, the tears, and the reproach) and may be understood as the thematic and structural keystone of the pericope. In short, verse 8aα is the rhetorical, thematic, and structural focal point of verses 7–8 and cannot be held to be secondary.

Another reason cited for the secondary status of verse 8aα is the argument that the ideological content of the quarter verse must be later than the original layer of the so-called Isaiah Apocalypse, to which 25:6–8 belongs. Joseph Blenkinsopp sums up this second reason in this way:

> The following verse, announcing the eschatological overcoming of death, is often assumed to be a later addition on the grounds that belief in a

---

15. As we discuss below, such things as "persecutions, oppression, need, and illness" were understood as "partial but real death" by the ancients (Tromp, *Primitive Conceptions of Death*, 213).

spiritually and morally meaningful postmortem existence only emerged clearly in the late biblical and early postbiblical periods—whether in the form of a selective resurrection of the dead (Dan 12:2) or some form of astral immortality (Eccl 3:21), or the Orphic-Platonic doctrine of the immortality of the soul (Wis 2:33–34).[16]

Several arguments can be made against this line of reasoning.

First, to cite Blenkinsopp, "it is rather risky to draw conclusions [about dating] on the basis of such partial and incomplete attestation, quite apart from the question whether we can claim that such an idea was unknown (e.g., to the authors of Pss 16 and 73) simply because [it was] not clearly articulated."[17] Blenkinsopp rightly questions whether the language of God swallowing death refers to postmortem existence or resurrection. He argues that "the wording seems to have been chosen to recall the old Canaanite myth of Mot" and that death here refers not to individual death but to "a force of disorder, negativity, and aridity, morally and physically."[18] The verse refers to an ancient myth and not necessarily to a later concept of postmortem existence. In addition, even if Isa 25:8aα refers to the idea of resurrection, it need not necessarily be dated late to a secondary layer. According to Blenkinsopp, the concept of postmortem existence or resurrection was not unknown to the author of the Isaiah Apocalypse. He argues that the theme is found in Isa 26:19.[19]

Second, Wildberger argues for the integrity of Isa 25:6–8 on the ground that there exists traditio-historical precedence for combining the theme of God's kingdom and death in Ps 22. Reading Ps 22:30a as "Indeed, to him [אך לו for MT אכלו] will bow down all who sleep [ישני for MT דשני] in the netherworld / all who go down to the dust will kneel before him," Wildberger notes that, in the kingdom of God, "the dead are brought into the relationship where they would be under the control of Yahweh."[20] The point is that speculations about YHWH's kingdom inevitably "stretch out over the whole world" and, therefore, must deal with "the problem of the dead—and death itself."[21] Thus, Wildberger finds "no valid reason for

---

16. Blenkinsopp, *Isaiah 1–39*, 359.
17. Ibid.
18. Ibid.
19. Ibid., 370–71.
20. Wildberger, *Isaiah 13–27*, 529.
21. Ibid.

treating this little phrase [He will swallow death] as an insertion by a later hand."[22] Rather, he argues that tradition history supports the combination of the theme of God's kingdom and death and that logic dictates that speculations about the kingdom of God, of necessity, include speculations about the fate of death. That God destroys death at the feast inaugurating his eschatological kingdom in Isa 25:6–8 is to be expected.

To these arguments, we can add a third reason that, to our knowledge, has escaped scholarly notice. As Blenkinsopp noted, it is not clear that our passage articulates a belief in postmortem existence or resurrection. What we do have in Isa 25:6–8, at the basic level, is the destruction of the figure of death within a feasting context. We have an analogous situation in *KTU* 1.23, what Mark S. Smith has recently called The Feast of the Goodly Gods. The text can be divided into two parts. The first part (lines 1–29) is a ritual text concerning a feast with embedded narrative and mythic elements. The second part (lines 30–76) is a narrative, mythic text about the double birth of El's children, Dawn and Dusk (*šḥr wšlm*), and the goodly gods ('*ilm n'mm*). It is a complex text that challenges generic boundaries, boundaries between inside and outside, and the binary understanding of destruction and death, on the one hand, and life and feasting, on the other.[23] For our purposes, it suffices to point out that within the ritual portion of the text concerning the feast is embedded a mythic episode that recounts the destruction of Mot, here referred to by a rare composite name: Mot and Shar (Death and Ruler). In the beginning of the text (lines 1–7), an unidentified speaker, perhaps a priest, invites the goodly gods, the king, the queen, and possibly others to a feast. The text about Mot's destruction follows immediately afterward:

Death-and-Ruler sits,
In his (one) hand a staff of bereavement
In his (other) hand a staff of widowhood.
The pruner prunes him (like) a vine,
The binder binds him (like) a vine,
He is felled to the terrace like a vine. (*KTU* 1.23.8–11)

We already know from the famous text in the Baal Cycle that Mot can be and is destroyed by Anat (*KTU* 1.6.ii.30–37). What The Feast of the

---

22. Ibid., 530.
23. See Smith, *Rituals and Myths of the Feast of the Goodly Gods*, 16–18, 145–66.

Goodly Gods teaches us that the Baal Cycle does not is that the destruction of death within the framework of feasting was a theme known in Canaan already in the second millennium. Therefore, that YHWH swallows death at his table shocks, but not necessarily due to its innovation. As with many biblical themes, what we find in Isa 25:8aα may be an Israelite transformation of a well-known Canaanite motif present in *KTU* 1.23: the swallowing or the destruction of death within a feasting context. Thus verse 8aα does not need to be excised as a late interpolation on the ground that its ideological content is late. Indeed, it may very well be early.

5. MULTIPLE ASPECTS OF DEATH

The task that remains before we turn to consider the frame of feasting within which death is destroyed is the identification of death in the passage. Our task here is expedited by the fact that we have touched on several aspects of death already and, for the most part, requires only a summary statement. One aspect we have not discussed and so will need to be covered in some detail is the relationship between death and the foreign nations.

The first aspect of death in Isa 25:8aα we must note is that of personified and deified death. As we argued in some detail above, the verb בלע and the figure of death are closely connected in biblical tradition, which likely reflects a more widespread Canaanite mythological tradition about the god of death. This chthonic deity is understood to be voracious and to have an insatiable appetite, which he tries to satisfy by swallowing all living things without discrimination. Naturally, Mot is also closely connected to the theme of feasting. In the Baal Cycle, he invites Baal to a feast and possibly devours him in that context (*KTU* 1.5.i.12–27). In The Feast of the Goodly Gods, the destruction of Mot is narrated within a feasting context. These analogies, the traditio-historical connection between death and the verb בלע, and the thematic connection between death and feasting make it likely that the death that appears in Isa 25:8aα evokes the god of death. Looking forward, it can be suggested that YHWH's swallowing of death has transformative, cosmic consequences. It is not merely figurative. Rather, it is a profound theological statement about the nature of YHWH's kingdom.

Second, death in Isa 25:8aα is also related more generally to life's ills. We noted above that verse 7aα and verse 8aα form an *inclusio*. This brings the images of YHWH swallowing "the covering" and "the veil" and of him swallowing "the death" into a close relationship with one another. In fact, the two actions may be interpreted as constituting two aspects of a single event. We know that ancient Israelites covered their faces and heads as a sign of mourning. David, for example, covers his head to mourn Absalom's coup (2 Sam 15:30), and he also covers (לאט, a biform of לוט; see Isa 25:7) his face to mourn Absalom's death (2 Sam 19:5). The example of David highlights an important distinction between ancient Israelite and our modern understanding of death. Death, for the ancient Israelites, did not necessary mean the absolute cessation of biological life. Death was anything that negates the full enjoyment of life, such as political trouble, bodily lack or sickness, or emotional distress. Wildberger puts it well:

> A person is in the realm of *mot* or in שאול (Sheol) already when being afflicted by a terrible illness. Mot is anything that causes trouble during one's life, is that which limits the way in which one lives life, is that which takes something away from one's prosperity and gets in the way of fellowship with other humans or with God.[24]

In short, "just as death in the strictest sense of the term is the weakest form of life, so any weakness in life is a form of death."[25] The destruction of death within a feasting context may, therefore, be interpreted as the destruction of the darkly powers over one's body, mind, or heart that prohibit the full participation in joyful celebration, such as an eschatological feast of Yнwн's kingship.

Third, death in Isa 25:8aα may also be associated with foreign nations that caused reproach for Israel. Isaiah 25:6–8 is characterized by a universal spirit, but it strikes a note of particularism in verse 8a: "He will remove the reproach of his people from all the earth." God here not only singles out his people Israel for special treatment but, it can be argued, also differentiates Israel from the foreign nations for purposes of judgment and vindication.

The motif of reproach (חרפה) is closely related to the antagonistic relationship between Israel and certain foreign nations in the Hebrew Bible. As Donald Polaski argues in detail, foreign nations are often portrayed as

---

24. Wildberger, *Isaiah 13–27*, 533. See also Shannon Burkes, *Death and Qoheleth and Egyptian Biographies of the Late Period* (SBLDS 170; Atlanta: SBL, 1999), 14–15 and n. 21.

25. Aubrey R. Johnson cited in Tromp, *Primitive Conceptions of Death*, 129.

agents who reproach Israel or turn Israel into a reproach.[26] An interesting example is found in Zephaniah:

> I [YHWH] have heard the reproach of Moab [מואב חרפת]
> and the revilings of the Ammonites,
> how they have reproached my people [את עמי חרפו]
> and made boasts against their territory. (Zeph 2:8 esv)

This verse is obviously of interest for Isa 25:10a–11, where "Moab is singled out, not for personal spite, but as the symbol of arrogance and pride that rejects the inclusion of all nations under the rule of Yahweh, Lord of hosts."[27] Does the introduction of the "reproach" motif anticipate the Moab oracle (Isa 25:10a–11)?[28]

We find another example of the connection between the theme of reproach and foreign nations in Lamentations:

> Remember, O YHWH, what has befallen us;
> look, and see our reproach [חרפתנו].
> Our inheritance has been turned over to strangers,
> our homes to aliens. (Lam 5:1–2, adapted from NRSV)

The author of Lamentations characterizes the loss of homeland that accompanied exile as a reproach and makes use of insider/outsider language. That outsiders occupy Israel is understood as a reproach.

Now, God sometimes himself causes reproach for Israel. "I [YHWH] will make them [Israelites] a horror, an evil thing, to all the kingdoms of the earth—a reproach [חרפה], a byword, a taunt, and a curse in all the places where I shall drive them" (Jer 24:9, adapted from NRSV). But more often, we find that, when the language of reproach is used, foreign nations are identified as the perpetrators (Pss 44:14; 74:22; 89:42, 51; Isa 51:7; Jer 24:9; Ezek 5:14, 15; 16:57; 22:4; 36:30; Joel 2:17, 19). Israel is usually the victim of reproach at the hand of foreign peoples (sometimes but not always at the request of God).

What this means for our passage, then, is that Isa 25:8 is not a neutral form of Israelite particularism within a universal horizon but a discerning

---

26. Donald C. Polaski, *Authorizing an End: The Isaiah Apocalypse and Intertextuality* (BibInt 50; Leiden: Brill, 2001), 188–92.

27. Brevard S. Childs, *Isaiah* (OTL; Louisville: Westminster John Knox, 2001), 185.

28. Polaski, *Authorizing an End*, 192–98.

one that differentiates between Israel and the foreign nations and between friendly and hostile nations. Though we do not want to press this identity too strongly, the allusion to antagonistic foreign nations that the language of "reproach" (חרפה) implies indicates a connection between foreign nations and death. Thus, for God to swallow death may suggest a scene of judgment against (some of) the foreign nations who have been invited to the eschatological feast. Here, we might mention the Targum of Isaiah, which reads:

> On this mountain the LORD of hosts will make for all peoples a feast and a festival; they think that it is of glory, but it will be to them for shame, strokes from which they will not be rescued, strokes by which they will come to an end. And the face of the great one who is master over all the peoples, and the face of the king who rules over all the kingdom will be annihilated on this mountain. They will forget death forever, and the LORD God will wipe away the tears from all faces and the reproaches of his peoples, he will take away from all the earth; for by the Memra of the LORD it is so decreed. (*Tg. Isa.* 25:6–8)[29]

According to the Targum, God invites the foreign nations not to a feast in which they are glorified, as replacements of the gods and kings who usually come to these feasts, but for judgment. The Targum, as with the Septuagint, lays bare perhaps a hidden meaning that falls deaf to our modern ears, a note of national particularism within a text otherwise marked by universalism. The Targum, in our mind, goes too far in condemning all the peoples to shame. We should likely distinguish between hostile and friendly foreign nations, between those who rebel and submit to YHWH's reign. Nevertheless, the Targum correctly warns against an easy tendency toward a universal reading of the text.

In sum, death in Isa 25:8aα may be understood as that composite power responsible for the termination of bodily life, the misfortunes one experiences between birth and death, and the national and personal reproach suffered by those forced to migrate by foreign powers from homeland into exile. Death, in other words, is a chthonic deity and the source of suffering in life, including the political and military powers that have and are doing harm to God's people.

---

29. Bruce D. Chilton, *The Isaiah Targum: Introduction, Translation, Apparatus and Notes* (ArBib 11; Wilmington, Del.: Michael Glazier, 1987), 49–50.

6. Feasting and Kingship

To this point we have focused on those aspects of death we deem important to the full understanding of Isa 25:6–8. We now turn our attention to the framing motif of feasting by first noting a number of general aspects of feasting that are relevant for our pericope, then analyzing the artistic interplay between the motif of death and feasting. As we set forth below, Isa 25:6–8 is an integrated whole that skillfully uses conventions related to feasting in order to overturn, in surprising and theologically significant ways, traditional conceptions of death in relation to the feast.

A feast, to be distinguished from both the exchange of food and drink and from the daily meal, is marked by, among other features, "the quantity of food, the number of participants, the length of the meal, [and] the social distance of the participants."[30] These elements will be important to the analysis below. Now, the ability to host a feast in itself was a sign of wealth, if not always of social prestige.[31] As such, as others have noted, feasting is closely connected to kingship in the Hebrew Bible.[32] For example, 1 Sam 25:36 makes an explicit connection between feasting and kingship: "[Nabal] was holding a feast in his house, like a feast of a king." Similarly, Pharaoh (Gen 40), Solomon (1 Kgs 3:15; 10:5), Belshazzar (Dan 5), and Ahasuerus (Esth 1), all kingly figures, are depicted as hosts of lavish feasts.

Accordingly, that Yhwh is depicted as hosting an extravagant feast for all nations in the Isaiah Apocalypse indicates his status as king. The eschatological writer claims Yhwh's kingship in other ways as well and makes the royal connotation of the feast more likely. For example, the closely related passage, Isa 24:21–23, depicts Yhwh exercising his kingly authority to judge the "host of heaven" and "the kings of earth" and pronounces

---

30. Nathan MacDonald, *Not Bread Alone: The Uses of Food in the Old Testament* (Oxford: Oxford University Press, 2008), 144. Michael Dietler ("Theorizing the Feast: Rituals of Consumption, Commensal Politics, and Power in African Contexts," in *Feasts: Archaeological and Ethnographical Perspectives on Food, Politics, and Power* [ed. Michael Dietler and Brian Hayden; Tuscaloosa, Ala.: University of Alabama Press, 2001], 65–114 [69–70]) writes: "To adapt a concept from linguistics analysis, feasts may be viewed as the 'marked' form of the 'unmarked' meal."

31. That Job's seven sons are able to hold a feast, "each on his day," is indicative of the hyperbolic wealth of the house of Job (Job 1:4).

32. MacDonald, *Not Bread Alone*, 134–65, esp. 154–60.

outright that "Yнwн of Hosts is king on Mount Zion and in Jerusalem."[33] Yнwн who hosts the feast "on this mountain," no doubt also Zion, is king.

The rich description of the feast in Isa 25:6 provides further details about Yнwн's kingship.

> Yнwн of Hosts will prepare,
> For all peoples, on this mountain,
> A feast of rich foods,
> A feast of aged wine,
> Of rich foods filled with marrow,
> Of aged wine well refined.

The details describing the foods and the participants in verse 6 underscore Yнwн's status as exalted king. As we noted above, "this mountain" on which Yнwн prepares a feast no doubt refers to Mount Zion, the royal mountain of God (24:23b).[34] Israel, and more specifically Jerusalem, is the seat of Yнwн's kingship. We should not fail to note the particularism of this claim. However, Yнwн's kingdom is not limited to Israel, his kingship subordinate to the kingship of a higher power (see Deut 32:8–9). In this light, it is to be noted that the feast is said to be for "all peoples." Nathan MacDonald writes that the "king's table was very important for creating and maintaining political support" and goes on to note that, on the one hand, to be invited to the king's table was an invitation "to join the royal

---

33. Isaiah 24:21–23 and 25:6–8, now separated by a psalm of praise (25:1–5), are closely related, as they both deal with Yнwн's kingship as demonstrated on "that mountain," that is, Zion. See J. Todd Hibbard, *Intertextuality in Isaiah 24–27: The Reuse and Evocation of Earlier Texts and Traditions* (FAT 2/16; Tübingen: Mohr Siebeck, 2006), 75; William R. Millar, *Isaiah 24–27 and the Origin of Apocalyptic* (HSM 11; Missoula, Mont.: Scholars Press, 1976), 65; Polaski, *Authorizing an End*, 161–62. The garden imagery of Isa 27:2–6 may be understood as referring to Yнwн's royal garden and thus to his kingship. Job Y. Jindo (*Biblical Metaphor Reconsidered: A Cognitive Approach to Poetic Prophecy in Jeremiah 1–24* [HSM 64; Winona Lake, Ind.: Eisenbrauns, 2010], 158) writes, "In the Bible, while the locus of the divine garden remains in the mytho-poetic sphere, the temple or the temple-city is conceived of as an earthly representation of the divine garden." He also writes that "the motif of the divine garden is modeled after the notion of the royal garden" (155). Note that there is an interplay between Israelite particularism and universalism in this verse as in Isa 25:6–8 (see Isa 27:6).

34. Jon D. Levenson, *Sinai and Zion: An Entry into the Jewish Bible* (NVBS; New York: HarperCollins, 1985), 122.

household," to eat "at the king's table like one of the king's sons" (2 Sam 9:11) and, on the other, to be excluded was an indication of "disfavour or political exclusion."[35] Thus, that YHWH's feast is for all peoples indicates that all peoples are invited to join YHWH's royal household, for foreign peoples to move from the outside to join the Israelites inside as the children of God.[36] Foreign participation, as a correlative to invitation, would then signal assent to YHWH as host and king. In this context, we might note that the royal banqueting tradition known from the ancient Near East reflects on the abundance of at least purported bounty. The most well-known of these, the feast of Asshurnasirpal II, records a banquet on the occasion of the founding of his capital, Nimrud/Kalhu, to which nearly seventy thousand people were invited.[37] YHWH's unusual bounty signals the inauguration of his universal kingship. From Zion, YHWH rules over all peoples.

The description of the food and drink on offer, and the artistic way in which this is set forth, is further indication of the glory of the host. The hyperbolically rich food and drink, first of all, point to the largesse and wealth of the host. Furthermore, the carefully crafted poetry of the verse underlines this fact.

A feast of rich foods,	AB (5)
A feast of aged wine,	AC (5)
Of rich foods filled with marrow	BD (7)
Of aged wine well refined.	CE (7)

---

35. MacDonald, *Not Bread Alone*, 157, 158.

36. See Janling Fu, "The Archaeological Signature of Feasting: Theoretical and Methodological Aspects" (paper presented at the annual meeting of the American School of Oriental Research, San Francisco, November 2011).

37. See the edition by D. J. Wiseman, "A New Stele of Assur-nasir-pal," *Iraq* 14 (1952): 24–44. We might add to this the iconographic attestations of the feast extending back to the third millennium B.C.E. to the Standard of Ur, then in the second and first millennium B.C.E. in the Megiddo ivories, and the later traditions of the Levant. On this, see, e.g., Frances Pinnock, "Considerations on the 'Banquet Theme' in the Figurative Art of Mesopotamia and Syria," in *Drinking in Ancient Societies: History and Culture of Drinks in the Ancient Near East: Papers of a Symposium Held in Rome, May 17–19, 1990* (ed. Lucio Milano; Padova: Sargon, 1994), 15–26; Irit Ziffer, "From Acemhöyük to Megiddo: The Banquet Scene in the Art of the Levant in the Second Millennium BCE," *TA* 32 (2005): 133–67.

Note, first, the patterned repetitions: AB/AC/BD/CE. "Feast" (A) is repeated at the head of the first paired lines, and the two elements paired with (A), "rich foods" (B) and "aged wine" (C), are repeated at the head of the second paired lines, each element intensified with further descriptions (D) and (E), creating an intricate and satisfying whole. It should also be observed that the first paired lines in Hebrew are identical save for one consonant (ר → נ): משתה שמרים // משתה שמנים. In addition, the paired metric scheme (5 / 5 // 7 / 7), the use of alliteration throughout ("m" and "sh"), the repeated vowel pattern between paired lines, and the fact that all four lines rhyme (-îm) mark these lines as high poetry. This is elevated language. Not only are the food and drink items themselves rich and distinctive, so too is the prosody employed to express their richness. The poetic quality of the verse draws attention to itself and, in turn, points to the splendor of the host of the feast.

In sum, the fact that Yhwh prepares a feast indicates that Yhwh is king. This is a feast to celebrate the inauguration of his eschatological kingship. Furthermore, the description of the feast itself, the guests who are invited and the foodstuffs on offer, point to the universal scope of God's kingdom and glory of the host. If the banqueting table is a microcosm of the kingdom, there can be little doubt that the eschatological kingdom of God, according to the prophet, is one of incomparable largesse, wealth, and prosperity.

7. "He Prepared for Them a Feast"

Before we discuss the theme of judgment, already adumbrated in the closely related passage in Isa 24:21–23, it is necessary to analyze the syntactical construction of the opening line: ועשה יהוה צבאות לכל־העמים... משתה (Isa 25:6a). The standard construction concerning the משתה feast follows a pattern: X (subject) + עשה (verb) + ל-Y (indirect object) + משתה (direct object). That is, this is the standard משתה construction: "host-X made for guest-Y a feast." Three illustrative examples of this construction are seen in Gen 19:3; 26:30; and 40:20.[38] In the first instance, Lot prepares a meal for two angelic guests:

---

[38]. That this construction, which we argue is the standard form, is infrequently attested is not problematic (see 1 Kgs 3:15; Esth 1:3; Dan 5:1). Partial attestations are explicable by the fact of ellipsis (see possibly Gen 21:8), and divergences from this

ויבאו אל־ביתו ויעש להם משתה ומצות אפה ויאכלו

And they entered his house. And he prepared for them a feast, and he baked unleavened bread. And they ate. (Gen 19:3)

In the second case, Isaac shows hospitality to Abimelech and his two officers within a covenantal context:

ויעש להם משתה ויאכלו וישתו

And he prepared for them a feast. And they ate and drank. (Gen 26:30)

These two examples illustrate that the preparation of the feast, as is logical, is often followed by its consumption. In the third example, the Pharaoh prepares a feast on the occasion of his birthday:

ויעש משתה לכל־עבדיו

And he prepared a feast for all his servants. (Gen 40:20)

The same standard syntactical construction is used in Isa 25:6a. Here, Yhwh plays the role of host and prepares (עשה) the feast (משתה) for his guests, "all peoples" (לכל־העמים). The use of the conventional syntactic construction establishes a number of expectations concerning the feast that are overturned in the following verses. First, one might expect, given the example from Gen 19 and, perhaps more vividly, Abraham's enthusiastic hospitality toward Yhwh and his divine company in Gen 18, that it should be the people who prepare a feast for Yhwh, those of inferior status for the superior. In contrast, Yhwh prepares the feast here. However, that Yhwh is the host is understandable, as we noted above, within the context of a royal feast in which the king distributes his wealth in exchange for the loyalty of his inferiors. We see the same situation in Gen 40 above and elsewhere in 1 Kgs 3:15; Dan 5; Esth 1; etc. The royal feast is an enactment of present political order used to maintain present relations, or, as is the case in Isa 25, it can be a vehicle for change, to create new relations between superior and inferior, lord and subject, as well as among the subjects.

Feasting also can have a covenantal nuance, as we see clearly in Gen 26. Even when a covenant is not in view, there are assumed strictures that govern the relationship between host and guests and define what actions

---

standard construction are normally understandable given the context (see Judg 14:10, 12, 17).

can and cannot be taken at the table.[39] Perhaps the greatest of such strictures is that the host show hospitality toward the guests or, negatively stated, that the host safeguard the guests from harm. For example, Abimelech says to Isaac,

> We see clearly that YHWH has been with you. So we say, Let there be an oath between us, between you and us, and let us make a covenant with you, that you will do us no harm just as we have not touched you and have done nothing but good, sending you away in peace. You are now blessed of YHWH (Gen 26:28–29).

Abimelech seeks a covenant explicitly related to protection. That Isaac hosts a feast in response is tacit agreement and an actualization of the proposed covenantal relationship. More dramatically, the lengths to which Lot goes to protect his visitors, whom he had invited into his house and for whom he prepared a feast, vividly illustrates the seriousness of a host's obligation to ensure the safety of his guests (Gen 19; cf. Judg 19). Thus, it is reasonable to assume that those who come to the royal feast come, not only in assent to the king's claim to power, but also under the assumption of protection. Those who come, especially in the case of former or potential rivals to the king, come in submission and under protection.

Another convention regarding the feast we need to mention is that the preparation of the feast is followed by its consumption. Isaiah 55:1–5 arguably describes an eschatological meal where God prepares a covenantal feast—the "everlasting covenant, my enduring covenant faithfulness for David" is mentioned (Isa 55:3b).[40] The focus lies on consumption:

> Hey, all who are thirsty, come to the waters!
> Even if you have no money,
> Come, buy, and eat.
> Come, buy wine
> Without money and without price. (Isa 55:1)

---

39. Cristiano Grottanelli, "The Roles of the Guest in the Epic Banquet," in *Production and Consumption in the Ancient Near East* (ed. Carlo Zaccagnini; Budapest: University of Budapest, 1989), 272–332.

40. See, e.g., Richard J. Clifford, "Isaiah 55: Invitation to a Feast," in *The Word of the Lord Shall Go Forth: Essays in Honor of David N. Freedman in Celebration of His Sixtieth Birthday* (ed. Carol L. Meyers and Michael O'Conner; Winona Lake, Ind.: Eisenbrauns, 1983), 27–35.

The act of eating and drinking is presented as the main event, the immediate benefit for the thirsty and hungry that comprises an entrance into a covenantal relationship. We see a like example in Exod 24:11, where the preparatory scene is elided and only the scene of consumption depicted. In contrast to Isa 55:1–5 and Exod 24:11, Isa 25:6 describes the foods and drinks in rich, descriptive poetry, thus heightening the reasonable expectation for the subsequent consumption of food and drink.

However, these last two expectations, that the host safeguard the guests and that the prepared foods be consumed, are seemingly, even spectacularly, broken. Consumption, to be sure, happens. But, in contrast to the expected scene of the guests enjoying their repast, it is the host who swallows "the cover that covers all the peoples and the veil cast over all the nations…[and] death" (25:7–8). Feasting begins with the host consuming what the guests, perhaps unwittingly, have brought with them to the table. And if we are correct to see in the figure of death a reference to nations hostile to Israel, then the feasting also begins with Yhwh seemingly reneging his duty as host to protect his guests. If Isa 25:6 follows the conventional syntactical construction in describing the preparation for the feast, the rest of the passage is a radical departure from the norm: Yhwh will prepare for all peoples a feast, and he will swallow (some of) the peoples!

8. Feasting and Judgment

Yhwh's surprising behavior at the table, quite apart from the fact that he swallows death, breaks conventional expectations concerning the feast but, at the same time, adheres to an important motif related to the trope of feasting, especially royal feasting: judgment. MacDonald, among others, has noted the strong connection between feasting and judgment in the ancient Near East and in the Hebrew Bible.[41] He writes, "In the Old Testament the table is the locus for judgment and vindication."[42] For example, Pharaoh's judgment of his cupbearer and baker in the Joseph story occurs at the table:

> On the third day, Pharaoh's birthday, he prepared a feast for all his servants. And he lifted the head of the chief cupbearer and the head of the chief baker among his servants. He restored the chief cupbearer to his

---

41. MacDonald, *Not Bread Alone*, 166–95.
42. Ibid., 194.

cupbearing, and he placed the cup in Pharaoh's hand; but the chief baker he hanged, just as Joseph had interpreted to them (Gen 40:20–22).

The king's judgment takes place in the context of his birthday banquet, the cupbearer returning immediately to the king's table upon being restored and the baker being hung.[43] The cupbearer and the baker represent the two sides of royal feasting, pardon and condemnation. To mention an example

43. The same connection between feasting and judgment is known from other ancient Near Eastern evidence. For example, this connection is iconically represented in the garden feast of Ashurbanipal. In this well-known scene, Ashurbanipal, accompanied by his seated wife, reclines within a garden setting. Yet hanging from a tree is the head of his enemy, the Elamite king Te-Umman. Dominik Bonatz ("Ashurbanipal's Headhunt: An Anthropological Perspective," *Iraq* 66 [2004]: 93–101 [98]) notes of this scene with Ashurbanipal looking at the severed head of Te-Umman: "This shows that the royal repast is also consecrated to the triumph over an enemy. We may notice how the head of Te-Umman had become a lasting trophy signifying that Ashurbanipal had actively and permanently gained control over his enemies." In Bonatz's view, this was an act of "ritual attention," a "political symbol" that maintains "ideological control of the past" (99). At the same time, it was an act of judgment, for Te-Umman was considered not to have honored the gods. See also David Stronach, "The Imagery of the Wine Bowl: Wine in Assyria in the Early First Millennium B.C.," in *The Origins and Ancient History of Wine* (ed. Patrick E. McGovern, Stuart J. Fleming, and Solomon H. Katz; London: Routledge, 1995), 175–95 (190). The connection of a celebratory banquet following a military victory should be kept in mind with Assyrian reliefs. Note the first two panels of the Black Obelisk of Shalmaneser III, which can be seen to telescope the portrait of war and of banqueting. The tradition, of course, extends back at least to the Standard of Ur. A number of recent works have commented on the connection between judgment and feasting. Besides MacDonald (*Not Bread Alone*), Irene Winter ("The King and the Cup: Iconography of the Royal Presentation Scene on Ur III Seals," in *Insight through Images: Studies in Honor or Edith Porada* [ed. Mariyln Kelly-Buccellati, Paolo Matthiae, and Maurits Van Loon; BMes 21; Malibu: Undena Publications, 1986], 253–68) shows that the king was often depicted as being at feast and that this was connected to his role in judgment. For the king at feast for Achaemenid Persia, see Pierre Briant, *From Cyrus to Alexander: A History of the Persian Empire* (Winona Lake, Ind.: Eisenbrauns, 2002); Wouter F. M. Henkelman "'Consumed before the King.' The Table of Darius, that of Irdabama and Irtaštuna, and that of His Satrap, Kartiš," in *Der Achämenidenhof: Akten des 2. Internationalen Kolloquiums zum Thema "Vorderasien im Spannungsfeld klassicher und altorientalischer Überlieferungen," Landgut Castelen bei Basel, 22.–25. Mai 2007* (ed. Bruno Jacobs and Robert Rollinger; Classica et Orientalia 2; Wiesbaden: Harrassowitz, 2010), 667–775 and "Parnakka's Feast: Šip in Pārsa and Elam," in *Elam and Persia* (ed. Javier Alvarez-Mon; Winona Lake, Ind.: Eisenbrauns, 2011), 89–166.

that has escaped scholarly attention, Solomon's famous judgment of the case of the two prostitutes and their babe (1 Kgs 3:16–28) immediately follows the notice that Solomon had "prepared a feast for all his servants" (1 Kgs 3:15a). Thus, it is likely that the judgment took place in the context of the feast. Another example of judgment taking place at the king's table occurs in Dan 5, where God usurps Belshazzar's place at the table and, in an ironic turn of events, judges the presumptuous royal host as the true king and host.

In light of this traditio-historical connection between feasting and judgment, what we have in Isa 25:7–8 may be interpreted as a scene of judgment taking place at the eschatological king's table. The fact that it is said in Isa 24:21 that YHWH will judge "the host of heaven" and "the kings of earth," who YHWH apparently incarcerates in a pit-prison (בור and מסגר; 24:22), only further supports the judicial interpretation of Isa 25:6–8. In fact, what we see in Isa 25:6–8 may be understood as the direct narrative continuation of 24:21–23. Reading these passages together, if death appears at the table, it appears in shackles, lifted up from the pit-prison for judgment, just as the Pharaoh's cupbearer and baker were in Gen 40. On the one hand, like Pharaoh's baker, death is unceremoniously condemned and as punishment swallowed, so that no question of its survival, no trace of its threat, can linger. "He will swallow death in perpetuity." On the other, Israel and all peoples are comforted and welcomed into God's kingdom: "And the Lord YHWH will wipe away the tears from all faces; and the reproach of his people, he will remove from all the earth." From among those called to the feast of rich foods and aged wine, some will be lifted up to glory and others for shame. The feast is a marked and public event, a political mechanism where some are marked for inclusion and others for exclusion from the kingdom.

In conclusion, the climax of the feast on that mountain, the eschatological feast on Mount Zion, is YHWH's swallowing of death. The scene shocks because death, traditio-historically the paradigmatic swallower, is himself swallowed. The scene further surprises because, if death represents some of those invited to the feast, YHWH seems to overturn standard conventions concerning the host's duty to protect his guests. However, interpreted in light of the contextual (Isa 24:21–23) and traditio-historical evidence that connects feasting and judgment, death's condemnation and destruction at the feast becomes understandable. Indeed, as Wildberger has noted, the inauguration of YHWH's glorious and universal kingdom calls out for death's death, and with it all sufferings that plague life. That YHWH will swallow death comes as a surprise, but it is a wholly appropriate first act of consumption that ushers in a new age. In fact, this triumph over death by consumption both symbolically and in fact enacts the inauguration of YHWH's kingdom.

Resurrection or Transformation?
Concepts of Death in Isaiah 24–27

Annemarieke van der Woude

1. Introduction: Death and Culture

"Die Kultur entspringt dem Wissen um den Tod und die Sterblichkeit."[1] According to Jan Assmann, culture is nothing more, and nothing less, than finding ways to deal with the knowledge that our life is limited and that we have to die.[2] Culture realizes an opportunity to think beyond the borders of our mortality. Every time, and every society, seeks its own answers to the problem of death.[3] In this respect, there is no difference between biblical times and, for instance, twenty-first century Dutch society.

---

1. Jan Assmann, *Der Tod als Thema der Kulturtheorie: Todesbilder und Totenriten im Alten Ägypten: Mit einem Beitrag von Thomas Macho: Tod und Trauer im kulturwissenschaftlichen Vergleich* (Erbschaft unserer Zeit 7; Frankfurt: Suhrkamp, 2000), 13.

2. See Angelika Berlejung and Bernd Janowski, eds., *Tod und Jenseits im alten Israel und in seiner Umwelt: Theologische, religionsgeschichtliche, archäologische und ikonographische Aspekte* (FAT 64; Tübingen: Mohr Siebeck, 2009), v; Gönke Eberhardt, *JHWH und die Unterwelt: Spuren einer Kompetenzausweitung JHWHs im Alten Testament* (FAT 2/23; Tübingen: Mohr Siebeck, 2007), 1 n. 2; Bernd Janowski, "JHWH und die Toten: Zur Geschichte des Todes im Alten Israel," in *Tod und Jenseits im alten Israel und in seiner Umwelt: Theologische, religionsgeschichtliche, archäologische und ikonographische Aspekte* (eds. Angelika Berlejung and Bernd Janowski; FAT 64; Tübingen: Mohr Siebeck, 2009), 447–77 (470–71); J. Schnocks, "Konzeptionen der Übergänge vom Leben zum Tod und vom Tod zum Leben," in *Biblische Anthropologie: Neue Einsichten aus dem Alten Testament* (ed. Christian Frevel; QD 237; Freiburg: Herder, 2010), 317–31 (317 n. 1). See also Bernd Janowski, *Der Gott des Lebens* (vol. 3 of *Beiträge zur Theologie des Alten Testaments*; Neukirchen: Neukirchener, 2003), 242–43.

3. For an extensive overview of the debate, focusing on the German society, see Franz-Josef Bormann and Gian D. Borasio, eds., *Sterben: Dimensionen eines anthropologischen Grundphänomens* (Berlin: de Gruyter, 2012).

Israel's answer to its finite existence is not to claim the immortality of the soul. Instead of looking forward, Israel looks back. The Israelites shape their desire to exist beyond biological death by the idea of a "historia sacra"[4]: people live on in their children and grandchildren.

In the last decennia, the multicolored palette of death in the Hebrew Bible has been in the spotlight: "es [wäre] unrealistisch, vom Alten Testament eine auch nur einigermassen konsistente theologische Stellungnahme zu Sterben und Tod zu erwarten."[5] Nowadays, scholars agree that during the long history of Israel's literary production concepts of death develop.[6] In this contribution, I will discuss in detail three passages from Isa 24–27 in order to investigate the way they present living and dying.

2. Textual Analysis

In Isa 24–27, three verses explicitly deal with death:

(1) He will swallow up death for good (Isa 25:8);

(2) They are dead, they live no more, mere shades, they do not rise (Isa 26:14);

---

4. Assmann, *Tod als Thema der Kulturtheorie*, 18. See also: Thomas Podella, "Totenrituale und Jenseitsbeschreibungen: Zur anamnetischen Struktur der Religionsgeschichte Israels," in *Tod, Jenseits und Identität: Perspektiven einer kulturwissenschaftlichen Thanatologie* (ed. Jan Assmann and Rolf Trauzettel; VIHA 7; Freiburg: Alber, 2002), 530–61, who indicates this phenomenon as the "anamnetische Struktur" of Israel's religion.

5. Walter Gross, "Zum alttestamentlich-jüdischen Verständnis von Sterben und Tod," in *Sterben: Dimensionen eines anthropologischen Grundphänomens* (ed. Franz-Josef Bormann and Gian D. Borasio; Berlin: de Gruyter, 2012), 465–80 (467). See also Kent Harold Richards, "Death," *ABD* 2:108–10.

6. The concept of the "Kompetenzausweitung JHWHs" is one of the proposals to deal with the changing relationship between the deity and the underworld. See Eberhardt, *JHWH und die Unterwelt*, esp. 3–32; Gönke Eberhardt, "Die Gottesferne der Unterwelt in der JHWH-Religion," in *Tod und Jenseits im alten Israel und in seiner Umwelt: Theologische, religionsgeschichtliche, archäologische und ikonographische Aspekte* (ed. Angelika Berlejung and Bernd Janowski; FAT 64; Tübingen: Mohr Siebeck, 2009), 373–95; Janowski, "JHWH und die Toten." See also: Wim Weren, *Uit stof en as: Bijbelse beelden van Gods relatie met de doden: Rede ter gelegenheid van zijn afscheid als hoogleraar in de Bijbelwetenschappen (Nieuwe Testament) aan de Universiteit van Tilburg op vrijdag 27 mei 2011* (Tilburg: Tilburg University, 2011).

(3) Your dead will live, my corpses will rise (Isa 26:19).[7]

In the following textual analysis, these verses will be discussed in detail. Special attention will be paid to the communication in these passages in order to gain insight into the way they present death.[8] Another focus will lie upon those concepts that serve as a "Negativfolie"[9] to death. What are the contrary terms death is related to? To give an example: death can point to not-life, but it can also point to not-God.[10] A presupposition is that a sketch of these opposite images sheds light on the specific meaning of death in a particular Isaianic passage.

Undeniably, in biblical times death has a spatial connotation.[11] To circumscribe this phenomenon, Thomas Podella coins the term

---

7. Unless otherwise noted, all translations of biblical texts are my own.

8. See also Archibald L. H. M. van Wieringen, " 'I' and 'We' before 'Your' Face: A Communication Analysis of Isaiah 26:7–21," in *Studies in Isaiah 24–27: The Isaiah Workshop–De Jesaja Werkplaats* (ed. Hendrick Jan Bosman and Harm van Grol; OtSt 43; Leiden: Brill, 2000), 239–51; Stefan A. Nitsche, *Jesaja 24–27: Ein dramatischer Text: Die Frage nach den Genres prophetischer Literatur des Alten Testaments und die Textgraphik der grossen Jesajarolle aus Qumran* (BWA[N]T 166; Stuttgart: Kohlhammer, 2006). Divergent other criteria can be used to analyze these chapters. See, for instance, Hendrick Jan Bosman, "Syntactic Cohesion in Isaiah 24–27," in *Studies in Isaiah 24–27: The Isaiah Workshop–De Jesaja Werkplaats* (ed. Hendrick Jan Bosman and Harm van Grol; OtSt 43; Leiden: Brill, 2000), 19–50, for a syntactic analysis; Harm van Grol, "An Analysis of the Verse Structure of Isaiah 24–27," in *Studies in Isaiah 24–27: The Isaiah Workshop–De Jesaja Werkplaats,* (ed. Hendrick Jan Bosman and Harm van Grol; OtSt 43; Leiden: Brill, 2000), 51–80, for a prosodic one. Brian Doyle, *The Apocalypse of Isaiah Metaphorically Speaking: A Study of the Use, Function and Significance of Metaphors in Isaiah 24–27* (BETL 151; Leuven: Leuven University Press, 2000) pays special attention to the metaphors used; J. Todd Hibbard, *Intertextuality in Isaiah 24–27: The Reuse and Evocation of Earlier Texts and Traditions* (FAT 2/16; Tübingen: Mohr Siebeck, 2006) uses the method of intertextuality; Reinhard Scholl, *Die Elenden in Gottes Thronrat: Stilistisch-kompositorische Untersuchungen zu Jesaja 24–27* (BZAW 274; Berlin: de Gruyter, 2000) focuses on the stylistic characteristics of these chapters in light of the composition of the book of Isaiah and of the Hebrew Bible. Christopher B. Hays, *Death in the Iron Age II and in First Isaiah* (FAT 79; Tübingen: Mohr Siebeck, 2011) explores the rhetoric of death in Isa 1–39 in its historical context.

9. Podella, "Totenrituale und Jenseitsbeschreibungen," 555.

10. See also Janowski, *Der Gott des Lebens,* 201–43.

11. See, for instance, Kathrin Liess, "'Hast du die Tore der Finsternis gesehen?' (Ijob 38,17): Zur Lokalisierung des Totenreiches im Alten Testament," in *Tod und Jenseits im alten Israel und in seiner Umwelt. Theologische, religionsgeschichtliche, archäo-*

"Jenseitslandschaften."[12] Podella emphasizes that these landscapes show divergent characteristics. They can be analyzed along the lines of periphery and center. Next to this horizontal axis, there is a vertical one that has to be taken into consideration; that is to say, the concepts of death deal with the opposite terms "high" and "low."[13] In the analysis, special attention will also be paid to these environmental connotations of death. To grasp these nuances, a close reading of the passages is necessary as well.

2.1. Isaiah 25:6–12

2.1.1. Translation of Isaiah 25:6–12[14]

(25:6a) Then YHWH Tseba'ot will prepare
(6b) for all peoples
(6c) on this mountain
(6d) a feast of fat dishes,
(6e) a feast of aged wines,
(6f) fat dishes filled with marrow,
(6g) aged wines filtered out;
(7a) then he will swallow up, on this mountain,
(7b) the face of the shroud that shrouds all peoples,
(7c) the sheet that sheets all nations:
(8a) he will swallow up death for good.
(8b) Then Adonai YHWH will wipe away
(8c) the tears from all faces
(8d) and the disgrace of his people
(8e) he will remove from all the earth.

---

logische und ikonographische Aspekte (ed. Angelika Berlejung and Bernd Janowski; FAT 64; Tübingen: Mohr Siebeck, 2009), 397–422.

12. Podella, "Totenrituale und Jenseitsbeschreibungen," 545. See also Jürgen Werlitz, "Scheol und sonst nichts? Zu den alttestamentlichen 'Jenseits'-Vorstellungen," in Das Jenseits: Perspektiven christlicher Theologie (ed. Stefan Schreiber and Stefan Siemons; Darmstadt: Wissenschaftliche Buchgesellschaft, 2003), 41–61.

13. See also Podella, "Totenrituale und Jenseitsbeschreibungen," 545–50; Janowski, Der Gott des Lebens, 244–66.

14. The translation is taken from Hendrick Jan Bosman and Harm van Grol, "Annotated Translation of Isaiah 24–27," in Studies in Isaiah 24–27: The Isaiah Workshop–De Jesaja Werkplaats (ed. Hendrick Jan Bosman and Harm van Grol; OtSt 43; Leiden: Brill, 2000), 3–12.

(8f) Yes, Yʜᴡʜ has spoken.
(9a) Then they will say on that day:
(9b) Behold, this is our God!
(9c) We yearned for him that he would save us.
(9d) This is Yʜᴡʜ! We yearned for him,
(9e) let us be glad and have joy in his salvation:
(10a) Yes, the hand of Yʜᴡʜ rests on this mountain!
(10b) Then Moab will be trampled down in its place,
(10c) as straw is trampled down in the water of a dung pit,
(11a) and he will stretch out his hands in the middle of it,
(11b) as a swimmer stretches out (his hands) to swim,
(11c) but he will bring down his pride despite the cleverness of his hands.
(12a) The fortification, your towering walls, he bends them,
(12b) he brings down, lets touch the ground, to the very dust.

2.1.2. Speech Situation in Isaiah 25:6–12

In order to gain insight in the meaning of death in this passage, it is necessary to demarcate it and to define subunits along the lines of the shifts in
communication.

Sʜɪꜰᴛs ɪɴ Cᴏᴍᴍᴜɴɪᴄᴀᴛɪᴏɴ ɪɴ Isᴀɪᴀʜ 25:6–12

subunit	speaker	speaker
Isa 25:6a–8f	I–figure →	
Isa 25:9a	I–figure →	
Isa 25:9b–10a		"we" [= "his people"] →
Isa 25:10b–11c	I–figure →	
Isa 25:12a–12b	I–figure → "you" [= "Moab"]	

In the passage that precedes the one under consideration (vv. 1–5), an
I-figure speaks, as the first person singular indicates (v. 1). He addresses a
second person masculine singular, the Lord, and shouts, "Yʜᴡʜ, my God
you are!" (v. 1). In our passage, the Lord is no longer spoken to but instead
is spoken about. A shift has taken place from an intimate conversation into
a more general one. The reader gets an helicopter view. A wide perspective

is sketched. It is an argument to consider the first five verses of this chapter as an independent unit and to isolate them from the verses that follow.[15] The closure of our passage is marked by the end of the conversation that addresses Moab as a "you" (v. 12a–b).

Our passage opens with a *weqatal* form (v. 6a). As a result of the isolated position of the preceding smaller unit (vv. 1–5), this verbal form should be connected to the *weqatal* forms at the end of chapter 24, starting with "then it will be on that day" (Isa 24:21). The utterance belongs to a smaller unit that declares that the Lord will be the king (Isa 24:23). All actions he is going to undertake emphasize his sovereignty. The closure of this sub-section is clearly marked. The *qatal* clause, "Yes, Yhwh has spoken" (v. 8f), concludes a chain of *weqatal* forms (vv. 6a–8e). These words confirm that all things are going to happen indeed, because the Lord has spoken it. His words are reliable.

Next to these arguments that are based upon a syntactical analysis, the communication situation also gives a clue to define the first smaller unit. In the first part (vv. 6a–8f), there is no direct speech. What is yet to come concerns everybody: "all peoples" (vv. 6b, 7b), "all nations" (v. 7c), "all faces" (v. 8c), "all the earth" (v. 8e). Nobody will be excluded from God's grace. The passage displays a universalistic tendency.

About the subject in this smaller unit there is no doubt: "Yhwh Tsebaot" (v. 6a), "Adonai Yhwh" (v. 8b), "Yhwh" (v. 8f), and "he" (vv. 7a, 8a) also refers to the Lord. The place of action is "on this mountain" (vv. 6c, 7a). At the end of the preceding chapter, the mountain is mentioned as well and is determined there: "on the mountain of Zion" (Isa 24:23). In other words, the mountain is the place to be, where God will organize a large feast: "Feel free to come and to participate!"

In the next subunit, direct speech is introduced: "Then they will say on that day" (v. 9a). The confession of a group of people, "Behold, this is our God!" (v. 9b), sounds like a refrain of the words at the beginning of this chapter (v. 1). But there is one important difference: the perspective in time. Whereas the nominal phrase at the beginning of this chapter expresses a state of affairs, the nominal phrase in the middle of the chapter is preceded by a *weqatal* form. Thus, it expresses a future situation.

---

15. The title "Das Danklied des Propheten" is a way to circumscribe the same observation of these verses as an independent unity. See Willem A. M. Beuken, *Jesaja 13–27* (HTKAT; Freiburg: Herder, 2007), 343–454.

Who are these people that speak as a "we" in the following lines: "our God" (v. 9b), "we yearned" (v. 9c, d), "would save us" (v. 9c), "let us be glad" (v. 9e)? The person who introduces the group that is going to speak (v. 9a) is the I-figure that praised the Lord in the preceding passage (vv. 1–5). The perspective has broadened now. The group that confesses that YHWH will be their savior (vv. 9b–10a) consists of men and women from a wide area (vv. 6a–8f). It refers to "his people" (v. 8d). The כִּי-yiqtol clause, "Yes, the hand of YHWH rests on this mountain!" (v. 10a), marks a closure.

In the following unit (vv. 10b–12b), the second person masculine singular "your" (v. 12a) is the most remarkable phenomenon. Moab is the addressee here (v. 10b). It is the only occurrence in this passage where somebody is addressed directly. The effect of addressing somebody as a "you" is that the words make a strong impact. Moab cannot escape the doom that is pronounced towards it. But who is the speaker in these verses? The weqatal form, "will be trampled down" (v. 10b), stands in coordination with the weqatal form, "will say" (v. 9a). The line of speech is interrupted by the shouting of the we-group (vv. 9b–10a), but is continued by the same I-figure that spoke at the beginning of the section (v. 9a) and at the beginning of this chapter (from v. 1 onwards).

2.1.3. Close Reading of Isaiah 25:6–12

Repetition is one of the structural features in the first verses (Isa 25:6–8). The adjective "all" appears five times (vv. 6b, 7b, c, 8c, e). In every case where the adjective "all" appears, a preposition is used.

PREPOSITIONS IN ISAIAH 25:6–8

	preposition	"all"
6b	לְ	"for all peoples"
7b	עַל	"[without translation] all peoples"
7c	עַל	"[without translation] all nations"
8c	מֵעַל	"from all faces"
8e	מֵעַל	"from all the earth"

The application of these prepositions underscores the totality of the Lord's interference. He acts in favor of his people (לְ); he delivers them (עַל); and there is no place imaginable that does not benefit from his deeds (מֵעַל).

"On this mountain" (vv. 6c, 7a), God's glory will be revealed. There he celebrates a feast (v. 6d–g). In this smaller unit (vv. 6a–8f), death stands in opposition to "feast."[16] The repetition of the verbal form "he will swallow up" (vv. 7a, 8a) indicates that the mountain is the place where death is conquered (v. 8a). The removal of death means the disappearance of sadness and tears. The image that emerges, is that the mountain functions as the center of the earth, where God's presence is discernible. He assembles people from the four corners of the world to participate in his celebration. In the next unit, the "mountain" is mentioned again (v. 10a). It confirms the impression that the height is a place blessed by God.

"On that day" (v. 9a) occurs several other times in Isa 24–27 (Isa 24:21; 26:1; 27:1, 2, 12, 13). The utterance belongs to the language of apocalyptic literature. Here, it is related to the moment that death has disappeared. As a consequence, dying and living does not only relate to space, as expressed in "on this mountain," but also to time, as expressed in "on that day." This aspect of time is noticeable in the word "for good" (v. 8a) as well.

At the end of this smaller unit, verbal forms that point to some kind of decline are in the majority: "will be trampled down" (v. 10b), "is trampled down" (v. 10c), "will bring down" (v. 11c), "bends" (v. 12a), and "brings down, lets touch the ground, to the very dust" (v. 12b). Most of all, "dust" bears the connotation of death (see also Isa 26:5, 19d). These actions of bringing down form a sharp contrast with the height of the mountain where the Lord will organize his feast.

2.2. Isaiah 26:7–27:1

2.2.1. Translation of Isaiah 26:7–27:1[17]

(26:7a) The path for the righteous is straightness,
(7b) straight, the track of the righteous you level.
(8a) Surely, in the path of your judgments, Yʜwʜ, we yearn for you,

---

16. See van Grol, "An Analysis of the Verse Structure of Isaiah 24–27," 68: "The feast is worked out as the swallowing up of death and the elimination of tears and disgrace."

17. The translation is taken from Bosman and van Grol, "Annotated Translation of Isaiah 24–27."

(8b) for your name and your memory is the longing of the soul.

(9a) My soul longs for you in the night,

(9b) surely, with breath strong in me I look for you.

(9c) Yes, when your judgments hit the earth,

(9d) they learn righteousness, the inhabitants of the world.

(10a) The wicked one may be shown mercy, but does not learn righteousness,

(10b) in a land of uprightness he distorts

(10c) and does not see the majesty of YHWH.

(11a) YHWH, your hand is lifted high, but they do not notice.

(11b) May they notice and be ashamed at (your) zeal for the people,

(11c) surely, may the fire for your enemies consume them!

(12a) YHWH, you establish peace for us,

(12b) yes, even all our achievements, you have done them for us.

(13a) YHWH, our God,

(13b) other masters besides you have ruled over us,

(13c) only of you do we keep in memory your name:

(14a) they are dead, they live no more,

(14b) mere shades, they do not rise;

(14c) indeed you have punished, you exterminated them

(14d) and wiped out all memory of them.

(15a) You have added to the nation, YHWH,

(15b) you have added to the nation from which you receive glory,

(15c) you have removed all borders of the earth.

(16a) YHWH, in their distress they have appealed to you,

(16b) they have poured out incantations when your discipline was on them.

(17a) Like a pregnant one

(17b) —she comes near to giving birth,

(17c) she writhes, she cries out in her pains—,

(17d) so we have been

(17e) because of you, YHWH:

(18a) we were pregnant, we writhed,

(18b) but when we gave birth: wind!

(18c) Salvation we can not achieve on the earth

(18d) and inhabitants of the world will not fall.

(19a) Your dead will live,

(19b) my corpses will rise,

(19c) wake up and exult,

(19d) dwellers in the dust!

(19e) yes, dew of the light-herb is your dew,

(19f) and the earth will let fall the shades!

(20a) Go, my people,

(20b) enter your rooms
(20c) and shut your doors behind you,
(20d) hide away for a short time
(20e) until the ordeal has passed by!
(21a) Yes, behold, YHWH is about to come out of his place
(21b) to punish the sin of the inhabitant of the earth upon him.
(21c) And the earth will disclose her bloodshed
(21d) and she will cover up her killed no longer.
(27:1a) On that day: YHWH will punish
(1b) with his fierce, great, strong sword
(1c) Leviathan, the swift serpent,
(1d) Leviathan, the coiling serpent,
(1e) and he will kill the monster that is in the sea.

2.2.2. Speech Situation in Isaiah 26:7–27:1

SHIFTS IN COMMUNICATION IN ISAIAH 26:7–18

subunit	speaker
Isa 26:7a–8b	"we" → "you" = "YHWH"
Isa 26:9a–9b	"I" → "you" [= "YHWH"]
Isa 26:9c–13c	"we" → "you" = "YHWH"
Isa 26:14a–16b	["we"] → "you" = "YHWH"
Isa 26:17a–18d	"we" → "you" = "YHWH"
Isa 26:19a–19f	
Isa 26:20a–e	
Isa 26:21a–d	
Isa 27:1a–e	

The passage that is now subject of our investigation is placed between two units that open with "on that day" (Isa 26:1 and 27:2, respectively). Although it seems to be a clear demarcation of the end of this passage, one question remains: What about the same utterance in the first verse of the chapter (Isa 27:1a)? Does not that clause indicate the beginning of a new subsection? The most decisive argument to draw a line between the two identical utterances has to do with the speaker: the Lord refers to himself as "I" (Isa 27:3). The speech situation has changed compared to the preceding verses where the Lord was spoken about as "he" (Isa 26:21a–27:1e).

The beginning of this unit is even more difficult to determine. The first part of the chapter is about a song that is going to be sung (v. 1). Where does this song end? The transition from song to text does not seem to be marked very clearly. But the communicative setting switches, where the Lord is addressed as "you" by people that speak as "we" (v. 8a). In other words, talking about the Lord as a third person masculine singular has ended (vv. 1–6). It is an argument to presume that the song comes to a close here.

In the lines that follow, there is a change of sender. A first person plural "we" (v. 8a) turns into a first person singular "I" (v. 9a, b). The shift from first person plural into singular effectuates intimacy. What was considered to be a general statement about longing for the Lord, changes into a personal confession: "Surely, with breath strong in me I look for you" (v. 9b). It is a sound conclusion that this I-figure is a member of the we-group from the preceding clauses (v. 8a–b).

In the subsequent lines (vv. 12a–13c), we return to a high density of first person plural personal pronouns. Again, a we-group is the sender of the message, as is the case in the lines in between (vv. 9c–11c). Needless to say, the addressee in these verses remains the same, namely, the Lord. The grammatical forms—second person masculine singular "you" (vv. 7b, 8a, 9a, b, 12a, b, 13b, c) and "your" (vv. 8a, b[bis], 9c, 11a, c, 13c)—point to him as the receiver of these words.

In what follows (vv. 14a–16b), the text displays a "they," a third person masculine plural, instead of a "we." The tone of the communication changes, although the setting remains the same. It is plausible to presume that the we-group still is speaking here. Numerous second person masculine singular grammatical forms detect God as the addressee (vv. 14c[bis], d, 15a, 15b[bis], c, 16a, b).

This communication situation is continued in the next lines (vv. 17a–18d). God remains the one that is spoken to. And a first person plural is the sender of these words. There is a chain of first person plural verbal forms: "so we have been" (v. 17d), "we were pregnant" (v. 18a), "we writhed" (v. 18a), "when we gave birth" (v. 18b), "we can not achieve" (v. 18c). What about the identity of this we-group? The first opportunity to detect a reference for the first person plural (from v. 8a onwards) is found at the beginning of this chapter: "A strong city is ours" (v. 1). The singers are those who sojourn in Judah. As a result, the camera has taken another standpoint.

Whereas the feast "on this mountain" (Isa 25:10a) concerns all inhabitants of the earth, in the next chapter (Isa 26) the focus lies upon the people of Judah. The reader gets the impression that the salvation pronounced by the Lord is viewed under different perspectives. These verses can be considered as "a reflection on the song that is announced in Isa. 26:1–6."[18]

Because the line of communication in Isa 26:19 is a highly debated issue, the last few verses of this passage (vv. 19a–27:1e) are analyzed together.

2.2.3. Speech Situation in Isaiah 26:19

The characteristics of the speech situation in Isa 26:19 deserve special attention. The clauses themselves offer little clues to be definite about who is talking to whom. For example, to whom does the first person singular "my corpses" (v. 19b) refer? Is this the same I-figure as the one who spoke in the preceding verses: "my soul" (v. 9a) and "I look for you" (v. 9b)? In other words, is this a member of the we-group that sang at the beginning of this chapter "a strong city is ours" (v. 1)? This question is even more urgent, since its answer relates directly to our topic: the concepts of death in Isa 24–27. Do we deal here with the idea of an afterlife?[19]

Let us consider divergent options for analyzing the speech situation in this smaller unit (v. 19a–f). The argumentation for the first possibility runs as follows. In the preceding passage, a group of people belonging to Judah is the speaker (from Isa 26:1 onwards). These people address the Lord. The sentences that follow (vv. 7a–19f) can be regarded as a continuation of that communication. "Your dead will live" (v. 19a) relate to those who have passed away, but are saved by God. God is the addressee. The

---

18. Bosman, "Syntactic Cohesion in Isaiah 24–27," 35.

19. See, for instance, Willem A. M. Beuken, "'Deine Toten werden leben' (Jes 26,19): 'Kindliche Vernunft' oder reifer Glaube?" in Schriftauslegung in der Schrift: Festschrift für Odil Hannes Steck zu seinem 65. Geburtstag (ed. Reinhard G. Kratz et al.; BZAW 300; Berlin: de Gruyter, 2000), 139–52; Klaus Bieberstein, "Jenseits der Todesschwelle: Die Entstehung der Auferweckungshoffnungen in der alttestamentlich-frühjüdischen Literatur," in Tod und Jenseits im alten Israel und in seiner Umwelt: Theologische, religionsgeschichtliche, archäologische und ikonographische Aspekte (ed. Angelika Berlejung and Bernd Janowski; FAT 64; Tübingen: Mohr Siebeck, 2009), esp. 437–39; Scholl, Die Elenden in Gottes Thronrat, 141–45; Klaas Spronk, Beatific Afterlife in Ancient Israel and in the Ancient Near East (AOAT 219; Neukirchen-Vluyn: Neukirchener, 1986), esp. 297–305. See also Philip S. Johnston, Shades of Sheol: Death and Afterlife in the Old Testament (Downers Grove, Ill.: InterVarsity Press, 2002).

first person singular in "my corpses" (v. 19b) designates the prophet. The boundary between the we-group and the prophet is fluid. Willem Beuken opts for this possibility.[20]

BEUKEN ON THE COMMUNICATION SITUATION IN ISAIAH 26:19

subunit	speaker
Isa 26:19a	we-group → "your" (= God)
Isa 26:19b	"my" (= prophet) → ["you"] (= God)
Isa 26:19c–d	[prophet] (= we–group) → "dwellers in the dust"
Isa 26:19e–f	we–group → "your" (= God)

A second option has as its point of departure the first person singular in "my corpses" (v. 19b). It should be connected to the last preceding grammatical form, first person singular: "my soul" (v. 9a) together with "I look for you" (v. 9b). As a consequence, the same member of the we-group that spoke there is the sender of a message in this verse. But to whom is it spoken? The Lord is one possibility; the we-group is another. For instance, Archibald van Wieringen defends this last option.[21]

VAN WIERINGEN ON THE COMMUNICATION SITUATION IN ISAIAH 26:19

subunit	speaker
Isa 26:19a–f	"my" (= member of we-group) → "dwellers in the dust" (= we-group)

A third possibility is to assume a shift in speech situation between what preceded and what is at stake now. In the foregoing smaller units (vv. 7a–18d), the Lord was addressed permanently. Does it make sense that he is the one who is supposed to react: "your dead will live" (v. 19a)? In that case, the addressees are the "we" (vv. 17d, 18a[bis], b, c). The *yiqtol* forms "will live" (v. 19a), "will rise" (v. 19b), and "let fall" (v. 19f) are the beads of one chain. The verbal forms in between, "wake up" (v. 19c) and "exult" (v. 19c), presuppose a different communicative setting. The speaker

---

20. Beuken, *Jesaja 13–27*, 380–85.
21. van Wieringen, "'I' and 'We' before 'Your' Face," 247.

remains the same; the address has changed into "dwellers in the dust" (v. 19d). Hendrik Jan Bosman suggests this speech situation.[22]

BOSMAN ON THE COMMUNICATION SITUATION IN ISAIAH 26:19

Subunit	speaker
Isa 26:19a–b	"my" (= God) → "your" (= we-group)
Isa 26:19c–e	[God] → "dwellers in the dust"
Isa 26:19f	[God] → ["your"] (= we-group)

In order to clarify the speech situation in this verse, it is worthwhile to investigate the way in which the communication proceeds (Isa 26:20a–27:1e). "Go, my people" (v. 20a), an imperative second person masculine singular, leaves no doubt. The Lord is speaking here; his people are addressed.

In what follows, the communicative situation changes. The Lord is no longer speaker, but is spoken about (Isa 26:21a). It is not immediately clear who is talking here. Nor are the addressees specified. The particle כִּי (v. 21a), opens a smaller unit that contains concluding remarks (v. 21a–d). Inasmuch as the circumscription "cantata"[23] is adequate for the literary structure of these chapters, one might imagine that a choir is singing here, to bring to a close a smaller unit and to summarize what has been said thus far: "YHWH is about to come out of his place" (v. 21a).

"On that day" marks the beginning of another subunit (Isa 27:1a–e). Again, God is referred to as a third person masculine singular (27:1a). And, as was also the case in the preceding smaller unit, in these clauses it is not clear who is addressed. It is true for these two units, that first and second person grammatical forms are absent. The tone of what is said differs from what has been said before. Here, the reader is confronted with two general remarks.

---

22. Bosman, "Syntactic Cohesion in Isaiah 24–27," 49.

23. Bosman, "Syntactic Cohesion in Isaiah 24–27," 35. See also Johannes Lindblom, *Die Jesaja-Apokalypse: Jes. 24–27* (LUÅ 34.3; Lund: Gleerup, 1938), 69–71. The concept of a "cantata" is taken from Lindblom, although Lindblom uses the term in a slightly different way. His thesis runs as follows: Isaiah 24–27 is a cantata that was performed on a festival to celebrate the destruction of a foreign city. Lindblom pointed to a historical phenomenon, not to a structural feature.

The topic under consideration still is the puzzling speech situation in "your dead will live" (v. 19a). The analysis thus far opens two possibilities. One is that this utterance prolongs the preceding dialogue (vv. 7a–18d) and presents the same communicative situation. As a consequence, the we-group is talking to God about his dead people. Another possibility is that the mentioning of dead people being alive serves as a starting point for a new conversation. In that case, the speaker here is the same as the one who says, "Go, my people" (v. 20a). The Lord addresses his people by indicating what will be their fate: they will live!

It is too early to draw a conclusion. The resemblance between two smaller units in this chapter is striking (vv. 14a–b and 19a–b, f). We take a closer look at them in order to investigate whether they can shed light on the communicative situation in the clauses under discussion (v. 19a–f).

ISAIAH 26:19 AND ISAIAH 26:14

19a	"your dead will live"	14a	"they are dead, they live no more"
19b	"my corpses will rise"	14bβ	"they do not rise"
19f	"and the earth will let fall the shades!"	14bα	"[they are] mere shades"

In the middle of this chapter (v. 14), the we-group, as sender in the communication process, is presupposed. The people that sing in Judah are meant (v. 1). The Lord is spoken to, as the oft-repeated vocative "YHWH" underscores (vv. 8a, 11a, 12a, 13a, 15a, 16a). But about whom is the passage speaking? These people are indicated with third person masculine plural forms (v. 14a[bis], b[bis]) referring to "other masters" (v. 13b).

The passage (vv. 7a–16b) is built upon several pairs of oppositions. Some of them are composed by negations. Thus, the text shows the positive and the negative sides of the same coin: the coming of God's judgments upon the earth.

PAIRS OF OPPOSITIONS IN ISAIAH 26:7A–16B

| 9d | "they learn righteousness, the inhabitants of the world" | 10a | "the wicked one ... does not learn righteousness" |
| 11a | "YHWH, your hand is lifted high" | 11a | "they do not notice" |

12a	"Yhwh, you establish peace for us"	13b	"other masters besides you have ruled over us"
13c	"we keep in memory your name"	14a	"[other masters] they live no more"
		14b	"[other masters] they do not rise"
15a	"you have added to the nation"	16a	"in their distress they have appealed to you"

Being alive means dwelling in close proximity to God. Opposing his judgments is the same as being dead. Two parties are the mirror image of one another: a we-group and a they-group. Righteous people are compared to the unfaithful. It is from this broader semantic context that the passage under consideration (v. 19a–f) receives its meaning.

"They are dead, they live no more" (v. 14a) is counteracted by "your dead will live" (v. 19a). Above, I advanced two hypothetical speech situations. One is that the former dialogue (vv. 7a–18d) is prolonged. This would mean that the we-group, who observes that other lords are dead (v. 14a), proceeds to address God by confirming that his people will be alive (v. 19a). Another is that these verses present different speakers. In that case, the communicative situation is turned upside down. Think of these chapters as a cantata, as was suggested above. Applied to the two verses that show a similarity in their terminology (vv. 14 and 19), it does make sense to suppose that these verses are uttered by different singing voices.

After the we-group has stated that the Lord has "wiped out all memory" (v. 14d) of other rulers, it becomes introspective. The people use the metaphor of a pregnant woman to describe their behavior. Although new life was growing within them and the day of their deliverance was ahead, they failed. They have betrayed the Lord's confidence. This passage is a confession of guilt (vv. 17a–18d). They evaluate their own conduct as even more severe than that of the masters they just described. Concerning the other rulers, the Lord cherished no hope. He had placed his hope in his people. And they have disappointed him.

Then, suddenly, the Lord interrupts their lamentation (v. 19a–f). As if he is shouting, he confirms, "*your* dead will live" (v. 19a), opposite to the masters who have died (v. 14a), "*your* dead" will be alive. "Dwellers in the dust" (v. 19d) is a paraphrase of people considered to be dead. Instead of imagining themselves as people without a future, the Lord affirms that salvation is achievable for them. As a result, there is no shift in communication between this verse and the following (vv. 19a–f and 20a–e). The Lord continues to speak and to address his people. The transition from one speaker to another has taken place between the metaphor of giving birth (vv. 17a–18d) and the Lord's encouraging words (v. 19a–f).

SHIFTS IN COMMUNICATION IN ISAIAH 26:19–27:1

subunit	Speaker
Isa 26:19a–f	"my" (= God) → "your" = "dwellers in the dust" (= we-group)
Isa 26:20a–e	"my" (= God) → "your" = "my people" (= we-group)
Isa 26:21a–d	speaker → ?
Isa 27:1a–e	speaker → ?

2.2.4. Close Reading of Isaiah 26:7–27:1

We start with some remarks on the first verses of the chapter (Isa 26:1–6). Here, several literary features of the last part of the preceding chapter (Isa 25:6–12) recur. The chapter opens with the same adjunct of time: "on that day" (v. 1). Although the mountain has not been mentioned, there are other determinations of place. As in the foregoing chapter, "height" has an ambiguous connotation. It is the place where the Lord dwells, but it is also the place from where the opponents are dethroned (vv. 5–6; see also Isa 25:10b–12b). The opposition "low" and "high" also occurs. It does not only relate to locations, but also to people: "the inhabitants of the high place" (v. 5) function as a mirror image of "an oppressed one" and "the poor" (v. 6). It is a challenging paradox; the highly placed persons are brought down by the people who are considered to be humble.

The scenery changes, when we arrive at the next unit (vv. 7a–13c). There is no mountain, nor a high place, but a "path" (vv. 7a, 8a) and a "track" (v. 7b). The "righteous" people (v. 7a, b; see also vv. 9d, 10a) are diametrically opposed to "the wicked one" (v. 10a), "your enemies" (v. 11c) and "other masters" (v. 13b). The external contrast between "high" and "low" in the previous units (Isa 25:6–12; 26:1–6) has become an internal one. It now concerns the people's behavior. Here, we encounter the language of wisdom literature. Two ways are sketched, one for those who are prepared to learn (v. 9d) and another one for those who are not (vv. 10a-11c). The Lord's "judgments" (vv. 8a, 9c) help to discriminate between the good and the bad.

Next to the disappearance of the mountain as location of God's presence, we have also lost the opposition between center and periphery. YHWH does not dwell at one fixed place, but orientation on his "name" (vv. 8b, 13c) and keeping his "memory" (vv. 8b, 13c) suffice to experience him. These two topics will be worked out in what follows.

Death is the focus of this contribution. What do we learn about that concept in the following subsection (vv. 14a-16b)? A group of people is said to be "dead" (v. 14a). The difference between being dead or alive has to do with "memory" (v. 14d). So, here we deal with a social aspect of being dead. This is true in a twofold way. On the one hand, one can declare somebody not alive anymore by rubbing out the reminiscence (v. 14d). On the other hand, cherishing the memory of somebody keeps the person alive (vv. 8b, 13c). Where death and "feast" were opposite terms in the preceding chapter, in these verses death and "memory" stand in opposition.

Whereas, in the former chapter (Isa 25:6–12), all men and women were invited to come from the edges of the world to the center in order to celebrate the Lord's feast on the mountain, we notice that there is a movement in the opposite direction in these verses. The center here resembles the eye of a storm; it is empty. All the more attention is paid to the outer parts: "you have removed all borders of the earth" (v. 15c) and "you have added to the nation" (v. 15a, b). The universalistic tendency is continued here. However, a new aspect is added in which another element of wisdom literature is discernible. These verses stress openness towards the Lord's liberating activities. Origin is not decisive. Everybody who shows willingness to be judged by God has access to his peace.

In two separate units (vv. 14a-16b and 19a-f), similar terms are used (see above, subsection 2.2.3). "Your dead will live" (v. 19a) contrasts with "they are dead, they live no more" (v. 14a). "My corpses will rise" (v. 19b) and "the earth will let fall the shades!" (v. 19f) counterbalance "mere shades, they do not rise" (v. 14b). In addition to the comparability of the terms, the latter concepts also belong to the field of "high" and "low." The terminology might be the same, but what about the meaning? For instance, it is difficult to determine whether the falling of the shades has a positive or a negative connotation (v. 19f).

The repetition of "the earth" catches the attention (vv. 18c, 19f, 21b, c, [d]). In these verses, the earth holds different functions. It acts as a location where liberation cannot exist (vv. 18c, 21b) and as a person who is responsible for certain deeds (vv. 19f, 21c, [d]). When we take into account the pattern these verses present (v. 19a–f), then the falling of the shades has a positive association, just as the living of the dead and the rising of the corpses have. I agree with those who stress that "to fall" is related to "to give birth."[24] As a result, a sharper contrast between the images evoked here is hardly imaginable. The Lord transforms the earth from a barren place into a life-giving woman.

In the preceding lines (vv. 7a–13c, 14a–16b), it was said that God is praised everywhere his name is kept in memory. In the passage under consideration "Yhwh is about to come out of his place" (v. 21a). The transition between these passages reveal a movement from periphery to center, although the reader receives no clue as to from what place the Lord is supposed to leave. At the same time, people are summoned to enter their rooms and shut their doors (v. 20b–c). These words recall "every house is shut off from entering" (Isa 24:10). It serves as a counterpart. There, the houses cannot function as a shelter, whereas in this passage the rooms are designated as safe haven. The overall picture evokes a choreography: whereas men and women are called to gather at a specific place, God is said to leave his location.

The connotation of memory in relation to death (vv. 7a–13c, 14a–16b) is not continued here. Nor does the reader envision a feast as a counterpart of death (Isa 25:6–12). What is the literary context that determines the content of death in this smaller unit (Isa 26:17a–27:1e)? Here, the opposite term of death is "giving birth." Death means the inability to produce life. Nevertheless, what is at stake here is more than just death and life as opposite terms. Living is formulated as a passage through death. It is a kind of transformation.[25] Those who were supposed to be dead are brought into life again: "Your dead will live!" (v. 19a).

---

24. See, for instance, Bosman and van Grol, "Annotated Translation of Isaiah 24–27," 10 n.16. See also: B. Doyle, "Fertility and Infertility in Isaiah 24–27," in *The New Things: Eschatology in Old Testament Prophecy: Festschrift for Henk Leene* (ed. Ferenc Postma et al.; ACEBTSup 3; Maastricht: Shaker, 2002). In the Dutch language, the affinity between these verbs is even more pronounced: "vallen" next to "bevallen."

25. On the same topic, see Schnocks, "Konzeptionen der Übergänge," 324–28. See also Podella, "Totenrituale und Jenseitsbeschreibungen," 560: "Es hat den Anschein,

3. SUMMARY

In the passages under consideration in this contribution (Isa 25:6–12 and Isa 26:7–27:1), death occurs three times.

DEATH AND OPPOSITE TERMS IN ISAIAH 24–27

Text	Death	Opposite Term
Isa 25:8a	"He will swallow up death for good"	feast
Isa 26:14a–b	"They are dead, they live no more, mere shades, they do not rise"	memory
Isa 26:19a–b	"Your dead will live, my corpses will rise"	birth

In these different literary contexts, death has divergent connotations. In the first unit (Isa 25:6–12), death stands in opposition to feast. What is said about death runs via a horizontal and a vertical axis. There is a movement from periphery to center, inasmuch as the Lord's feast will take place on the mountain and everybody is invited to participate. The line from "high" to "low" has as its poles "mountain" in opposition to "dust." Finally, next to the spatial connotation of death, these verses also reveal a temporal one, as the clause "on that day" indicates.

In the second unit (Isa 26:7–16), death contrasts "memory." "High" and "low" no longer refer to an external opposition, but to an internal one. It concerns the people's behavior. The opposition between center and periphery functions, compared to the preceding unit, in an opposite way. The Lord is not recognizable at one fixed place, but everywhere his name is remembered. A social aspect has been introduced: death relates to being ignored.

In the third unit (Isa 26:17–27:1), death has "birth" as its contrary concept. Death relates to infertility. Again, there are dynamics on the horizontal line. Whereas God is said to leave his place, people are summoned to take shelter at one specific place. In this subsection, death is sketched as a passage: through death, one is brought to life again.

---

als ob … der Tod im gesamten Alten Testament nur als ein Übergangsstadium zu einer anderen Existenzform verstanden wurde."

3.1. Concepts of Death in Isaiah 24–27

What does the outcome of our investigation tell us about the concepts of death in Isa 24–27? One of the passages discussed draws our attention (Isa 26:7–16). These verses stress the value of remembering. It functions as a confirmation of Assmann's characterization of Israel's dealing with history as a sacred history.

Another topic that deserves an answer has to do with the supposed presentation of an afterlife in these texts (Isa 26:19). In the textual analysis presented in this contribution, it has been made evident that a dimension of time, in relation to death, is undeniable. Undoubtedly, this is an apocalyptic feature of these passages. Anyhow, the picture that "feast," "memory," and "birth" as mirror images present brings me to another conclusion. More than related to time, death is related to God. Instead of "resurrection,"[26] what these verses present about death is "transformation." In biblical times, the Israelites solve the problem of their mortality by sketching the contours of a new existence in God's neighborhood.

---

26. Richards, "Death," 2:109: "there was little if any vision of an afterlife in Israel." See also Podella, "Totenrituale und Jenseitsbeschreibungen," 531: "das grosse Schweigen des Alten Testaments über ein Leben nach dem Tod."

Deliverance as Fertility and Resurrection: Echoes of Second Isaiah in Isaiah 26

Stephen L. Cook

A corpus of authoritative, sacred writings was in place by postexilic times, to which Israel's early apocalyptic visionaries, such as the authors of the so-called Isaiah Apocalypse (Isa 24–27), made ready reference.[1] In a text such as Isa 26, we see a new medium of revelation emerging that relies on the mantic study and cross-referencing of Scripture. Here, apocalyptic prophecy forges a new symbolic universe through the study and reactualization of an emergent scriptural corpus. The role of intertextuality in the development of Israelite apocalypticism was not isolated. As Marvin Sweeney writes, illusions to preceding biblical texts "play a key role in every proto-apocalyptic text."[2]

In Isa 26, the Bible's early apocalyptic visionaries reach into Israel's new sacred corpus to reuse Isa 44, Isa 54, and Isa 66. God's purposes revealed in Second and Third Isaiah are received as constants, but now extend in a radically totalizing fashion. On this mantic foundation, Isa 26 includes faith in a bodily resurrection of the faithful within Israel's restoration hope. Daughter Zion's end time labor pangs and subsequent birthing

---

1. For a good, brief bibliographic note on the scholarly attempt to pin down a postexilic date for Isa 24–27, recognized for over a century as a distinct section within Isa 1–39, see Philip C. Schmitz, "The Grammar of Resurrection in Isaiah 26:19a–c," *JBL* 122 (2003): 145 n. 1. I use the term "Isaiah Apocalypse," a commonplace rubric, as a label of convenience for this section of Isaiah. The text is not, of course, a full-blown Hellenistic apocalypse. Its character as early "apocalyptic prophecy" should become clear below.

2. Marvin A. Sweeney, *Form and Intertextuality in Prophetic and Apocalyptic Literature* (FAT 45; Tübingen: Mohr Siebeck, 2005), 240.

of new miracle children is interpreted as nothing other than a rising to life again of dead Israelites. This is the thesis I intend to defend here.

In this essay I apply the relatively new scholarly lens of intertextuality specifically to the controverted problem of interpreting the language of resurrection in Isa 26. I take as my foil the argument of some scholars that the text is metaphorical, entailing national restoration not physical resurrection. It does not envision a real rising to life of dead corpses. Rather, the Judeans, having "died" when they lost their land and kingdom, "come back to life" as they return to their land to reestablish their nation. As John Collins puts it, Isa 26 "does not necessarily involve an actual resurrection of dead Israelites."[3]

I approach Isa 26 as a unified piece of poetry in its present canonical form, a self-contained section of the Isaiah Apocalypse. Its first part in verses 1–6 is an eschatological and processional song of thanksgiving, which echoes a similar song in Isa 12. The song will be sung by Israel "on that day," the day of God's decisive victory on earth (26:1; cf. 12:1). The chapter's second, longer section in verses 7–21 is a communal lament and petition for God's intervention against the wicked on behalf of the righteous. Here, the victory of the preceding poem still lies unachieved. The section contains three strophies, verses 7–10, verses 11–19; and verses 20–21. The resurrection of the dead occurs in verses 19–21 as part of two salvation oracles responding to the people's supplication.[4]

---

3. John J. Collins, *Daniel* (Hermeneia; Minneapolis: Fortress, 1993), 395. The view is more common among scholars than one might imagine. For sample proponents, see Schmitz, "The Grammar of Resurrection," 148; John Day, *Yahweh and the God's and Goddesses of Canaan* (JSOTSup 265; Sheffield: Sheffield Academic Press, 2000), 124; Hans Wildberger, *Isaiah 13–27* (trans. T. H. Trapp; CC; Minneapolis: Fortress, 1997), 567–60; Ronald E. Clements, *Isaiah 1–39* (NCB; Grand Rapids: Eerdmans, 1980), 16.

4. For a persuasive division of the chapter, see Marvin A. Sweeney, *Isaiah 1–39 with an Introduction to Prophetic Literature* (FOTL 16; Grand Rapids: Eerdmans, 1996), 469–70. Donald C. Polaski makes a somewhat simpler division of the poem into two units of unequal length: Isa 26:1–6 and Isa 26:7–21. See his *Authorizing an End: The Isaiah Apocalypse and Intertextuality* (BibInt 50; Leiden: Brill, 2001), 207, 216. J. Todd Hibbard offers the same division but includes Isa 27:1 in the second, lament section. He divides the lament into essentially the same subunits that Sweeney identifies: 26:7–10; 26:11–19; 26:20–27:1. See his *Intertextuality in Isaiah 24–27: The Reuse and Evocation of Earlier Texts and Traditions* (FAT 2/16; Tübingen: Mohr Siebeck, 2006), 123–24. For additional discussion of the role of verses 19–21 within the chapter's structure, see n. 11 below.

The lament's first strophe, verses 7–10, pines for God and expresses the wisdom that righteousness will always have the upper hand. The second strophe, verses 11–19, expresses confidence that God will redeem Israel from the possession (בעל) of enemy husbands (v. 13). Israel's true husband is returning, and marvelous fertility will replace the current sterility. In a striking counterpoint to the grim fate of the enemy dead (v. 14), Israel's own dead, who rely on God, will rise and reinhabit the earth (v. 19). The poem's final strophe in verses 20–21 expands the oracle of salvation with an assurance that God *will* come forth to destroy the enemy. The remnant of Israel had best duck and cover.

Given its vision of contrasting fates for God's enemies and God's friends along with its hope of corporeal, bodily resurrection of individuals, Isa 26 shows marked resonances with the phrasing and hope of Dan 12. True, reference to individual, bodily resurrection is more clear-cut in the latter text. That Isa 26 is more mythopoetic and imagistic than Dan 12, however, does not obviate the larger points of similarity.[5]

Daniel 12:1–4 did not interpret Isa 26:19 as mere politics, sensing instead the expansive, potent valence of its language of remarriage and fertility. For Isa 26, the rules of the old age are collapsing; the land of shades is catching its first rays of sun. Watered by God's dew, it is releasing and rebirthing its dead. The exuberant poetic mood of the text resists positivism and pushes back against distinctions between rebirthing Israel and rebirthing individual bodies. The point is the radical passing away of the present age, including death's sterile, dusty darkness.

The theme occurred earlier in Isaiah in 8:16–9:7, where a deathly, sepulchral world gives way to newborn peace and abundance. At the time of Isa 8, Isaiah's opponents are consulting spiritualists, tapping into the world of the dead. Such consultation with the deceased lacks power; the prophet warns that it has "no dawn" (Isa 8:20). Those who rely on necromancy are doomed. They will cross over to Sheol themselves, where they will languish, oppressed, starving, and wrathful (Isa 8:21).[6]

---

5. That Dan 12 represents an innerbiblical interpretation of Isa 26 is uncontestable. See, e.g., George W. E. Nickelsburg, *Resurrection, Immortality, and Eternal Life in Intertestamental Judaism* (exp. ed.; HTS 56; Cambridge: Harvard University Press, 2006), 30–33, 37–38.

6. As Christopher B. Hays puts it, "such pursuits lead only to darkness, suffering, and distress—that is, the condition of the uncared-for-dead" (*Death in the Iron Age II and in First Isaiah* [FAT 79; Tübingen: Mohr Siebeck, 2011], 276). Note that the verb

The "unhappy dead" of Isa 8 see no hope (v. 22).[7] Isaiah 26:18 maintains the selfsame theme. The people, fast in Sheol's clutches, complain: "We cannot produce deliverance on the earth; people to populate the world are not born" (NET). In both 8:21–22 and 26:19, ארץ should be translated as "underworld" or "netherworld." This is the likely referent of the feminine pronoun in the term בה in 8:21. By contrast, when Isa 26:18 speaks of the world of the living, it uses the term תבל, differentiating the world of life and reproduction from the world of dead spirits.

Just as Isa 8 spoke of a world being swallowed alive by death, so also Isa 26 speaks of a people forlorn, up against insurmountable sterility. Although powerless in and of themselves to infuse Israel's family tree with life (v. 18), God's oracle of salvation in verse 19 startles them to hope. In shocking words of encouragement, it cries out: But friends, your dead ones will live! Israel, still alive and in prayer, receives assurance that their faithful dead (a plurality in the Hebrew, not a "collective" singular) will miraculously return to earth. The dead and buried will hear the command as a corpse: "Wake up! Sing!" Hearing the call, the people's dead ones revive and shout for joy. God's earth revives as a place of birth and fresh growth.[8]

עבר may easily signal passing on to the grave (e.g., Job 33:28; 33:18; see George C. Heider, *The Cult of Molek: A Reassessment* [JSOTSup 43; Sheffield: JSOT Press, 1985], 330). Ezekiel 16:21; 20:26; 23:36–42 use the root to describe passing children to the beyond at the valley of Hinnom (alluded to in Ezek 39:11). Gog's apocalyptic horde thus consists of "passers-on," those traversing the boundary between earth and underworld (Ezek 39:11). On Sheol's inhabitants as hungry, and thus wrathful, see Hays, *Death in the Iron Age II*, 44–45, 120.

7. Hays, *Death in the Iron Age II*, 277.

8. On the dead as a plurality, not a collective and political entity, see Jon D. Levenson, *Resurrection and the Restoration of Israel: The Ultimate Victory of the God of Life* (New Haven: Yale University Press, 2006), 197–200. For the translation "as a corpse," see Schmitz, "Grammar of Resurrection," 147–48. I am reading verse 19 as God's promise spoken to Israel, given in response to the prayer and lament of the preceding verses. As Hibbard observes, a salvation oracle is a recognized feature of the lament form (*Intertextuality in Isaiah 24–27*, 124). It is also possible, however, to understand God's response as beginning in verse 20, with verse 19 still addressed to God: "Oh that Your dead will live, [O Lord]" (see LXX, NJPS, NIV, NLT). (Targum Jonathan likewise makes God the subject of the action, bringing the dead to life.) Note that Robert Martin-Achard (followed by Jon Levenson) takes the "you" of the verse as being God, but still argues that Isa 26 is "thinking only of certain members of the Chosen People, of those to whom the words 'Thy dead' refer" (*From Death to Life: A Study of the Development of the Doctrine of the Resurrection in the Old Testament* [trans. John P.

Whereas in its distress Israel could only whisper and murmur incantations (לחש, 26:16 NJPS, NET, NASB), now even their silent dead (see Pss 6:5 [MT: 6:6]; 30:9 [MT: 30:10]; 88:10–11 [MT: 11–12]; 115:17; Isa 38:18) shout and sing for joy (רנן, 26:19). These newly vocal members of Israel are merely the worst-off subset of the people as a whole, Israel's "dead ones" (מתיך). Robert Martin-Achard believes that the authors are "doubtless thinking first and foremost of Jews who died for the sake of remaining faithful to Yahweh—in short, of the martyrs."[9] This would fit with the tone of Isa 26:2, but the text may be referring more generally to all who died at the Babylonian conquest, whether considered "righteous" and "faithful" (26:2) or not (see Isa 27:8; see also Lam 1:1; 2:20–21; Ezek 9:8). It was primarily at the time of the exile that Daughter Zion fell into bereavement according to Isaiah's book (Isa 49:20–21; 51:18–20).

At the time of the Babylonian conquest, Judah's foes became the masters as in Isa 26:13 (see also Isa 63:19; Lam 1:5). Foreign masters continued in power over Israel through the Persian era, when the Isaiah Apocalypse was composed. Both Isa 63:19 and Neh 9:36, 37 join Isa 26:13 in lamenting before God how foreign, imperial power has replaced the Lord's rule over Israel. Even Persian rule, considered favorably in some biblical texts (e.g., Isa 44:28; 45:1–4; Ezra 1:1–4; 6:3), could be experienced as slavery.[10]

The final colon of verse 21 may support this line of interpretation.[11] It appears to reveal, at least partially (see below), which dead Israelite family

Smith; Edinburgh: Oliver and Boyd, 1960], 131; see Levenson, *Resurrection and the Restoration of Israel*, 197).

9. Martin-Achard, *From Death to Life*, 131. Note that Jerome's paraphrase of Isa 26:19 is parallel to that of Martin-Achard: "Thy dead, who were slain for Thy sake."

10. See the comments and bibliography in Francesca Stavrakopoulou, *Land of our Fathers: The Roles of Ancestor Veneration in Biblical Land Claims* (LHBOTS 473; New York: T&T Clark, 2010), 25 n. 97.

11. Some critics have argued that Isa 26:20–27:1 was originally an independent unit, separate from the poem in Isa 26:1–19. See Bernhard Duhm, *Das Buch Jesaia: Übersetzt und Erklärt* (HKAT 3.1; Göttingen: Vandenhoeck & Ruprecht, 1922), 183; George Buchanan Gray, *A Critical and Exegetical Commentary on the Book of Isaiah, I–XXXIX* (ICC; New York: Scribner's Sons, 1912), 437 (commentary on chapters 1–27 only is extant); Claudia D. Bergmann, *Childbirth as a Metaphor for Crisis: Evidence from the Ancient Near East, the Hebrew Bible, and 1QH XI, 1–18* (BZAW 382; Berlin: de Gruyter, 2008), 122 n. 21. If they are later additions, it is probably best to regard them as created for their present context as interpretive expansions of verses 7–19. They fill out the oracle of salvation in verse 19 by responding directly to the supplication in verse 11. Hibbard follows this tack and treats the expansions separately

members verse 19 has in mind. The netherworld, the verse declares, will soon cease covering over *the murdered*. These "slain," the murdered ones of verse 21, would appear to be those killed by God's adversaries (v. 11), that is, by the "other lords" of verse 13. The casualties of the Babylonian destruction of Jerusalem and of the exile might well be center stage in the authors' minds.

According to Isa 26:21b, the bloodstains of the slain will be disclosed by death's own confession. Sheol will cease any longer to hide those who have been killed. Christopher Hays renders the verse's final bicolon as follows: "The underworld will uncover her blood, and will conceal her slain no longer."[12]

Does this reference to earth's "revealing" of the dead constitute another reference to bodily resurrection? The translation of the NLT is highly suggestive: "They [i.e., those killed] will be brought out for all to see" (v. 21). Martin-Achard writes that the shed blood of verse 21 is doubtless that of those "whom Yahweh recognises as His dead and for whom He will accomplish the miracle of the resurrection."[13]

The reference to רפאים ("rephaim"; NRSV: "those long dead"; GNT, GNB: "those who have long been dead") at verse 19's end is significant. A "democratization" of the term in Hebrew usage allowed it to apply to all the living dead, including those of recent memory.[14] Despite this broadening of the term's meaning, however, language of rephaim continued to conjure thoughts of heroes of yore and of dead, divinized kings, not merely thoughts of the undifferentiated deceased (see 2 Sam 21:15-22; 1 Chr 20:6, 8).[15]

---

from verses 7-19, because of their mythological style (again, he is including 27:1) and because they have a different intertextual character (they draw on the Noah narrative and on Mic 1:3a). See his *Intertextuality in Isaiah 24-27*, 135, 162-63, 166-67.

12. Hays, *Death in the Iron Age II*, 325. Hays sees the line's two parts pointing to the underworld's giving up of *both* perpetrators *and* victims (333). The first colon speaks of Sheol giving up those with bloodguilt due to violence (cf. Amos 9:2). The second colon speaks of earth finding release in disclosing the unjustly slain (cf. Gen 4:11).

13. Martin-Achard, *From Death to Life*, 136.

14. On the rephaim as the general class of the dead in biblical psalms and wisdom literature, see Ps 88:10 (MT: v. 11); Prov 2:18; 9:18; Job 26:5.

15. Also see Deut 3:11; Josh 12:4. Note how Ezek 32:17-32 highlights the place of kings, princes, and past war heroes among the hordes of living dead in the world below. The ancient tradition of the special, honorable interment of the elite of yore was familiar to Israelites (Ezek 32:27). On the term "rephaim" in biblical texts as associated

Five verses earlier in Isa 26, we find a striking memory of the term's older, more narrow application—an understanding that it refers to the divinized royal dead (26:14; see also Isa 14:9). This memory is still resounding in the mind as the reader reaches verse 19. The larger context of chapter 26 thus tends to lure the reader away from the thought that merely the contemporary political Israel, conceived collectively, is in mind in 26:19.

In the wider Semitic world, the rephaim were group founders, royal patrons. In their persons, individual and group interests coincided. As deified royal or heroic dead, they were guarantors of dynastic succession, protectors of their city and its virility.[16] To think about group identity and vitality was necessarily to think about the fate after death of these individuals. As the rephaim rose from the underworld, the living king of Ugarit was exalted in their gathered assembly and his subjects greatly blessed.

In using vocabulary of rephaim, Isa 26:19 likely finds communal and individual prospects to be coincident. The text speaks of the rising of dead rephaim in part to convey nuances of Israel's ancient founders and patrons leading a stream of rebirths up from the netherworld. Israelite founders and rulers, such as Abraham, Jacob, and Josiah, will lead the deceased children of Daughter Zion out from the burial chambers. Such a belief fits the era of the Isaiah Apocalypse. In Third Isaiah, the community explicitly laments Israel's alienation from the living-dead souls of its founding ancestors. The people of the early restoration era are in the sorriest of straits, since "Abraham does not know us and Israel does not acknowledge us" (Isa 63:16).[17]

---

with figures of the mythic past and with the royal ancestors of rulers, see Matthew J. Suriano, *The Politics of Dead Kings: Dynastic Ancestors in the Book of Kings and Ancient Israel* (FAT 2/48; Tübingen: Mohr Siebeck, 2010), 159–65.

16. At Ugarit the rephaim were an elite class, whose members were kings and heroes. The publication of a syllabic version of Ugarit's King List has confirmed the divinization of dead kings in Ugaritic religion (see Hays, *Death in the Iron Age II*, 108, 120). Across the ancient Near East, the royal line played the crucial role of supreme officiants in the ancestor cult (see Georgio del Olmo Lete, "The Ugaritic Ritual Texts: A New Edition and Commentary; A Critical Assessment," *UF* 36 [2004]: 539–648 [645]).

17. The supplication in Isa 63:15–19 is tied to our passage by the reverberation between Isa 26:13 and Isa 63:19. Both texts lament the absence of God's direct rule and both cling to Israel's special possession of God's invocation name. Note also how the plea for the Lord to manifest קנאה ("zeal") in 26:11 echoes the same entreaty in 63:15 (see Hibbard, *Intertextuality in Isaiah 24–27*, 142 n. 110). On Abraham and Israel as actual living-dead ancestors in Isa 63:16, see Stavrakopoulou, *Land of our Fathers,*

The likes of Abraham, Jacob ("Israel"), and the Davidic kings must rise from the netherworld first. They are those elaborately and carefully buried (e.g., Gen 25:9–10; 49:29–30; 50:13; 1 Kgs 2:10; 11:43; 14:31; 22:50 [MT: 22:51]; 2 Kgs 23:30). They are those having undertaken "the passage from life to significant status as an ancestor."[18] The rising of iconic patrons, however, cannot be separated from the entire community's salvation. In royal patrimonial ideology, the sacral blessings borne within the royal line extend directly to the populace (Ps 89:49). It is nothing other than God's sure love for David that manifests itself in an everlasting covenant with all God's servants in Isa 55:3.

The renewed vitality of ancestral founders spells beneficence for all. Thus, Zion's godly people will shout for joy when God "will make David's strength thrive" (Ps 132:16–17 CEB). By the same token, New Testament texts insist that Jesus's resurrection was a particularistic phenomenon that from the start had collective ramifications (Matt 27:51–53; 1 Cor 15:20; Col 1:18).[19]

According to the prayerful hope of Isa 26:13–14, God must wipe out all memory of the earthly dynasties who have oppressed Israel. Not only are living enemies slated for death (v. 11), but all the departed, deified dead will soon lie beyond the reach of their descendants' needs. Their invocation names (זכר) will be forever abolished; the normal blessing and intervention functions of the royal shades are permanently lost.[20]

42–44; Lena-Sofia Tiemeyer, *Priestly Rites and Prophetic Rage: Post-exilic Prophetic Critique of the Priesthood* (FAT 2/19; Tübingen: Mohr Siebeck, 2006), 63; Duhm, *Jesaia*, 469; Ignác Goldziher, *Der Mythos bei den Hebräern und seine geschichtliche Entwickelung* (Leipzig: Brockhaus, 1876), 229–30; Karel van der Toorn, "Echoes of Judaean Necromancy in Isaiah 28,7–22," *ZAW* 100 (1988): 199–217 [216]; Thomas Kelly Cheyne, *Introduction to the Book of Isaiah* (London: A&C Black, 1895), 352–53; J. Skinner, *The Book of the Prophet Isaiah* (2 vols; CBSC; Cambridge: Cambridge University Press, 1917), 2:224.

18. Baruch Halpern and David S. Vanderhooft, "The Editions of Kings in the 7th–6th Centuries B.C.E.," *HUCA* 62 (1991): 179–244 (188 n. 25); see Suriano, *The Politics of Dead Kings*, 167 n. 67.

19. On the coincidence of the interests of the individual, the collective, and even nature itself in the biblical expectation of resurrection, see Kevin J. Madigan and Jon D. Levenson, *Resurrection: The Power of God for Christians and Jews* (New Haven: Yale University Press, 2008), 197–98.

20. See Rüdiger Liwak, "רפאים," *TWOT* 13:607–11. Calling a name to memory in biblical Israel did not entail mere recollection but a dynamic encounter. Without invocation of the name among the living, the descendants are deprived of the ances-

Isaiah 26:13 assures us that faithful Israel would never invoke the deified dead of their foreign overlords, nor for that matter the names of any
claimants to power other than the Lord. "Loyal to you alone, we invoke
[זכר] your name" (NJB). Verse 8 had earlier affirmed the same commitment: God's name, the means of invoking God's presence (זכר), is the soul's
desire. As the NJPS renders the verse, "We long for the name by which You
are called." The commitment to calling forth only the Lord leads directly
into verse 14's theme. According to verse 14, foreign powers hope in vain
to invoke the preternatural.

There seems little doubt that verse 14 continues the judgment on
enemy rulers in the preceding verses.[21] First, verses 13 and 14 are in dialog
over which preternatural power it pays to invoke (זכר). Invoking the foreign rephaim is futile, the pair of texts declare, for God has made sure these
"shades do not rise."[22] Second, the two verses adhere together in repeating
a pattern seen in Isa 14, where a grim fate in Sheol attends the judgment of
a wicked ruler. A glance at Isa 14 is highly relevant. As Klaas Spronk notes,
"The term רפאים ... does not occur anywhere else in the book of Isaiah
except in 14:9 where it is used in a similar context."[23]

In Isa 14:20–22, as in Isa 26:11–14, God finishes off the opposing
tyrant; he kills him a second time by eliminating the invocation of his
name. Isaiah 14:20 states, "Let him never be named, that offshoot of evil!"
(NABre). Isaiah 14:20 and Isa 26:14 thus join in declaring ancient expecta-

---

tor's blessing and intervention, and the ancestor is cut off and the soul withers (see Pss
9:5 [MT: 9:6]; 41:5 [MT: 41:6]; 109:13). Note the use of the root זכר in Prov 10:7; Job
18:17; Jer 11:19; and the particularly illuminating comments of van der Toorn on the
meaning of the *hiphil* of זכר in 2 Sam 18:18 (*Family Religion in Babylonia, Ugarit, and
Israel: Continuity and Changes in the Forms of Religious Life* [SHCANE 7; Leiden: Brill,
1996], 208). On an ancestor's "second death" when his name is lost on earth, see Brian
B. Schmidt, "Memory as Immortality: Countering the Dreaded 'Death After Death'
in Ancient Israelite Society," in *Death, Life-after-Death, Resurrection and the World
to Come in the Judaisms of Antiquity* (vol. 4 of *Judaism in Late Antiquity*; ed. Alan J.
Avery-Peck and Jacob Neusner; HO 55; Leiden: Brill, 2000), 87–100.

21. Wildberger, *Isaiah 13–27*, 564–5; Sweeney, *Isaiah 1–39*, 340; Joseph Blenkinsopp, *Isaiah 1–39: A New Translation with Introduction and Commentary* (AB 19; New
York: Doubleday, 2000), 370; Polaski, *Authorizing an End*, 238–39.

22. Hibbard reads verse 14a differently than I do, but we agree on verse 14b: "While
the community has continued to memorialize (נזכיר) YHWH's name, all remembrance
(זכר) of the foreign rulers will cease" (*Intertextuality in Isaiah 24–27*, 144).

23. Klaus Spronk, *Beatific Afterlife in Ancient Israel and in the Ancient Near East*
(AOAT 219; Neukirchen-Vluyn: Neukirchener, 1986), 300.

tions about the royal dead to be defunct.[24] God is tying the hands of the enemy ruler. In life, the foreign lord cannot count on his ancestors' succor; in death, the rephaim will advise him to abandon all hope (see Isa 14:11).

The dead souls of enemy rephaim in Isa 14 and Isa 26 are no metaphor. Until their names are eliminated, the rephaim retain power to help living members of the royal line. Their ostensive divine power and knowledge can function just as it did at Ugarit. In Isaiah's book, there are those within Israel who consider death and its minions a literal force in competition with the Lord (e.g., Isa 8:19; 14:9–10; 19:3; 28:15; 57:6; 65:4).[25] "Why should the dead suddenly appear in this context," Hays writes, "unless it is because they were seen as a competing source of divine power and knowledge?"[26]

The "death after death" of the enemy rephaim in verse 14 paves the way for the miracle of verse 15. God's extermination of the royal dead allows Israel's population to multiply dramatically and the borders of the land to extend. Just as when Israel destroyed the rephaim at the conquest of Canaan, the land's present owners/occupiers must be disenfranchised. As Francesca Stavrakopoulou observes, "To destroy the dead, as this text [Isa 26:14–15] suggests, is to replace their continued 'life after death' with a permanent 'death after death'—to wipe out all memory of them. In this

---

24. Like Isa 26:14, Isa 14:20–22 also speaks of evil royalty (here, possibly Sargon II of Assyria) cursed to never more be invoked upon earth. The Ugaritic royal funerary text (*KTU* 1.161) uses the same vocabulary as Isa 14:20 for invoking the rephaim. Note how plainly Isa 14:20–22 attests to how a lineage's health depended directly upon proper burials, secure inheritances, and the preservation of deceased persons' names (see Suriano, *Politics of Dead Kings,* 162 n. 49; Hays, *Death in the Iron Age II,* 211).

25. The observation holds even for the postexilic portions of Isaiah. On texts such as Isa 57:6 and 65:4 as related to cults of the dead, see William H. Irwin, "'The Smooth Stones of the Wadi'? Isaiah 57:6," *CBQ* 29 (1967): 31–40; Theodore J. Lewis, *Cults of the Dead in Ancient Israel and Ugarit* (HSM 39; Atlanta: Scholars Press, 1989), 149; Philip S. Johnston, *Shades of Sheol: Death and Afterlife in the Old Testament* (Downers Grove, Ill.: InterVarsity Press, 2002), 175; Tiemeyer, *Priestly Rites and Prophetic Rage,* 63–64, 151–52. On the general cultic history of the restoration era, see Brooks Schramm, *The Opponents of Third Isaiah: Reconstructing the Cultic History of the Restoration* (JSOT-Sup 193; Sheffield: Sheffield Academic Press, 1995).

26. Hays, *Death in the Iron Age II,* 326. I am unclear why Hays later distances himself from linking the enemy lords in Isa 26:13 with the dead who do not rise in 26:14 (336).

way, their hold on their land is released. This appears to be a pervasive motif ... of the biblical conquest traditions."[27]

We may now return to verse 19's meaning. In this context of wrestling over the fate of real souls, Israel's corpses, buried in the dust (v. 19), cannot be mere symbols. Verse 19's dead Israelites are no more figurative of something else than are their counterparts, the putatively divinized shades of enemy kings (v. 14). The text holds the two sets of souls in antithetical tension. In each case, the living dead are at issue.

George Nickelsburg correctly notes the "contrast between the raising of the dead of Israel and the fact that their enemies will not rise." The language of rising in both cases is realistic; the rephaim are individual lords' souls. An interpretation of a mere national restoration of Israel is "untenable."[28] So too, Martin-Achard writes, "Vs. 19 is the answer to v. 14"[29]; Rüdiger Liwak states, "Antithetical to v. 14 is the salvation oracle in v. 19.... It draws on the language of v. 14 but arrives at the opposite conclusion by omitting the negative particle."[30]

The souls of enemy kings will not rise to the aid of their people (v. 14); they are slung away from all relevance to the living as from the hollow of a sling. Israel's dead, by contrast, continue in remembrance and relevance. Their ancestral lands, which bind them to the world of flesh and blood, are still claimed by their lineages, and will be restored to rightful "borders" (v. 15). The Israelite rephaim of verse 19 are the remains of real individuals, bundled together with the living in the concern of God.[31]

---

27. Stavrakopoulou, *Land of Our Fathers*, 68. For the conquest traditions in mind, see Num 21:33–35; Deut 3:3, 11, 13; Josh 12:4; 13:12; 17:15; 18:16.

28. Nickelsburg, *Resurrection, Immortality, and Eternal Life*, 31. By the same token, Levenson writes, "the coming revival of the dead is the mirror [i.e., flipped] image of the fate of the idolatrous lords whom the true LORD has dispatched" (*Resurrection and the Restoration of Israel*, 198; see also Madigan and Levenson, *Resurrection*, 186). Paul L. Redditt puts it this way: "The verse clearly distinguishes God's dead from the would-be masters of v. 13, who are also dead" ("Isaiah 26," *RevExp* 88 [1991]: 195–99 [198]).

29. Martin-Achard, *From Death to Life*, 135. He explains, "the Ḥasidim who have paid for their faithfulness to the God of Israel with their lives cannot suffer the same lot as their adversaries, who are Yahweh's enemies as well; the latter vanish for ever, the former will be restored to life."

30. Liwak, *TWOT* 13:611; see Spronk, *Beatific Afterlife*, 301.

31. This is all the more true if Hays's alternative reading of the end of verse 19 is correct. He understands the final colon to double back for a final comment on the fate

Isaiah 26 pushes this contrast in the fate of souls to an extreme. It is not just that Israel's dead remain invoked on earth, connected to the living. Mere ongoing remembrance and communion beyond the grave (see Isa 14:9; 2 Sam 12:23; Gen 37:35) is *not* the vision of the salvation oracle. Instead, Israel's dead will rise reembodied on God's coming day, alive again in corporeal form. They are blessed with the hope of bodily resurrection, of returning to concrete living, breathing, communal life on earth.

Isaiah 26 cares about international affairs and the repatriation of the exiles of Israel. In light of its stunning concern with the fate of dead souls, however, it cannot be reified as bare politics. I part company with J. Todd Hibbard in his view that Isa 26 is read most "naturally" as speaking to "immediate concerns," as anchored in a "moment of despair."[32] God's salvation in Isaiah's book—even in the preapocalyptic Second Isaiah—goes well beyond political dimensions and *zeitgeschictliche,* history-moored concerns. It encompasses an expectation of the stupendous flourishing of nature and humanity. Across the passages of Second Isaiah, the ideal future Zion is well watered and fructified, her waste places springing with growth, teeming with life (Isa 41:18; 43:20; 49:19; 51:3; 52:9). There is a great blossoming forth throughout nature.

The vision of verdant fecundity in Second Isaiah reverses descriptions of Daughter Zion as presently a grieving widow, bereft of all her children (Isa 49:21; 43:6; 54:1; cf. 66:8). God responds to Zion's tragedy by making her supernaturally prolific (44:4; 48:19; 49:22–23; 54:2–3; cf. 66:8). Seeing her new fertility, Zion is wrapped up in awe. A penniless, exiled mother, she is unnerved to discover herself restored with a plethora of perfectly reared children. "Where on earth did these children come from?" Zion asks in 49:21.[33] The ambiguity of the phrase בְנֵי שִׁכֻּלָיִךְ ("children of your

---

of the rephaim of verse 14. Whereas Israel's dead will live, God will "bring down the Rephaim into the underworld" (Hays, *Death in the Iron Age II,* 324). "The final line of v. 19," Hays writes, "contrasts the lot of Yhwh's dead with that of the supposedly powerful divinized dead" (331).

32. Hibbard, *Intertextuality in Isaiah 24–27,* 148. In early apocalyptic prophecy, such as that in Isa 26, the long-range purposes of God, demanding resolution, come into their own. "The ultimate concern," Job Jindo writes, is "not history as such, but the predetermined ending of world history, i.e., the reign of God" (Job Y. Jindo, "On Myth and History in Prophetic and Apocalyptic Eschatology," *VT* 55 [2005]: 412–15 [413]).

33. Zion is enthralled at something beyond explanation, something manifestly greater than herself. By fronting the pronoun אֵלֶּה ("these") twice, the poetry brings

bereavement") in Isa 49:20 suggests a miracle even more extravagant than profuse fertility. One interpretation, found already in the LXX and in Rashi, understands the text to speak of the astonishing return to life of Zion's original children who had perished (see NAB, NJB, NASB, NJPS)![34]

The authors of Isa 26 were doubtless familiar with these motifs and themes. Second Isaiah's vision of new, miracle life on earth must have profoundly touched them. They were prodigious students of Isaiah's book. As Hibbard demonstrates, they were "steeped in the Isaiah tradition."[35]

The Isaianic trajectory toward life's supernatural triumph over sterility and death that begins in Second Isaiah comes to a head in Isa 25:6–8, a text found somewhat earlier within the Isaiah Apocalypse than chapter 26's lament. In Isa 25:6–8, death meets its match in God. Here again, the vision does not limit its purview to Israel's political recovery. Its scope is universal, not national. It speaks of all souls on earth feasting with the God who saves them. The Lord's feast on Zion is for "all peoples" (v. 6); God destroys the shroud cast over "all peoples," "all nations" (כל־הגוים, v. 7). God accomplishes a literal eradication of death on earth.[36] Premodern Jewish commentators rightly point to this passage as a warrant for the rabbinic doctrine of life after death.

Isaiah 26 exhibits intertextual relationships with two specific passages of Second Isaiah of immediate relevance for this essay. Each insists that the ultimate triumph of the God of life involves a miracle of fundamental human and ecological transformation. First, Isa 26 takes up and interprets

---

out how preternatural the children really are: "these—who has reared them?" and "these—where are they from?" Such awe at miraculous, effortless fertility is echoed in Isa 66:8, "Who ever heard the like? Who ever witnessed such events?" (NJPS).

34. See Stephen L. Cook, "The Fecundity of Fair Zion: Beauty and Fruitfulness as Spiritual Fulfillment," in *Daughter Zion: Her Portrait, Her Response* (ed. Mark J. Boda et al.; SBLAIL 13; Atlanta: Society of Biblical Literature, 2012), 77–100.

35. Hibbard, *Intertextuality in Isaiah 24–27*, 140. He notes, for example, that the term ארח ("path") found in both 26:7 and 26:8 appears eight times in Isaiah's book. I am struck by the rare term גאות ("sublimity," "illustriousness") in Isa 28:10 and its echo of Isa 12:5. Based on an in-depth study of Isa 26, Hibbard finds that "the texts that are reused most often in this chapter come from elsewhere in the Isaian tradition." There is likely evidence here of "a growing Isaianic exegetical and interpretive tradition" (119; see also 166).

36. Here I must disagree with Hays's view that Isa 25:6–8 is not eschatological (*Death in the Iron Age II*, 322–23).

Isa 44:1–5, which envisions God's deliverance as life springing up from a newly watered earth. Verses 3–5 of the text read:

> For I will pour water on the thirsty land, and streams on the dry ground; I will pour my spirit upon your descendants, and my blessing on your offspring. They shall spring up like a green tamarisk, like willows by flowing streams. This one will say, "I am the LORD's," another will be called by the name of Jacob, yet another will write on the hand, "The LORD's," and adopt the name of Israel. (NRSV)

The thematic flow of the lament in Isa 26 mirrors the movement from dry barrenness to lush fertility in Isa 44:1–5. God's chastening was upon Israel (26:16; see also 43:28), leaving the people bereft of vitality. They were giving birth "only to wind"; "no one is born" (26:18). Their loved ones were "dwellers in the dust" (26:19), sucked dry by the "thirsty land" (Isa 44:3). Soon, though, infused by God's dewy blessing, the land becomes a *womb*. Isaiah 44:2 says the Lord forms Israel "in the womb." Isaiah 26:19, in turn, makes the earth a womb that "gives birth."[37] In Isa 44:4 those newly birthed sprout like grass; in Isa 26:18 they "populate the world" again (NET). Isaiah 26 repeats the general flow of Isa 44:1–5, but it pushes its motifs significantly farther. It presents a shockingly literal reading of God's vivifying of the barren land. The earth will birth nothing other than Israel's buried dead.

Second Isaiah's vision bears a universalizing thrust that bursts beyond the sphere of nationalism and politics. The thrust is firmly rooted in the tradition, appearing in texts such as 42:6; 45:22; 49:6; 56:3–6; 56:7. It is plain to see in Isa 44:5, where the new progeny springing up from the ground are not natively Israelite but adopt both the name of Israel and the embrace of Israel's Lord. The language of Isa 44:5 is that of foreigners choosing to become servants of the Lord. The same openness to all earth's inhabitants embracing the Lord appears in Isa 26:9. As Hibbard notes, "The inhabitants of the world have the opportunity to 'learn righteousness' (26:9) just like the Judean community."[38]

Isaiah 26:19 has an even more demonstrable relationship with a second text of Second Isaiah, Isa 54. Isaiah 26 takes up Isa 54's image of the barren woman Zion receiving the miracle of abundant children. Chapter 26 not

---

37. See n. 43 below.
38. Hibbard, *Intertextuality in Isaiah 24–27*, 151.

only forwards the earlier chapter's images and themes but also repeats several of its keywords.[39]

In 54:1, God transforms a desolate, barren Zion, devastated by judgment. She is plagued with sterility, having borne no child (ילד) and having no prospect of labor (חול). Isaiah 26:16–17 repeats the verbs, but gives them an intensive, *apocalyptic* spin. Zion strains toward a reversal of her barrenness, toward a fulfillment of God's promises of chapter 54. At first, however, she languishes in the attempt. Pregnant and ready to deliver (ילד), she writhes (חול) with labor pangs (26:17). Though she writhes (חול), she gives birth (ילד), as it were, only to wind (26:18). In short, she remains barren, and her crisis has come to a head. She is in agony as the power of death bears down upon her.[40] As Hibbard argues, the joyful shouting (רנן) of the resurrected in Isa 26:19 is an intertextual allusion to Isa 54:1. There, Zion, no longer barren, shouts for joy.[41] Joy at effortless fertility in Isa 54 becomes joy at apocalyptic victory over sterility and death in Isa 26. Israel must rejoice at the ultimate victory of the God of life over dusty, barren death's threat to lush, verdant human community.

Daughter Zion is not in labor for nothing (Isa 26:17); miracle children will be (re)born (Isa 26:19, 21).[42] The God of history *and* nature is about to triumph decisively. As Spronk observes, "the answer to the complaint

---

39. In different ways, several scholars have argued for reverberations between Isa 54 and Isa 26. Of particular interest are Reinhard Scholl, *Die Elenden in Gottes Thronrat: Stilistisch-kompositorische Untersuchungen zu Jesaja 24–27* (BZAW 274; Berlin: de Gruyter, 2000), 129–30, 216; Polaski, *Authorizing an End*, 252–53; Hibbard, *Intertextuality in Isaiah 24–27*, 150–52.

40. John Day has argued for a different intertextual connection here, namely, a connection with Hos 13:13. This is one of eight parallels he finds between Isa 26:13–27:11 and Hos 13:4–14:10. See his "A Case of Inner Scriptural Interpretation: The Dependence of Isaiah XXVI.13–XXVII.11 on Hos XIII.4–XIV.10 (Eng. 9) and its Relevance to Some Theories of the Redaction of the 'Isaiah Apocalypse,'" *JTS* 31 (1980): 309–19; Day, *Yahweh and the Gods*, 58–59,122.

41. Hibbard, *Intertextuality in Isaiah 24–27*, 151.

42. The futile travail in labor of Isa 26:17–18 represents an image at opposite extremes from that in Isa 66:7–8, which describes Zion's effortless delivery of an entire nation of progeny. For Isa 66:7–8, "as soon as birth pangs came, Zion bore her children" (CEB). It is difficult to establish which text is earlier, Isa 26 or Isa 66. If Isa 26 is drawing on Isa 66, the community is pointedly reminding God that the promised miracle of easy birthing seems distant indeed. In fact, the community's present writhing under foreign domination feels like futile labor! For discussion, see Hibbard, *Intertextuality in Isaiah 24–27*, 156.

that 'no inhabitants of the world were born (נפל qal)' (v. 18bβ) is that the earth shall give birth (נפל hif.) to the dead residing in the netherworld (v. 19bβ)."[43] The miraculous fertility of chapter 54 must blossom in mother earth sprouting verdant, resurrected life.

Weighty, cumulative evidence backs up the claim that Isa 26 draws on and interprets Isa 54. The influence of Isa 54 is first felt in Isa 26:7, which twice identifies the community with the "righteous" (צדיק). They are the righteous who occupy the new Zion (26:2), the fortress God establishes in "righteousness" (צדקה, 54:14).[44] Reverberation continues in Isa 26:12 (see also 26:3), which echoes the language of "peace"—stability and blessing—in 54:10. What God calls "my covenant of peace" (ברית שלומי) in 54:10 is God's unshakeable pact in which those of "firm purpose" (26:3 NABre) trust.

Echoes of Isa 54 continue when Isa 26:13 complains that God does not yet fully possess Zion as God's betrothed. Other lords besides God rule (בעל, 26:13), when God should be embracing Israel in marriage (בעל, 54:5). Verse 20's command to shut the doors and wait for God's judgment to pass appears to take its cue from Isa 54:9's reference to the Noah flood. As Noah's family once did, Israel must now seal themselves off from the effects of God's coming wrath. Finally, verse 20's note that God's coming wrath will last but a "little while" may draw on the idea in Isa 54:7–8 that outbursts of divine anger last but a moment (both Isa 26:20 and Isa 54:7–8 use the term רגע).

---

43. Spronk, *Beatific Afterlife*, 301. The Israelite imagination knows of "*mother earth*" (Sir 40:1; 16:30; Gen 2:7; 3:19; Qoh 5:15) and links the mysterious operations of the womb with the goings on in earth's depths. Psalm 139:15 speaks of the human embryo as knit together in the "recesses of the earth" (NJPS), that is, "in the dark of the womb" (NLT). Job 1:21 reads: "Naked I came from my mother's womb, and naked shall I return there."

44. As Hibbard observes, the claims about being "righteous" here are neither exclusivist nor triumphalist. Isaiah 26:9 is clear that all earth's inhabitants may "learn righteousness" (Hibbard, *Intertextuality in Isaiah 24–27*, 151). We have observed Isaianic notes of universalism above in Isa 44:4–5 and 25:6–7. Against Hibbard, I would not privilege these texts over against Isa 54:3, with its hope to "possess [ירש] the nations." Rather than chauvinism, Isa 54:3 reflects close attention to the tradition that God's blessing and multiplication of Abraham's descendants also entails their inheriting (ירש) the gate of their enemies (Gen 15:5–8; 22:17; 24:60; 28:4; Exod 34:24). The same tradition of inheriting the land of the hostile enemy sounds in Isa 26:15, which, I suggested above, pictures God granting lands held by enemy rephaim to Israel.

According to Isa 26, chapter 54's hopes of intimate reunion with God as husband are still unfulfilled. Neither has the vision of a joyful explosion of progeny materialized. Nevertheless, as Hibbard writes, "what had been stated earlier would indeed come to pass; the community need only to continue to wait on YHWH (קוה; 26:8)."[45]

Among all of chapter 26's reverberations with Isa 54, echoes of the theme of fertility ring loudest. The text's climax and its most surprising revelation occur when 26:19 echoes the shout of joy over new birth that opens Isa 54. The twice-repeated term טל ("dew") in 26:19 also stands out, a poetic encapsulation of divine power to revive life (see esp. Hos 4:5–7 [MT: 6–8]; Ps 110:3; *KTU* 1.19.i.38–46).[46] What is more, the repeated reference to the rephaim reinforces chapter 26's emphasis on deliverance as fertility. As noted above, at Ugarit departed members of the royal house are invoked precisely in order to vouchsafe vitality to the throne and city. In the rephaim texts, the departed are able to assure offspring for King Danil. Isaiah 26, of course, transfers the productive power of fertility from the rephaim to the Lord.

It is this preoccupation with ideal fecundity infusing humanity and nature, as this hope is received from Isa 44 and Isa 54, that pushes Isa 26 beyond concerns with mere political deliverance. Mantic study of the Isaiah tradition has lead instead to a vision of Zion supernaturally infused with God's dew, granting rebirth to Israel's powerless, deceased rephaim (Isa 26:19). Despite all scholarly doubts, Isa 26 is indeed about the rising from death of individual Israelites.

In a stunning reversal of common belief, Isa 26 insists that God's salvation alone can fulfill the archetypal hope for life and bounty—for ennobling fertility—that infused Canaanite royal ideology.[47] God's apocalyptic

---

45. Hibbard, *Intertextuality in Isaiah 24–27*, 151, see also 166–67.

46. John F. Healey, "Dew," *DDD* 249–50; Day, "A Case of Inner Scriptural Interpretation," 309–10; idem, "טל אורת in Isaiah 26 19," *ZAW* 90 (1978): 265–69; Spronk, *Beatific Afterlife*, 299 n. 3; Hays, *Death in the Iron Age II*, 331. Hibbard writes, "dew, often used in parallel with rain, was considered to have powers of renewal, and was, therefore, a great blessing on the land (cf. Deut 33:28; Mic 5:6 [7]; Hag 1:10; Zech 8:12; Ps 133:3; Prov 19:12)" (*Intertextuality in Isaiah 24–27*, 148). The resurrecting power of dew is clear in Jewish midrash. Rabbi Tanḥuma of Edrei said that "the dew of the resurrection descends from the head of the Holy One, blessed be he. In the future he will shake his head [cf. Cant 5:2–3] and make a life-giving dew descend and the dead live again" (Pirqe R. El. 34 [81a])

47. See Liwak, *TWOT* 13:611. He cites *KTU* 1.22.i.5; 1.17.vi.20, 32–33. See also

blessing is world inverting, assuring the lineage of the servants of the Lord an awesome, continuing vitality. "You have increased the nation, O LORD, You have increased the nation; You are glorified" (Isa 26:15 NRSV). "All that we have done, you have done for us" (26:12 NRSV).

Spronk, *Beatific Afterlife*, 300.

Isaiah 24–27 and Trito-Isaiah: Exploring Some Connections[*]

J. Todd Hibbard

1. Introduction

In recent years, several publications have explored intertextual elements of Isa 24–27.[1] Most of these studies have examined how the author(s) of these four late chapters of Isaiah engage(s) with other texts, primarily from within the Hebrew Bible, though there is some acknowledgement that other nonbiblical texts and traditions have been utilized as well. These studies have noted that intertextual connections between Isa 24–27 and elsewhere in the Hebrew Bible do not seem to privilege one portion of the canon, though it is safe to say that several intertexts are found within Isaiah itself. This is not surprising, since most Isaiah scholars recognize that the development of the book over the many centuries of its composition involved, among other things, the creation of an inner-Isaianic discourse. That is, later texts in Isaiah often interact with earlier texts in the book.[2] As one of the later large additions to the book, Isa 24–27 stands theoretically near the end of this process.

---

* This short study originated as a presentation to the Formation of the Book of Isaiah Group meeting at the annual meeting of the SBL, San Francisco, Calif., 19 November 2011. My thanks to the participants there for their incisive comments and questions.

1. See, e.g., Reinhard Scholl, *Die Elenden in Gottes Thronrat: Stilistisch-kompositorische Untersuchungen zu Jes 24–27* (BZAW 274; Berlin: de Gruyter, 2000); Donald C. Polaski, *Authorizing an End: The Isaiah Apocalypse and Intertextuality* (BibInt 50; Leiden: Brill, 2001); J. Todd Hibbard, *Intertextuality in Isaiah 24–27* (FAT 2/16; Tübingen; Mohr Siebeck, 2006).

2. Jacques Vermeylen, *Du Prophète Isaïe à l'apocalyptique, I–XXXV, miroir d'un demi millénaire d'expérience religieuse en Israël* (2 vols; EBib; Paris: Gabalda, 1977–

Uncertainty over the dating of Isa 24–27 necessarily complicates the attempt to describe and understand this intertextual dimension of these chapters. Proposals for dating this material range from the eighth century B.C.E. to the second century B.C.E., with suggestions for every century in that span.[3] As anyone who has worked on these chapters will attest, the difficulty is not only what date to assign them, but *on what basis* any date should be assigned. This section lacks clear references to historical matters that often serve as guideposts for dating prophetic literature, especially Isaiah. Additionally, if one accepts, as most scholars do, that these chapters contain evidence of redactional expansion, the issue of dating becomes even more complicated: Are discusssions about dating directed at the earliest or latest redactional formations of these four chapters or of the entire redactional process?[4]

Given this current state of the situation, the method(s) and criteria used to date this material are important matters of consideration. Prior efforts to date Isa 24–27 have proceeded along several different lines. Arguments for an eighth century date linked to Isaiah himself are based generally on negative assessments of differences in language and style that are marshalled

---

1998), described this as *relecture*, "rereading." Odil Hannes Steck and others preferred the idea of *Fortschreibung*, "updating"; see Odil H. Steck, *Studien zu Tritojesaja* (BZAW 203; Berlin: de Gruyter, 1991). However one describes it, most agree that the book contains instances of earlier texts being reinterpreted by later texts. For an approach to this question that focuses on Deutero-Isaiah's role in this, see Hugh G. M. Williamson, *The Book Called Isaiah: Deutero-Isaiah's Role in Composition and Redaction* (Oxford: Clarendon, 1994).

3. For a more complete treatment of the dating of Isa 24–27, see Polaski, *Authorizing an End*, 51–62; Hibbard, *Intertextuality in Isaiah 24–27*, 32–36.

4. For example, Bernard Duhm's interpretation of the material separated an original core from later additions; see Bernard Duhm, *Das Buch Jesaia* (4th ed.; HKAT 3.1; Göttingen: Vandenhoeck & Ruprecht, 1922), 172. Vermeylen's argument for three stages of the material's composition is consistent with his overall interpretation of the book, which highlights its growth through a process of *relecture* (rereading); Jacques Vermeylen, "La composition littéraire de l'apocalypse d'Isaïe (Is. XXIV–XXVII)," *ETL* 50 (1974): 5–38. Additionally, Joseph Blenkinsopp suggests that "the text has undergone a process of successive restructuring over a significant period of time" and mentions "several drafts," the first of which may have been written soon after Cyrus's conquest of Babylon in 539 B.C.E.; however, he also mentions a plausible date for Isa 24–26 in the century of the Ptolemies; Joseph Blenkinsopp, *Isaiah 1–39: A New Translation with Introduction and Commentary* (AB 19; New York: Doubleday, 2000), 346–48.

to ground a later date.[5] In the absence of a good reason to date the text later, the default position among these interpreters is an early date. Others seek an eighth century date on traditional historical-critical grounds.[6] At the other end of the dating spectrum, Bernard Duhm, who was one of the first to identify the section or parts of it as the Isaiah Apocalypse,[7] dated it based on what he saw as late religious ideas similar to those found in Daniel.[8] Of course, nearly all scholars now recognize that the date assigned to the earliest Isaiah materials among the Dead Sea Scrolls on paleographic grounds rules out dating the section as late as Duhm did (second half of the second century B.C.E.). Dating the texts to the Hellenistic period based on notions of allegedly late religious ideas (e.g., protoapocalypticism, resurrection of the dead) has, however, persisted up to the present.[9] In writing about the date of Isa 24–27, Paul Redditt reminds us, however, that the "presence or absence of certain ideas in an Old Testament passage is an unreliable guide to its date."[10] Linguistically-oriented approaches have also been used to date the material as well. For example, William Millar based his dating of the text on a prosodic approach in which it compared favorably with Deutero-Isaiah.[11] He dated his highly reconstructed text to the second half of the sixth century B.C.E. His approach required extensive textual surgery which, in the view of many, undermined its helpfulness

---

5. John N. Oswalt, *The Book of Isaiah 1–39* (NICOT; Grand Rapids: Eerdmans, 1986), 23–28; A. H. van Zyl, "Isaiah 24–27: Their Date of Origin," 57 in *New Light on Some Old Problems: Papers Read at the 5th Meeting Held at the University of South Africa, Pretoria 30 January –2 February 1962* (ed. A. H. can Zyl; Potchefstroom : Pro Rege, 1962), 44–57.

6. John H. Hayes and Stuart A. Irvine, *Isaiah the Eighth-Century Prophet: His Times and Preaching* (Nashville: Abingdon, 1987), 293–320.

7. See also Rudolf Smend, "Anmerkungen zu Jes. 24–27," *ZAW* (4): 161–224.

8. Duhm, *Das Buch Jesaia*, 172. In his view, Isaiah could as well have written Daniel as Isa 24–27.

9. E.g., Otto Kaiser, *Isaiah 13–39* (trans. R. A. Wilson; OTL; Louisville: Westminster John Knox, 1974), 177–79. Otto Plöger also dated them to the Ptolemaic period based on these religious or theological grounds, but also on his assessment that the chapters reflect sectarian conflicts of the later Second Temple period; Otto Plöger, *Theocracy and Eschatology* (trans. Stanley Rudman; 2nd ed.; Richmond: Westminster John Knox, 1968), 53–78, esp. 77–78.

10. Paul Redditt, "Isaiah 24–27: A Form Critical Analysis" (Ph.D. diss., Vanderbilt University, 1972), 234.

11. William Millar, *Isaiah 24–27 and the Origin of Apocalyptic* (HSM 11; Missoula, Mont.; Scholars Press, 1976), 117.

for dating the text. A more potentially promising linguistic approach is that of Christopher Hays in the present volume, who argues for a seventh century B.C.E. date based on a diachronic approach to Hebrew linguistics.[12] His essay attempts to locate these chapters historically in light of recent research on the development of Hebrew. Unfortunately, in my view, much of the argument is an argument against certain later dates rather than an argument in favor of the proposed date. Though this may in time provide a way forward, more work remains to be done.

To be sure, however, the most common approach to dating this material involves identifying the oft-mentioned anonymous city (24:10; 25:2; 26:1, 5; 27:10) and then using that identification as a basis for dating.[13] Several scholars interpret the material about the anonymous destroyed city as corresponding to a particular city's destruction (e.g., Jerusalem, Babylon, etc.) at a particular historical moment and then assign a date to the text corresponding to that identification. Though several cities have been mentioned as possibilities, the most oft-mentioned candidate for the anonymous city is Babylon. However, even this does not solve the problem, since Babylon was attacked and sacked at various points during the first millenium B.C.E. So, Marie Louise Henry identified this text with the capture of Babylon by Cyrus in 539 B.C.E.,[14] Johannes Lindblom with the Xerxes I's alleged attack on Babylon in 485 B.C.E.,[15] and Wilhelm Rudolph suggested the attack of Alexander in 332 B.C.E.,[16] among others. This highly selective presentation of the interpretive diversity surrounding the identity of the

---

12. Christopher B. Hays, "The Date and Message of Isaiah 24–27 in Light of Hebrew Diachrony," pages 7–24 above.

13. It is unlikely that all of these references are to the *same* city, though some (e.g., Duhm) assumed so. At a minimum, the city in 26:1 does not appear to be the same as the city in 26:5. On the contrasting images of the city in Isa 24–27, see Micaël Bürki's essay ("City of Pride, City of Glory: The Opposition of Two Cities in Isaiah 24–27") in this volume.

14. Marie-Louise Henry, *Glaubenskrise und Glaubensbewahrung in den Dichtungen der Jesaja-apokalypse: Versuch einer Deutung der literarischen Komposition von Jes. 24-27 aus sem Zusammenhang ihrer religiösen Motivbildungen* (BWA[N]T 86; Stuttgart: Kohlhammer, 1967), 17–34; Dan G. Johnson, *From Chaos to Restoration: An Integrative Reading of Isaiah 24–27* (JSOTSup 61; Sheffield: JSOT Press, 1988), 17.

15. Johannes Lindblom, *Die Jesaia-Apokalypse, Jes. 24–27* (LUÅ 34.3; Lund: Gleerup, 1938), 110.

16. Wilhelm Rudolph, *Jesus 24–27* (BWA[N]T 9; Stuttgard: Kolhammer, 1933), 62–63.

city simply confirms what Willem Beuken has recently emphasized: the ambiguity in the description of the city precludes any positive identification of the city, let alone dating of the text on such grounds.[17]

What this brief survey of attempts to date Isa 24-27 reveals is that there is little consensus about the matter. The intertextual approaches to these chapters mentioned above[18] have attempted to establish a date for these chapters based on a different approach. It must be conceded that their results are hypothetical, but arguably no less so than attempts to date the material on other bases. This study follows the recent works of Beuken and Donald Polaski and dates the material to the fifth century, somewhat proximate to the time of Ezra and Nehemiah and their reforms. I hope to establish how certain links with Isa 56-66 support this view. Given the nature of the task, however, we can only hope to elevate a possibility into a probability.

Because of methodological complications arising from questions over dating, most of the studies on Isa 24-27's use of earlier material in Isaiah have avoided exploring links between these four chapters and Isa 56-66 (hereafter, T-I).[19] It has proved difficult—some would say impossible—to stratify the compositional dates of these two Isaianic corpora in a convincing way, making it problematic to talk about one section's use or interaction with the other. This is true whichever one imagines was composed first. Nevertheless, as several scholars have noted, there are a number of interesting similarities and, therefore, possible connections between the two sections.[20] Both are often dated to the Persian period or later, and, therefore, both are part of late layers of the Isaiah tradition. Additionally, there are several areas of verbal and thematic overlap between the two sections that may be noted:

---

17. Willem A. M. Beuken, *Jesaja 13-27* (HTKAT; Freiburg: Herder, 2007), 313-14.

18. See n. 1.

19. The relationship between Isa 40-55 and 56-66 continues to be debated. In my view, the last eleven chapters of the book contain diverse materials from multiple authors originating in a later time than chapters 40-55. The most recent attempt I am aware of to defend the unity of chapters 40-66 is that of Shalom Paul, but it is not persuasive in my view (*Isaiah 40-66: Translation and Commentary* [ECC; Grand Rapids: Eerdmans, 2012], 5-12).

20. Marvin A. Sweeney, *Isaiah 1-39 with an Introduction to the Prophetic Literature* (FOTL 16; Grand Rapids: Eerdmans, 1996), 323; Blenkinsopp, *Isaiah 1-39*, 348.

(1) both use childbirth imagery (Isa 26:17–18; 66:7–9)
(2) both use the language of waiting (קוה) for YHWH/salvation (Isa 25:9; 26:8; 59:9, 11; 60:9)
(3) both speak extensively about salvation (Isa 25:9; 26:1, 18; 56:1; 59:1, 11, 16, 17; 60:16, 18; 61:10; 62:1, 11; 63:1, 3, 5, 8, 9)
(4) both mention a ברית עולם ("eternal covenant," Isa 24:5; 61:8)
(5) both mention Jerusalem/Zion as the holy mountain (Isa 24:23; 25:6, 7; 27:13; 56:7; 57:13; 65:11, 26; 66:20)
(6) both contain communal laments (Isa 26:7–27:1; 59:9–20; 63:7–64:11)
(7) both envision the defeat of a national enemy (Isa 25:10b–12 [Moab]; 63:1–6 [Edom])
(8) both discuss transgression (פשע) (Isa 24:20; 57:4; 58:1; 59:20)
(9) both inveigh against false worship (Isa 27:9; 57:1–13; 66:1–5)
(10) both portray God's judgment through devouring fire (Isa 26:11; 66:15–16)
(11) both divide the community into the righteous and wicked (Isa 26:2, 7, 10 [cf. 24:16]; 57:1, 20; 58:6; 60:21)

Perhaps any one of these taken on its own would be insufficient to note a connection between the two sections, but when taken cumulatively, one plausible hypothesis is that they are associated in some way. The question is how to test this hypothesis and determine how such an association might be understood. It is not my contention that they share common authorship; their differences are too much in evidence to conclude that. Rather, this brief study will defend the thesis that portions of Isa 24–27 are responding to elements of T-I. It is hoped that this will shed light on some of the concerns motivating the author(s) of Isa 24–27. The results here are provisional and open to revision given the necessarily speculative nature of the task. We will explore two examples in order to make the case.

2. Isaiah 26 and Trito-Isaiah

Much in T-I deals with expectations and hopes about the restoration of Jerusalem and Judah in the first half of the Persian period.[21] Of impor-

---

21. Joseph Blenkinsopp, *Isaiah 56–66* (AB 19B; New York: Doubleday, 2003), 51–54. This is not unique to Isaiah, as Haggai and Zech 1–8 express similar sentiments.

tance are issues such as the rebuilding of Jerusalem and its temple, the repopulation of the city and its surroundings, and articulating who could have standing within the reestablished community, an issue that touched on civic, religious, and economic realities. In chapter 66, one reads that Jerusalem's reestablishment will occur with astonishing speed.

> Before she was in labor
> she gave birth;
> before her labor pains came
> she gave birth to a boy.
> Who has heard of something like this?
> Who has seen such things as these?
> Shall a land be born in one day?
> Or a nation be delivered all at once?
> Yet as soon as Zion was in labor
> she delivered her children.
> Shall I open the womb and not deliver? says Yнwн.
> Shall I, the one who delivers, close the womb? says your God. (Isa 66:7–9)[22]

In an oracle using first person divine speech, the restoration is presented here as occurring with such speed that it will be like a pregnant woman who gives birth before going into labor.[23] Though one would expect the restoration to take some time, Zion's return to prominence is envisioned as occurring at an unthinkable pace. Additionally, this restoration will not end prematurely; it will be complete, just as childbirth does not conclude without the actual birth of the child. The passage concludes by presenting Yнwн as a national obstetrician who delivers the child (i.e., Zion) himself.

As archaeological evidence has indicated, however, such a return to predestruction vitality did not materialize for Jerusalem during this period.[24] Rather, the city remained a relatively small town that was overshadowed by Samaria and Damascus (much as it had been in the predestruction era). Large portions of the predestruction city were uninhabited in

---

22. Unless otherwise noted, all translations of biblical texts are the author's own.

23. As Blenkinsopp notes, the passage concerns two issues of major concern in the first century of Persian rule: land and population (*Isaiah 56–66*, 305).

24. Ephraim Stern, *The Assyrian, Babylonian, and Persian Periods (732–332 B.C.E.)* (vol. 2 of *Archaeology of the Land of the Bible*; ABRL; New York: Doubleday, 2001), 434–38.

this period and large portions of the city wall remained unreconstructed.[25] Even though the temple was eventually rebuilt and cultic life restarted, social and economic life in the city apparently lagged. Nehemiah 11:1–2 notes that repopulating the city was done by casting lots, an indication that most persons were not enthusiastic about residing there. The evidence indicates, then, that the optimism of the earliest generation or two of the restoration era gradually gave way to frustration over the difficult realities of life in the fifth century and beyond.

This disappointment may be inscribed, in part, in the communal lament of Isa 26:7–19.[26] This lament starts by contrasting the righteous and the wicked (vv. 7–10) and goes on to note that the community (note the first person plurals of vv. 8, 12, 13, 17, and 18) has experienced some measure of success (v. 15). Ultimately, however, they continue to await lasting triumph. Beyond the evidence of the lament itself, this fact is confirmed by the juxtaposition of this passage with the victory psalm about Jerusalem in 26:1–6, which is set in the future (ביום ההוא, "on that day"; see below). A future hopefulness is balanced by a recognition of the grim realities of the present. A key passage of this lament uses childbirth language, but unlike 66:7–9, the passage utilizes it to describe a failure to produce anything of substance.[27] Isaiah 26:17–18 states,

> Like a woman with child, who writhes and cries out in her pangs
> when she is near her time, so were we because of you, Yhwh;
> we were with child, we writhed, but we gave birth only to wind.
> We have won no victories on earth, and the inhabitants of the world have
> not fallen.[28]

Though the passage is not without exegetical and linguistic challenges, the point is straightforward enough: the community ("we") was ready to give

---

25. David Ussishkin, "The Borders and Size of Jerusalem in the Persian Period," in *Judah and the Judeans in the Persian Period* (ed. Oded Lipschits and Manfred Oeming; Winona Lake, Ind.: Eisenbrauns, 2006), 147–66.

26. I understand 26:20–21 and 27:1 to be later redactional elements associated with the preceding lament but not part of it. See Hibbard, *Intertextuality in Isaiah 24–27*, 120–24.

27. The childbirth language appears also in Isa 13, a passage that Isa 24–27, especially chapter 24, appears to have taken up.

28. This last phrase, ובל יפלו ישבי תבל, is often rendered differently. For example, NRSV translates: "No one is born to inhabit the world." See Beuken, *Isaiah 13–27*, 382.

birth, but when the time came birthed nothing but wind. In other words, the community's expectation of fecundity and triumph has been cruelly replaced by a very different reality. Additionally, the emotional impact of the language is clear. The image of childbirth ordinarily results in joy and elation, but here is used to communicate sadness and despair.

The childbirth imagery here is reminiscent of Isa 66:7–9, but the passage reverses the meaning. The first person speech of Isa 66 uses the imagery to communicate the certainty of the community's recovery and restoration. This is particularly emphasized in the rhetorical questions of verse 9: "Shall I open the womb and not deliver?" and "Shall I, the one who delivers, close the womb?" The first person speech emphasizes that YHWH vouchsafes the certitude of the restoration, an expression of the community's confidence. Isaiah 26:17 uses the birth imagery to express the community's disappointment and subtly indicts YHWH for the lack of success. YHWH brought the community to the cusp of joy: "Like a woman with child, who writhes and cries out in her pangs; when she is near her time, *so were we because of you, Yhwh*" (emphasis added). Because of the common imagery, I read this as a commentary on Isa 66:7–9. In other words, Isa 26 claims that the community's expectation has its point of origin in YHWH.

If, as Joseph Blenkinsopp contends, Isa 66:7–14 was originally the ending to chapters 56–66, it increases the likelihood that a later author might begin with this passage to express disappointment over the restoration effort.[29] What makes this reflection all the more interesting is the acknowledgement in the lament that the nation (presumably Judah [Yehud]) has enjoyed some success: "but you have increased the nation, YHWH, you have increased the nation; you are glorified; you have enlarged all the borders of the land" (v. 15). Apparently, however, this enlargement of geographic boundaries has not translated into lasting success.[30] The inversion of the birthing imagery drives home the point vividly and provides plausible evidence of a connection between Isa 24–27 and T-I.

---

29. Blenkinsopp, *Isaiah 56–66*, 304.

30. Ulrich Berges, *Das Buch Jesaja: Komposition und Endgestalt* (HBS 16; Freiburg: Herder, 1998), 193–94. For an assessment of changes in Persian period settlement, or lack thereof, see Oded Lipschits and Oren Tal, "The Settlement Archaeology of the Province of Judah: A Case Study," in *Judah and the Judeans in the Fourth Cenutry B.C.E.* (ed. Oded Lipschits, Gary N. Knoppers, and Rainer Albertz; Winona Lake, Ind.: Eisenbrauns, 2007), 33–52.

Another aspect of this connection may be noted in the last line of 26:18, which notes that the community has not achieved ישׁועת, one of only two uses of the plural of ישׁועה in Isaiah (the other is 33:6). The term ישׁועה is an important *Stichwort* in both Isa 24–27 and 56–66.[31] In T-I it appears in the section's very first verse, where it is part of the motivation for doing משׁפט and צדקה.[32] It also sounds an important theme in chapters 60–62, the core of T-I, where it appears twice: in 62:1 the anonymous prophet announces his intentions not to keep silent until Jerusalem experiences ישׁועה,[33] and in 60:18 we read that the walls of the restored Jerusalem will be symbolically named "salvation" (along with gates, which are symbolically named "praise," תהלה). In these two passages, it is expressive of the ideas associated with the restoration of Jerusalem. Of course, as we have noted already, the optimism of Isa 60–62 eventually gave way to a different expression, one based on a different reality. This decidedly more pessimistic view is already found in T-I and includes passages using ישׁועה. In particular Isa 57 and 59 offer a much more somber tone, one which notes the failure of any such salvation to materialize. For example, as part of the communal confession of 59:9–15a,[34] 59:11 notes that though the community has waited for salvation, it has not come because of their sin (vv. 12–15a). In the hopeful response that follows in 59:15b–20, the lack of justice and failure of anyone to intervene to remedy the situation of 59:9–15a prompts Yhwh to clothe himself as a warrior to intervene himself. Part of his armor includes a "helmet of salvation." Other forms using the root term ישׁע also occur in chapter 59 (vv. 1 and 16), making clear this theme's importance in this chapter.

When Isa 26:18 laments that the community has not achieved instances of salvation, then, it echoes the language of Isa 59, as well as the chronologically earlier ישׁע discourse in T-I. Even in this instance, however, we may note that Isa 26:7–18 takes a more pessimistic view: where 59:15b–20 answers the lament with a portrait of Yhwh as warrior who

---

31. It also plays an important role in Isa 40–55, but not in a way that impacts the dating of Isa 24–27.

32. On the importance of this verse, see Rolf Rendtorff, "Isaiah 56:1 as a Key to the Formation of the Book of Isaiah," in *Canon and Theology* (trans. Margaret Kohl Minneapolis: Fortress, 1993), 181–89.

33. In 62:1 and 56:1, it is paired with צדקה, with the meaning of vindication or victory.

34. For the form and content of Isa 59, see Blenkinsopp, *Isaiah 56–66*, 184–203.

intervenes to bring salvation, 26:7–18 notes that YHWH's hand is upraised but apparently to no avail (v. 11). Indeed, the passage is rounded off with an admonition to the community to "take cover" because YHWH's punishment of the earth's inhabitants portends danger (26:20–21).[35] On the other hand, one might argue that the song of 26:1–6, which celebrates the future strong city of Judah (read: Jerusalem), is meant to counterbalance the lament that follows. This song also uses material from T-I, taking up language and themes from Isa 60 in order to reuse them here. The notice in 60:18 about the gates and walls of restored Jerusalem—the latter of which is called ישועה, "salvation," appears to be taken up by 26:1–2. The strong city (עיר עז) of this chapter also has walls associated with salvation (v. 2). Additionally, 60:17 notes that, among other things, "peace"(שלום) will be established as the overseer (פקדתך) over the new city. The role of peace in the life of the new community is taken up by 26:3 where it is given new coordinates: instead of its role for the city generally, it is here envisioned as a benefit for those within this newly established city who trust in YHWH. This leads to the last element of overlap between these chapters, the portrayal of the city gates: 60:11 and 26:2 use remarkably similar language:

Open the gates [פתחו שארים], so a righteous nation, one that observes faithfulness, may enter [ויבא גוי צדיק]. (Isa 26:2)

Your gates shall be open [פתחו שעריך] continually; day and night they will not be shut, in order to bring [להביא] to you the wealth of nations [חיל גוים] with their kings being led.[36] (Isa 60:11)

In this case, Isa 26 appears to have taken up this verse about the restored city's gates in order to recast who enters. The idea that the subjugated nations come bearing their wealth to the restored city in Isa 60 (see also 66:12) is replaced with the notion that it is a righteous nation or people who enters the city. This is related, of course, to the lament that follows, which questions why the wicked still prevail over the righteous (esp. 26:10). Additionally, we may note that the future role of the nations

---

35. This passage rounds off Isa 24–26, since it forms an *inclusio* with the concerns of Isa 24. Isaiah 27:1 represents a mythic reinterpretation of the ideas of 26:20–21, with the remainder of Isa 27 expressing matters of different concern.

36. On the form נהוגים, see Paul, *Isaiah 40–66*, 527.

is imagined differently in Isa 24–27 than in Isa 60–62: the idea that the nations serve the restoration community is replaced with the portrayal of the nations along with the Judean community as participants in the banquet on Zion prepared by YHWH (25:6–8).

The foregoing has sought to demonstrate that elements of Isa 26 have taken up passages and ideas from T-I in order to recast them. The cause for this appears to be that the community has not experienced the successful restoration envisioned in much of T-I (though as was noted, certain passages in T-I echo this). Why has the restoration fizzled out? To that question we turn in the next section of this study.

3. A BROKEN ברית עולם: ISAIAH 24:5 AND 61:8

Nearly all exegetes of these chapters have noted that the reference to the broken ברית עולם in 24:5 is an important element of these chapters.[37] Most studies have attempted to identify the ברית עולם in question, since the Hebrew Bible contains a limited number of such designations. Given the universal frame of reference in Isa 24, many have noted that the reference is likely connected in some way to the ברית עולם in Gen 9:16 established by YHWH with Noah in the aftermath of the flood (Gen 9:8–17), a covenant that is also universal in scope.[38] The idea in Isa 24, then, would be that the violation of the similarly designated covenant has universal ramifications. While a connection with Gen 9 is not entirely without difficulty, recognition of a connection between these two texts does not seem unwarranted.[39]

---

37. E.g., Kaiser, *Isaiah 13–39*, 183; H. Wildberger, *Isaiah 13–27* (trans. Thomas H. Trapp; CC; Minneapolis: Fortress, 1997), 500; Johnson, *From Chaos to Restoration*, 27; Donald C. Polaski, "Reflections on a Mosaic Covenant: The Eternal Covenant (Isaiah 24.5) and Intertextuality," *JSOT* 77 (1998): 55–73; Blenkinsopp, *Isaiah 1–39*, 351–2; Steven D. Mason, "Another Flood? Genesis 9 and Isaiah's Broken Eternal Covenant," *JSOT* 32 (2007): 177–98.

38. See, e.g., Erich Bosshard-Nepustil, *Vor uns die Sintflut. Studien zu Text, Kontexten und Rezeption der Fluterzählung Genesis 6–9* (BWA[N]T 5; Sttutgart: Kohlhammer, 2005), 248–59.

39. There are two problems with associating these two texts. First, it is not altogether clear what the covenant stipulation in Gen 9 is, which would make any accusation that the covenant is broken difficult to substantiate. Second, if one reads the prohibition of bloodshed in Gen 9:5–6 as the stipulation (an identification found frequently in antiquity), it must be noted that Isa 24 does not state that bloodshed forms the evidence of covenant violation.

The question is, is this the only connection one should make here in this reference to covenant? The Hebrew Bible recognizes more than just one ברית עולם of course. Genesis 17 uses this language to describe the Abrahamic covenant, with male circumcision as its requirement (vv. 10–14). Additionally, Exod 31:16 identifies the Sabbath as a ברית עולם, and Lev 24:8 specifies that the priestly bread offered each Sabbath is also a ברית עולם. Could these other pentateuchal references also be important for understanding the broken covenant in Isa 24? Given Isa 24–27's relatively late composition and intertextual character, Beuken has argued that the reference likely "bundles up" (bündelt) all these existing contexts of meaning.[40] As such, it refers not just to events in the past, but also to the present. He goes on to note that the inhabitants of the earth are included in this covenant.[41] This has ramifications for how it is understood and when this text was composed. How this is so requires us to return to the last eleven chapters of Isaiah.

Though it is rarely mentioned by interpreters in their efforts to understand the broken covenant of Isa 24, there is another ברית עולם in Isaiah that may have some bearing on that of Isa 24.[42] Isaiah 61:8 notes the establishment of a ברית עולם as part of the expectation of a restored Jerusalem found in the literary core of T-I (i.e., Isa 60–62).[43] Here we read:

> I will faithfully give them their reward (פעלתם), and I will make an everlasting covenant (ברית עולם) with them. (Isa 61:8b)

Using divine first person speech, the text reports the establishment of a ברית עולם with the inhabitants of Zion and Judah as part of a speech from an anonymous prophet who announces his call and message (61:1–11).

---

40. Beuken, *Jesaja 13–27*, 323–24; see also, Polaski, *Authorizing an End*, 71–145. My view on this issue has changed somewhat since my earlier publication on this subject; Hibbard, *Intertextuality in Isaiah 24–27*, 56–68, esp. 68.

41. Beuken argues that, in light of 24:21–23's emphasis on the future reign of YHWH, it also has the future in view; *Jesaja 13–27*, 323–24.

42. There is actually another ברית עולם in Isa 55:3, but I am not persuaded it has any direct bearing on Isa 24. For its impact on the construction of the covenant in Isa 61, see Jacob Stromberg, "The Second Temple and the Isaianic Afterlife of the חסדי דוד (Isa 55,3–5)," *ZAW* 121 (2009): 242–55.

43. For Isa 60–62 as the earliest layer of Third Isaiah, see most recently Jacob Stromberg, *Isaiah After Exile: The Author of Third Isaiah as Reader and Redactor of the Book* (Oxford: Oxford University Press, 2011), 11–13.

This covenant in perpetuity has moral coordinates: verse 8a speaks of
YHWH's love of משפט ("justice") and hatred of גזל בעולה (best understood
as "robbery with injustice").[44] The covenant in perpetuity is in parallel with
פעלתם ("their reward"), a term used elsewhere in Isa 40–66 in contexts
that speak of YHWH's restoration of Jerusalem and its community (40:10;
62:11; cf. 49:4). The idea is that as part of the restored life in Jerusalem,
YHWH will establish a ברית עולם with the community there, an act that
will signal its renewed status with God.[45] The larger context of chapter 61
also includes reference to the nations as those who acknowledge that these
covenant participants are blessed by YHWH (v. 9). This is reminiscent of
Gen 12 and the Abrahamic blessing, which also includes the idea that the
nations will be blessed through the Abrahamic community (12:1–3).[46] This
announcement stands at the center of Isa 60–62, itself the center of T-I. As
such, its importance is also structurally apparent.

Isaiah 56–66 contains other dialogue about covenant (though not
designated as an "eternal" one) that informs both the idea of covenant
in T-I and Isa 24. Such passages take up the role of the nations or non-
Judeans within the covenantal economy. In Isa 56, part of the outer frame
and, therefore, arguably among the latest portions of T-I, one finds an
attempt to define the covenant in such a way that foreigners and eunuchs
are permitted to join the covenant community (56:3–8). The requirement
specified for covenant inclusion is to keep the Sabbath (56:2, 4, 6).[47] On
this basis, then, non-Judeans would be granted standing in the temple
(56:7–8).[48] This is important for the understanding of covenant within T-I
and Isa 24–27, because it broadens the possible membership within the
covenant community. The placement of this passage *before* the passages
about the role of the nations as those who play a support role only in the
restoration life (e.g., 60:10–14) invites the reader to think in other ways
about the possibility of non-Judeans as covenant participants. We may say,

---

44. Paul, *Isaiah 40-66*, 545–46. The term בעולה has been interpreted in several
ways. Here עולה is read as denoting wrongdoing; cf. Job 5:16; Pss 58:3; 64:7.

45. It is noteworthy that both Jeremiah (32:40; 50:5) and Ezekiel (37:26) contain
very similar notions.

46. Blenkinsopp, *Isaiah 56-66*, 228–31.

47. Though Gen 17 mentions circumcision as a covenant requirement, it is not
mentioned here, nor anywhere else in Isaiah. In fact, it is not mentioned beyond the
book of Joshua at all (except at Jer 9:25 [MT 9:24], where physical circumcision is contrasted with circumcision of the heart).

48. See Paul, *Isaiah 40-66*, 456–57.

provisionally, that the final form of Isa 56–66 is one which defines the covenant participants, including the eternal covenant, in categories that are not exclusively ethnic but rather primarily cultic.[49] To put the matter differently, it presents a universalized notion of covenant community, inclusion in which is contingent on the performance of religious requirements not ethnic identification.[50]

This is the starting point for understanding the message of Isa 24. Isaiah 24:5's reference to the broken eternal covenant takes up the idea of covenant espoused by Isa 61 and 56 in order to make the case that its requirements—here understood as open to all—have not been met. Following Beuken and others, we might say that the use of ברית עולם here invokes *all* of the covenant traditions mentioned above to create a rich understanding of what is meant by covenant and what its requirements are. The Abrahamic covenant (Gen 12 and 17[51]) now opened to all humankind (Gen 9), the requirement of which is Sabbath observance (Exod 31; Isa 56)—this covenant that is a hallmark of restoration Jerusalem (Isa 61) has now been broken (Isa 24). Isaiah 61's use of moral language as part of its construal of the establishment ברית עולם invites the reader to connect it with idea in Isa 24:5 that such a covenant is now broken. Though the language in Isa 24 is different from Isa 61, the differences may be explained by noting that Isa 24 offers a broader and more expansive assessment of how this covenant is broken, one that includes but is not limited to what is said in Isa 61:8a. Additionally, this broader language explains, in part, the depiction of the covenant violations as having worldwide ramifications. A covenant community now open to all implies that violation of the covenant can affect all.[52]

---

49. See the discussion in Christophe Nihan, "Ethnicity and Identity in Isaiah 56–66" and Jill Middlemas, "Trito-Isaiah's Intra- and Internationalization: Identity Markers in the Second Temple Period," in *Judah and the Judeans in the Achaemenid Period* (ed. Oded Lipschits et al.; Winona Lake, Ind.: Eisenbrauns, 2011), 67–104 and 105–25, respectively.

50. This understanding of the Yhwh community is anticipated already in Isa 40–55; see, e.g., 44:5.

51. I recognize that including Gen 17 here may appear inconsistent since it mentions circumcision (מול, 17:11). However, its inclusion in this list is because of the association with Abraham, not circumcision. It is on this basis, that I would contend, that it plays any role in covenant discourse in Isaiah. Indeed, circumcising (מול) is never mentioned in Isaiah.

52. The image in Isa 25:6–8 of the meal on Zion in which Yhwh swallows (בלע)

Though it is impossible to be certain, it appears that Isa 24's understanding of the broken eternal covenant fits well with the period of Ezra and Nehemiah, that is, the late fifth century. Though the issues are addressed differently in those books, the basic matters appear similar. Where Ezra–Nehemiah takes a restrictive view of who has standing in the covenant community, defined principally on ethnic grounds, Isa 24 is in essential agreement with the position laid out in Isa 56—that the covenant community is open to all. This radical redefinition of the covenant community fits well with Isa 24's universalizing tendency. In this case, however, it recognizes that the covenant stipulations have been violated and depicts the effects of such violation in cosmic and cataclysmic terms. The lament in Isa 26:7–18 noting the success of the wicked and failure of the righteous along with the enumeration of cultic violations in 27:9–10 contributes to this portrayal. Read in this way, the reference to the deserted fortified city in 27:10 looks quite likely to be further reflection on the shame engendered in the community over failure to restore its former prestige. As such, hopes for Jerusalem remain situated in the future (25:6–10a; 26:1–6). To put the matter differently, in the period of the mid- to late fifth century, the author(s) of Isa 24–27 lamented the woeful and disappointing state of Jerusalem and understand the cause of its condition to be covenant violations. Whereas Ezra and Nehemiah took the view that the proper response was to expel foreigners (at least foreign women and children; Ezra 9–10), Isa 24–27 lamented these conditions and re-presented its hope for Jerusalem's future exaltation.

If Isa 24–27 is, in fact, reacting to material in T-I, why was it placed in its current location in the book rather than at the end of the book, adjacent to T-I itself? As several scholars have noted in recent years, Isa 24–27's placement in the book of Isaiah must be viewed in relation to the preceding oracles against the nations (Isa 13–23).[53] Isaiah 24–27's theological canvas is one of universal and cosmic scope, and, as such, it links well with the international concerns of the preceding eleven chapters. To the degree that the proposal here has merit, it offers an additional aspect of that asso-

---

death (המות) may have covenantal overtones as well, since meals are often depicted as part of the ceremony establishing covenants (e.g., Exod 24). In this case, then, the meal to which the nations are invited may augur the establishment of a new relationship (read: covenant) between Yhwh and the nations at Zion. See the essay by Cho and Fu in this volume.

53. See, e.g., Beuken, *Jesaja 13–27*, 311.

ciation with the nations in Isa 13–23: they are now possible participants in the covenant community, and the placement of Isa 24–27 at this point in the book makes this clearer.

Yahweh Regenerates His Vineyard: Isaiah 27

John T. Willis

Isaiah 27 is a very difficult text. At least four people appear in this chapter (Yahweh, the composer or prophet, the inhabitants of the fortified city, and Jacob or Israel or the people of Israel), sometimes in the first person, sometimes in the second person plural, and sometimes in the third person. The composer refers to Yahweh in the third person in 27:1, 7a, 8b, 9c, 11d–e, 12a, 13b. Yahweh speaks in the first person in 27:2–5. The composer refers to Jacob or Israel in the third person in 27:6, 9a–b and to "the fortified solitary city" in 27:10–11c. He addresses a group of people in the second person plural, once specifically addressing the "people of Israel" (27:8a, 12b). The MT of 27:6a reads הבאים ("Those who come [Jacob will take root...]"). Several scholars conjecturally emend this to בא היום ("the day has come [comes]") without any ancient manuscript support. The NRSV reads "In days to come." These variations in Isa 27 make it very difficult to follow the flow of thought. At the same time, alterations of this type are quite common throughout prophetic literature.

Many scholars have attempted to determine the historical setting of Isa 27. Several clues appear in this chapter, but none is absolutely conclusive. First, 27:6a–b, 9a, 12b specifically refer to or address Israel and Jacob. This might suggest Isa 27 pertains to north Israel. Second, "the fortified city" that is "solitary" in 27:10a–b might be Samaria, since the surrounding context is Israel and Jacob. However, other scholars insist this fortified city must be Jerusalem, because 27:13b specifically alludes to "the holy mountain at Jerusalem." Depending on the way in which one interprets the entire chapter, some scholars have proposed that this "fortified city" is Nineveh or Babylon. Still others connect 27:10a–b with an anonymous world capital mentioned in 25:2; 26:5 that Yahweh will destroy. Third, 27:9 announces that Yahweh will destroy Asherim or sacred poles and incense altars, a statement that assumes the worship of Asherim and incense altars was currently in use when this setting occurred. This fits the historical situation of north Israel, in particular Samaria, in 2 Kgs 17:9–12, 16, and also Jerusalem during the reign of Manasseh in 2 Kgs 21:3–5, 7. Fourth, 27:12–13 says Yahweh will gather the lost and driven out from Assyria and Egypt and bring them back to Jerusalem to worship Yahweh there, which calls to mind the Babylonian exile in 587 (or 586) B.C.E.

One's evaluation of the structure of Isa 27 depends on whether a researcher approaches this chapter diachronically or synchronically. Diachronically, some sharply partition Isa 27 into as many as seven independent units: 27:1, 2–5, 6, 7–8, 9–11, 12, 13; others divide it into 27:1, 2–6, 7–8, 9–11, 12–13; others separate it into 27:1, 2–6, 7–11, 12–13. In all these distinctions, scholars who understand Isa 27 diachronically think of each unit as independent and separate from the rest of the chapter. Synchronically, certain terms, metaphors, and ideas run as themes throughout Isa 27. (1) "On that day" occurs in 27:1, 2, (conceivably 6), 12, 13. (2) Agricultural or horticultural terms, ideas, and related terms permeate the entire chapter: serpent (v. 1); vineyard (v. 2); keep or guard (v. 3); water (v. 3); briers and thorns (v. 4); protection (v. 5); take root, blossom, put forth shoots (v. 6); fruit (vv. 6, 9); calves graze (v. 10) and strip branches (v. 10); dry boughs (v. 11); thresh (v. 12). (3) Violent, warlike, militant expressions, and ideas run throughout Isa 27: Yahweh will punish Leviathan with a cruel and great and strong sword and kill him (v. 1); Yahweh will "march to battle against" thorns and briers that threaten the vineyard (v. 4); the vineyard will cling to Yahweh "for protection" (v. 5); Yahweh "struck down" and "killed" those who opposed Yahweh's people (v. 7); "by exile" Yahweh's people struggled against their enemies (v. 8); with Yahweh's "fierce blast" he removed his enemies in the day of the east wind (v. 8); Yahweh will "crush to pieces" the incense altars so that none will remain standing (v. 9); "the fortified city is solitary" (v. 10); "on that day," "a great trumpet will be blown," summoning the lost and driven-out exiles to return from their captivities to Jerusalem (v. 13). (4) Several groups of people appear consistently throughout Isa 27: Jacob (vv. 6, 9), Israel (v. 6), "those who struck" (v. 7a), "their killers" (v. 7b), "you" (plural) = the people of Israel (vv. 8a, 12b), "the fortified city [that] is solitary" (v. 10), women (v. 11), a people without understanding (v. 11c–e), those lost and those driven out (v. 13). From a coherent rhetorical perspective orally, one may think of 27:1 and 12–13 as an *inclusio* in prose declaring that "on that day" Yahweh will overthrow the enemies of his people. Within the *inclusio*, 27:2–11 falls into two parts: in 27:2–6, Yahweh assures his penitent people that he will

sustain and protect them; in 27:7–11, Yahweh explains that his chastisement was essential to bring his people back to Yahweh, and now he has
removed his sin. Unlike Jerusalem (v. 13), "the fortified city" (probably
Samaria, but also possibly Babylon or an anonymous city) is forsaken and
deserted (vv. 9–11). Hence, Isa 27 presents a positive encouraging message
to Judah.[1]

The language in 27:1 is mythological. Leviathan, the fleeing serpent,
the twisting serpent, and the dragon in the sea are terms familiar in Ugaritic texts. Lotan (Leviathan), Yamm, Tannin, and similar terms appear as
enemies of Baal and Anat. Mythological language occurs several times in
the book of Isaiah: Tannin (51:9), Rahab (30:7; 51:9), Yam/"sea" (5:30; 9:1
[MT 8:23]; 10:26; 11:15; 17:12; 23:4, 11; 50:2; 51:19) and elsewhere: Leviathan (Job 3:8; Ps 74:14), Tannin (Job 7:12; Pss 74:13; 148:7), Rahab (Job
9:13; 26:12; Pss 87:4; 89:10 [MT 89:11]), Yam/"sea" (Job 3:8; 7:12; 26:12; Pss
74:13; 89:9 [MT 89:10]). Leviathan is a symbol of the autonomous, recalcitrant force of evil in a general sense, while some scholars suggest it refers
to Egypt, Tyre, Assyria, or Babylon.[2]

---

1. Note this emphasis by Brevard S. Childs, *Isaiah* (OTL; Louisville: Westminster
John Knox, 2001), 195.

2. (a) For evil in a general sense, see Paul Auvray, *Isaie 1–39* (SB; Paris: Gabalda,
1972), 239 (possibly); Otto Kaiser, *Isaiah 1–39* (trans. R. A. Wilson; OTL; London:
SCM, 1974), 221–23 (and yet, Kaiser says the biblical composer may have used a secret
language to refer to the kingdom that he really intended or possibly the nations in gen-
eral); Ronald E. Clements, *Isaiah 1–39* (NCB; Grand Rapids: Eerdmans, 1980), 218;
Joseph Jensen, *Isaiah 1–39* (OTM 8; Wilmington, Del.: Michael Glazier, 1984), 208;
John N. Oswalt, *The Book of Isaiah 1–39* (NICOT; Grand Rapids: Eerdmans, 1986),
491; John Day, "Leviathan," *ABD* 4:295–96; J. Alec Motyer, *The Prophecy of Isaiah: An
Introduction and Commentary* (Downers Grove, Ill.: InterVarsity Press, 1993), 221–22;
Walter Brueggemann, *Isaiah 1–39* (Westminster Bible Companion; Louisville: West-
minster John Knox, 1998), 210–11; Childs, *Isaiah*, 196–97; Patricia K. Tull, *Isaiah 1–39*
(Macon, Ga.: Smyth & Helwys, 2010), 400. William R. Millar wrote a monograph on
Isa 24–27, in which he parallels these texts with *KTU* 1.5.i.1–5. He argues that there is a
pattern in Isa 26:20–27:13 of threat, war, victory, and feast (he deliberately omits 27:7–
11, because it is corrupt and contains no solid clue for a probable reconstruction).
The composer of Isa 24–27 did his work after the flourishing of a royal festival at Zion
(587 B.C.E.) and the conflict that emerged in early postexilic Israel between two groups
vying for supremacy in the reconstruction of the destroyed nation. William R. Millar,
Isaiah 24–27 and the Origin of Apocalyptic (HSM 11; Missoula, Mont.: Scholars Press,
1976), 1–22, 54–63, 69–102, 104–8, 114, 119–21. (b) Egypt: Hans Wildberger (*Isaiah
13–27* [trans. Thomas H. Trapp; Minneapolis: Fortress, 1997], 578, 593–96) argues

Isaiah 27:2-6 completely and intentionally counters 5:1-7. "The song [27:2-6] is a conscious counterpart to the first one [5:1-7]."[3] Gene M. Tucker goes so far as to say: "The close parallels to the language indicate that the writer of 27:2-6 has Isa 5 before him."[4] (1) In 5:1, the prophet declares he will "sing" (שיר) about Yahweh's vineyard; in 27:2, the prophet summons his audience to "sing" (ענה) about Yahweh's vineyard. (2) Isaiah 5:1 describes Yahweh's vineyard as "on a very fertile hill"; in 27:2 Yahweh's vineyard is "pleasant." (3) In 5:2, 4, Yahweh expected his vineyard to yield good grapes but it yielded wild grapes, but in 27:6, Yahweh declares that Jacob will take root, Israel will blossom and put forth shoots, and fill the whole world with fruit. (4) In 5:5-6, Yahweh declares he will judge or punish the unproductive grapes, but in 27:3, Yahweh declares he will guard his vineyard day and night so that no one can harm it. (5) In 5:6d-e, Yahweh announces he will command the clouds so they can rain no rain upon his vineyard, but in 27:3b, Yahweh declares he will "water" his vineyard every moment. (6) In 5:6c, Yahweh proclaims his vineyard will be overgrown with "briers and thorns" (שמיר ושית), but in 27:4, Yahweh declares he will march to battle against the "briers and thorns" (שמיר שית) and burns them up. (7) In 5:5c, 5e, 6a, Yahweh declares he will remove the vineyard's hedge, break down its wall, and make it a waste, but in 27:5b, c summons the vineyard to make peace with Yahweh.[5]

The horticultural metaphor of Yahweh as a vinedresser or husband-man or viticulturist and Israel or Judah as a vine or vineyard appears in Hos 9:10, 16; 10:1, 11-13; 14:4-7; Isa 3:14; 32:12-16; Jer 2:21; 5:10; 6:9; 12:10; Ezek 15:1-8; Ps 80:8-19, communicating essentially the same spiritual story based on the metaphors of:

---

that the dragon in 27:1 is Egypt and that 27:1 dates from the time of the campaigns of Artaxerxes III in 342 B.C.E.; Auvray, *Isaie 1-39*, 239; Day, "Leviathan," *ABD* 4:295-96, both as a possibility. (c) Tyre: John D. W. Watts, *Isaiah 1-33* (WBC 24; Waco, Tex.: Word, 1985), 298-99, 348, 349, 351, with a chiastic chart suggesting that 27:1 is the counterpart of Isa 23 concerning Tyre. (d) Assyria: This is the view of John H. Hayes and Stuart A. Irvine, *Isaiah: The Eighth-Century Prophet: His Times and His Preaching* (Nashville: Abingdon, 1987), 315. (e) Babylon: Johann Fischer, *Kapiten 1-39* (vol. 1 of *Das Buch Isaias*; HSAT 7.1; Bonn: Hanstein, 1937), 180.

3. Watts, *Isaiah 1-33*, 349.

4. Gene M. Tucker, "The Book of Isaiah 1-39: Introduction, Commentary, and Reflections," in *The New Interpreter's Bible* (ed. Leander E. Keck; 12 vols; Nashville: Abingdon, 2001), 6:226.

5. See the careful observations of Wildberger, *Isaiah 13-27*, 583.

- Yahweh as husband and Israel or Judah as wife
- Yahweh as parent and Israel or Judah as children
- Yahweh as doctor or physician or healer and Israel or Judah as ill patient
- Yahweh as shepherd and Israel or Judah as sheep or flock
- Yahweh as potter and Israel or Judah as clay
- Yahweh as king and Israel or Judah as people or kingdom or nation.

This spiritual story falls into five (in some metaphors six) stages or scenes, as reconstructed in the story of Yahweh as the vinedresser and Israel or Judah as the vine or vineyard in Isa 5:1–7 and 27:2–6:

(1) Yahweh plants or transplants his vine or vineyard (from Egypt to Canaan).
(2) The vine or vineyard becomes degenerate or fails to produce good grapes.
(3) Yahweh punishes or prunes the vine or vineyard.
(4) Yahweh still sustains and preserves the vine or vineyard.
(5) Yahweh waters the vine or vineyard to cause it to bear good fruit.

The figure of "thorns and briers" appears in Isa 5:6; 7:23–25; 9:18 (MT 9:17); 10:17; 27:4; 32:13; Ezek 2:6; 28:24. Some scholars suggest this figure has in mind foreign invaders, the Assyrian oppressors (citing 10:17),[6] or Samaritan opponents.[7] Others argue that in the song of the vineyard in 5:1–7 and 27:2–6 this figure fits best of an internal process or decay and degeneration, thus the sin or rebellion of Israel or Judah against Yahweh. Benjamin J. M. Johnson reasons persuasively that the preferable reading in 27:4b–c is: "*Whoever* gives me thorns and thistles, I will march *with* her." Yahweh will be present with the vineyard in its war against the thorns and thistles. In light of the use of thorns and thistles in 9:18 (MT 9:17) and 10:17, thorns and thistles may refer to external or internal

---

6. Hayes and Irvine, *Isaiah*, 316.

7. Joseph Blenkinsopp, *Isaiah 1–39: A New Translation with Introduction and Commentary* (AB 19; New York: Doubleday, 2001), 374. Kaiser (*Isaiah 1–39*, 225) proposes that the enemies are future schisms within Judah that will have no hope of reconciliation.

enemies, possibly the Assyrians and opposing Israelites. The plea to the audience in 27:5–6 to cling to Yahweh's stronghold and be at peace with Yahweh could be an appeal both to foreign nations and Israel.[8]

Isaiah 27:7–11 contain the most difficult portion of Isa 27. The overall context of this chapter indicates that 27:7–11 presents an encouraging message for Israel (Jacob) and Judah. The synonymous parallel questions in 27:7—"Has he [Yahweh] struck them [Israel and Judah] down as he struck down those who struck them [Babylon]? Or have they [Israel and Judah] been killed as their killers [Babylon] were killed?"—call for a negative response. Yahweh has not punished Israel and Judah as much has he has punished Babylon and other enemies of Yahweh's people (v. 7).[9] By exile, "you" (plural; Yahweh's people) struggled against "her" (feminine singular; Babylon); with his (Yahweh's) fierce blast, he removed them in the day of the east wind (the sirocco) (the Babylonian exile) (27:8). "Therefore" (לכן) "by this" (בזאת), namely, Yahweh's punishment of his people by the Babylonians, Yahweh "will expiate" (יכפר, pual imperfect of כפר) the "iniquity" (עון) of Jacob and "remove" (הסר) the "sin" (חטאת) of Jacob by destroying the pagan Asherim and incense altars still standing among Yahweh's people (27:9).[10] Then Yahweh will overthrow "the fortified city [which] is solitary, forsaken." Paul Auvray, Otto Kaiser, Ronald Clements, Hans Wildberger, Walter Brueggemann, and Gene Tucker think this city is probably Samaria, "a people without understanding," because of their idolatry (27:9) contrasted with Jerusalem, the pleasant vineyard which experiences peace (27:2, 5).[11] Several scholars agree with this view, but emphasize that this refers to the Samaritans who came into conflict with the Judeans return-

---

8. Benjamin J. M. Johnson, "'Whoever Gives Me Thorns and Thistles': Rhetorical Ambiguity and the Use of *my ytn* in Isaiah 27.2–6," *JSOT* 36 (2011): 105–26 (107, 110, 118–23, 124).

9. Fischer (*Buch Isaias*, 181) reasons that, because Yahweh did not annihilate Israel like foreign nations but sent Judah into exile, Isa 27 must be dated after the Babylonian devastation of Jerusalem in 586 B.C.E. However, Hayes and Irvine (*Isaiah*, 317–19) argue that these questions call for an affirmative response, meaning that Yahweh has now smitten Assyria as Assyria used to smite Israel as a purging of his sinful people, and the destruction of the cult places in 27:9 was due to the reforms of Hezekiah which Isaiah is supporting (2 Kgs 18:4).

10. Brueggemann, *Isaiah 1–39*, 214; Blenkinsopp, *Isaiah 1–39*, 377.

11. Auvray, *Isaie 1–39*, 242–43; Kaiser, *Isaiah 13–39*, 230; Clements, *Isaiah 1–39*, 220–22; Wildberger, *Isaiah 13–27*, 578, 593–96; Brueggemann, *Isaiah 1–39*, 215; Tucker, "Book of Isaiah 1–39," 227.

ing from Babylon to rebuild the Jerusalem temple.[12] Christopher Seitz and Joseph Blenkinsopp believe this city is Babylon, because the Babylonians are "a people without understanding." Yahweh will have no compassion or favor on Babylon (27:10–11).[13] Johann Fischer and Patricia K. Tull think the fortified city is Jerusalem, which the Babylonians destroyed.[14] Several scholars conclude that this city is "the world city" or a symbol of earthly power and oppression without specifically giving a location.[15]

In 27:12–13, the composer or prophet announces that "on that day" Yahweh will thresh from one end of the ancient Near East to the other, separating the wheat of Yahweh's faithful servants from the chaff of Yahweh's enemies "one by one" in order to redeem his people (v. 12).[16] And "on that day" a great "ram's horn" (שׁוֹפר) will be blown (יתקע) not to summon Yahweh's people to enter into battle (a common use of the ram's horn; see Josh 6:4–21; Judg 7:16–22; Amos 2:2; 3:6; Hos 5:8–9; 8:1; Jer 4:5–6; 6:1), but to go to worship Yahweh on the holy mountain at Jerusalem (v. 13; see Pss 47:5 [MT 47:6]; 81:2–3 [MT 81:3–4]; 98:5–6).

---

12. Jensen, *Isaiah 1–39*, 210–11.

13. Christopher R. Seitz, *Isaiah 1–39* (Interpretation; Louisville: John Knox, 1993), 197–200; Blenkinsopp, *Isaiah 1–39*, 378–79.

14. Fischer, *Buch Isaias*, 184; Tull, *Isaiah 1–39*, 412.

15. This is the view of Kaiser, *Isaiah 13–39*, 228; Oswalt, *Book of Isaiah*, 496–97; Motyer, *Prophecy of Isaiah*, 224–25; Childs, *Isaiah*, 198.

16. Oswalt, *Book of Isaiah*, 500, argues that the Hebrew word means "beat off," and the harvest is not of wheat but of olives.

WORDS OF WOE, VISIONS OF GRANDEUR: A LITERARY AND HERMENEUTICAL STUDY OF ISAIAH 24–27*

Carol J. Dempsey

Isaiah 24–27 has long been considered the "Apocalypse of Isaiah," since material in these chapters possesses some similarities to apocalyptic literature. Recent scholarship, however, argues against assigning this block of material to the apocalyptic genre.[1] Although the precise genre of these four chapters has yet to be determined, one thing is clear: Isa 24–27 is a block of material rich in literary form and technique, whose poet used exceptional rhetorical skill to communicate a provocative message that is sure to evoke a response from the text's listeners and readers.

With respect to the dating of Isa 24–27, these four chapters seem to be late additions to Isa 1–39 and seem to have originated sometime during the Persian Period, though clues within the text that would suggest such a dating, or even another date, are few.

In addition to questions surrounding the genre and dating of Isa 24–27, questions have also surfaced with regard to the material's unity. Is this block of material a series of loosely strewn together passages, or is the material arranged in such a way so as to suggest a subtle unity among these chapters? Joseph Blenkinsopp argues that Isa 24–27 is composed of a "number of loosely connected passages of uneven length, the sequence

---

* This essay contains both new information as well as some thought that was first introduced in my commentary on Isaiah (see *Isaiah: God's Poet of Light* [St. Louis: Chalice, 2010]).

1. For further discussion on the question of the literary form and genre of Isa 24–27, see Marvin A. Sweeney, *Isaiah 1–39 with an Introduction to Prophetic Literature* (FOTL 16; Grand Rapids: Eerdmans, 1996), 313; see also Patricia K. Tull, *Isaiah 1–39* (Macon, Ga.: Smyth & Helwys, 2010), 367.

of which manifests no immediate logical order."[2] Blenkinsopp's argument invites a closer look at Isa 24–27, and hence, this essay aims to: (1) explore the literary and rhetorical dimensions of the material at hand in order to uncover the literary richness of these four Isaian chapters and to argue for an inherent unity within Isa 24–27; (2) examine the place and function of Isa 24–27 in relation to Isa 1–39; (3) evaluate how the texts' literary and rhetorical dimensions help to develop the theological themes present in Isa 24–27; and (4) consider the hermeneutical aspects of Isa 24–27 and how the material can speak to contemporary audiences today.

1. Isaiah 24: A Harrowing Yet Hopeful Vision

Isaiah 24 consists of three main units: a judgment speech (vv. 1–3); a vision of sadness and hope (vv. 4–20); and a judgment proclamation (vv. 21–23). The mix of material and sentiments conveyed within this first chapter sets the tone for all of Isa 24–27. Judgment and devastation will occur but such tragic experiences have the purpose of paving the way for a new world order, one that will include not only salvation for Zion/Israel (Isa 24:1–27:13) but also a divine plan for Jerusalem that will entail the announcement of the coming of a promised royal savior (Isa 28:1–33:24). Of note, the "city" mentioned in verses 10 and 12 is nameless, which suggests that the poet of Isa 24 could be doing two things at the same time: (1) reflecting on the destruction that happened to Jerusalem at the time of the Babylonian Empire and (2) commenting on the Persian takeover of Babylon that was foreshadowed earlier in Isa 13 (see specifically 13:17).

Verses 1–3 open with a judgment speech on a cosmic scale: the whole earth is about to be laid waste and made desolate by God (v. 1). The speaker of these verses is the prophet Isaiah, who offers his listeners a poetic vision of impending disasters that are about to take place. Strains of the Noachic flood story (see Gen 7) resound in the background of this opening judgment speech. Like the time of the great flood, this impending disaster will be cosmic and catastrophic. The image of Israel's God laying waste the earth, making it desolate, twisting its surface, and scattering its inhabitants makes clear that this God is not simply a tribal deity interested in a small

---

2. See Joseph Blenkinsopp, *Isaiah 1–39: A New Translation with Introduction and Commentary* (AB 19; New York: Doubleday, 2000), 346.

group of people. No, this God as personified by the poet is the Lord of creation and the Lord of history who works on grand scales.

In verse 2 the use of a catalogue that contains several antitheses adds to the breadth and scope of God's intended actions introduced in verse 1. The six pairs of people to be affected by the imminent disaster include: the people and the priest, the servant and the servant master; the maid and her mistress; the buyer and the seller; the lender and the borrower; the creditor and the debtor. Collectively, these six antithetical pairs of people highlight the fact that no social class, no religious group, and no specific gender will escape God's judgment, a curse that will be applied universally. The use of the catalogue with its antithetical pairs of people also serves to foreshadow the message of verse 3: "The earth will be utterly laid waste and despoiled."[3] This phrase recalls verse 1, but now the use of the *niphal* absolute paired with the *niphal* imperfect verb בקק adds a sense of totality to the impending devastation that the prophet announced earlier in verse 1. The phrase "for the Lord has spoken this word" closes this first unit. This phrase represents an appeal to divine authority that assures the prophet's audience that indeed all that has been spoken will in fact happen. Thus, the poet's rhetoric has created a unit that is woven together tightly to deliver a horrifying message sure to rattle the bones of Isaiah's listeners.

Verses 4–20, the second unit, are a vision of sadness and hope. Throughout the unit, the word ארץ serves as a keyword. Its repetitious use (fourteen times: vv. 4 [twice], 5, 6 [twice], 11, 13, 16, 17, 18, 19 [three times], and 20) keeps the prophet's audience's attention on the earth while providing a link between verses 1–3 (where ארץ appears in v. 1 and v. 3) and verses 4–20. The use of a series of perfect and converted perfect verb forms as present tense verbs makes clear that the impending devastation is inevitable. These tense forms are consistent with prophetic vision. Thus, the tragic events about to befall the people are reported as if they have already occurred (see, e.g., v. 4).

In verses 4–5, the earth is personified as a living entity capable of expressing itself. Here in these verses, earth is mourning,[4] and even the heavens are languishing together with the earth (v. 4). These verses hint at a severe drought that has or is about to take place in the land. The image of

---

3. Unless otherwise noted, all translations of biblical texts follow that of the NRSV.

4. For a detailed discussion on earth mourning, see Katherine M. Hayes, "*The Earth Mourns*": *Prophetic Metaphor and Oral Aesthetic* (Atlanta: Society of Biblical Literature, 2002).

the earth lying polluted under its inhabitants (v. 5a) is an indirect indictment against some members of the community who are guilty of bloodshed resulting from murders, wars, and executions that have contaminated
the land. The statement may also be not only an allusion to the Babylonian
invasion of the land but also a foreshadowing of the Babylonians being
conquered by the Persians. Verse 5b is the climax not only of verses 4–20
but also of the entire poem (vv. 1–23). Until now, the prophet has given no
reason for the divine wrath that is about to befall the people. The prophet
has kept his audience in wonderment and suspense to hold their attention
and to capture their imaginations. Only now does the poet allow the audience to see the reason behind the divine judgment speech, namely, that
some within the community have transgressed laws, violated statutes, and
broken the everlasting covenant. The use of three verbs in rapid succession
in verse 5b depicts a progression of action on the part of the community
while capturing the severity of the people's waywardness that results in the
suffering of the land and all its inhabitants.[5]

Finally, the mention of ברית עולם in verse 5b harks back to covenants
made with Noah (Gen 9:1–17), Abraham (Gen 15 and 17), David (2 Sam
7:1–17), the Israelite people in the days of Jeremiah (Jer 32:40), and Ezekiel
(Ezek 16:20). The reference to an everlasting covenant also recalls Sabbath
rest, a ברית עולם between God and the Israelites (Exod 31:16; see also Lev
24:8). The covenant reference here in Isa 24:5b is most likely a reference to
a cosmic covenant first introduced in verses 1–3.

In verses 6–12, the poet develops more fully the images introduced in
verses 4–5. Verse 6 is a pivotal verse that looks backwards to verses 4–5 and
forward to verses 7–12. The double use of the phrase על־כן (v. 6a and 6b)
links verses 4–5 to verses 7–12. The indictment and theological message
become clear: the people will now experience a divine curse, because they
have transgressed the law and broken the covenant (see Deut 28:15–68).
The divine curse is personified as an entity that has a rather large mouth,
one large enough to "devour" the entire earth (6a). A simple statement in

---

5. In the ancient world, people believed that disasters happened in the natural
world as a result of God's judgments. God would strike the land with droughts, floods,
pestilence, and blithe in order to punish the people for their transgressions (see, e.g.,
Amos 4:6–12; see also Deut 28:15–68). Hermeneutically, while these metaphorical
acts of divine judgment may have been justified to chastise an unjust people, the acts
would be unjust from the perspective of the natural world, which is not responsible
for human transgressions.

verse 6b captures the severity of the curse: "therefore the inhabitants of the earth dwindled and few people are left."

Verses 7–12 expand on verse 6. In verses 7–12, the prophet outlines very clearly what is to take place as a result of the divine curse and chastisement. Because the land is cursed, the "wine dries up," "the vine languishes," and "all the merry-hearted sigh" (v. 7). Mardi Gras has now ended. The curse of the land affects its vegetation, which in turn affects the people. The image of the wine drying up and the vine languishing harks back to verse 4, where the land mourns and the world and the heavens languish together with the earth. Thus, the poet has picked up images from verse 4 and moved them in a different direction in verses 7–9. Images from verse 7 also recall Isa 5:12, 14 and Joel 1:10, 12. Verses 8–9 pick up the dispiritedness of the people expressed in verse 7. Festivities, normally celebrated when the vintage is completed, come to a halt.[6] There is no music, no wine, no song. Thus, the imagery of suffering associated with sin pervades Isaiah's message.

In verses 10–11, the progression of the curse and chastisement mentioned in verse 6 continues through the use of imagery. The countryside scene created by the use of vineyard imagery in verse 6 now shifts to an urban setting. The audience's attention is now directed to the "city of chaos." This city is nameless. The reference to this city links Isa 24:10–12 to Isa 25:2–5; 26:1–6; and 27:10–11. All of these passages make mention of a "city." Here in Isa 24:10 the "city of chaos" could be an allusion to Damascus or Samaria (Isa 7:8–9; Isa 17), Babylon (Isa 13 and 21), and Tyre (Isa 23). It is most likely a reference to Jerusalem as well. Thus, the image of the city links Isa 24 to other parts of Isa 1–39. John D. W. Watts points out that

> It is not the cities themselves that are important here, but what they stand for. They have represented an era in which cities dominated the political scene. They were the seats of influence and wealth, and they were often the real power within the small nations. Sometimes foreigners simply seized the city and were thereby able to control the larger countryside for generations.[7]

In this era, the city of chaos is broken down, houses are shut up, people begrudge the lack of wine, all joy has reached its eventide, and the glad-

---

6. For further discussion on the cessation of the vintage festivals, see Ronald E. Clements, *Isaiah 1–39* (NCB; Grand Rapids: Eerdmans, 1980), 202.

7. See John D. W. Watts, *Isaiah 1–33* (WBC 24; Waco, Tex.: Word, 1985), 319.

ness of the earth no longer exists. The city is left desolate; even the gates are "battered into ruins." Human sinfulness has affected not only the land but also civilization as a whole.

Verse 13 is a summary of verses 4–12. Here the prophet links the land and the people together. The shift from the prophetic perfect in verses 4–12 to the imperfect in verse 13 serves as a shift in time and focus. The vision of devastation (vv. 4–12) within the prophetic proclamation (vv. 1–24) has come to an end, and the prophet now states that what he has envisioned for the people in verses 4–12 will indeed come to pass. Two similes from the natural world common to the people of Isaiah's day (see v. 13b) intensify the prophet's message and hold his audience's attention. The future verb tense used in verse 13 is similar to those used in verses 1–3. Thus, the message that Isaiah proclaims and the vision that he describes to the people as part of his message will indeed come to pass.

Following a descriptive vision of cosmic catastrophe comes a vision of hope in verses 14–16a. These verses describe a group of jubilant people who are joyful over God. This jubilation is captured by a series of three phrases: "they lift up their voices," "they sing for joy," "they shout from the west" (v. 14). Isaiah does not name the jubilant ones or suggest who "they" are who lift up their voices and sing for joy. Scholars offer a variety of suggestions.[8] In the context of verses 1–15, the jubilant ones could be the ones who are the righteous ones among all the people who remain faithful to their relationship with God and with each other. Perhaps they are the few in verse 6 who remain after all else is cursed and chastised. Perhaps they are the "remnant." Looking at verses 14–15, perhaps the ones who are jubilant over God's majesty are those who were once oppressed and sinned against, who now witness the demise of their oppressors—the sinners. One problem, however, still remains. How can the people sing when the land has been devastated and people are wasted because of their sinfulness? Should not their song be a song of mourning as well as joy? These two questions posed to the text anticipate verses 16b–20.

Once again the picture and tone shifts in verses 16b–20. In these verses, the prophet laments. Unlike the jubilant ones who sing for joy in verses 14–16a, the prophet sings a mourning song (vv. 16b–20) that begins, "I pine away, I pine away. Woe is me" (v. 16b). He laments how treacherously

---

8. See, e.g., Clements, *Isaiah 1–39*, 204; G. B. Gray, *A Critical and Exegetical Commentary on the Book of Isaiah, I–XXVII* (ICC; New York: Scribner's Sons, 1912), 417.

the treacherous deal; he grieves that terror, the pit, and the snare are upon the inhabitants of the land (v. 17) and how no escape will be possible (v. 18). The image of the windows of heaven being opened and the foundations of the earth trembling recall the flood story (Gen 7:11). Finally, very poignantly Isaiah mourns for the land in verses 19–20:

> The earth is broken,
>> the earth is torn asunder
>> the earth is violently shaken.
> The earth staggers like a drunkard
>> it sways like a hut
> its transgression lies heavy upon it
>> and it falls, and will not rise again.

The use of personification brings the plight of the earth to life. The land—the earth, אֶרֶץ created and named by God, אֶרֶץ who has cared for and welcomed so many people, אֶרֶץ who is home to everything living—is on its last leg and is destined to fall, never to rise, all because of humankind's sinfulness.

Verses 21–23, the poem's third and last unit, are a judgment proclamation rich in personification and similes. The eschatological phrase "on that day" (v. 21) signals this new unit. For the prophet, the vision that he envisioned for the people has come to a close, but for the people, the vision is about to unfold. The day of the Lord is coming; God's justice is about to take place (vv. 1–3, 4–20, 21–22), beginning with the host of heaven in the heights and then the kings of the earth who, because of their office, should have been exercising their responsibility of assuring justice among the inhabitants of the land (see Mic 3:1–12). Finally, in a cosmic setting and with the luminaries personified (v. 23), Isaiah proclaims that God, the Lord of hosts, will reign in the land—on Mount Zion and in Jerusalem. And the city of chaos, with Jerusalem implied, will once again become glorious.

2. Isaiah 25: A Prophet's Prayer and a Vision of Celebration

With the coming of the reign of God now proclaimed, the prophet now offers a word of praise to God (vv. 1–5). A vision of a great celebration follows Isaiah's prayer (vv. 6–8), and a statement of confidence expressed by Isaiah closes this next poem (vv. 9–12).

Isaiah's prayer in verses 1–5 opens with a vocative, "O Lord," which is followed by a confession: "you are my God." Two short phrases capture Isaiah's exuberance: "I will exult you"; "I will praise your name" (v. 1a). Following the prophet's initial words of praise is a more detailed confession in which the prophet describes all the wonderful things that God has done. Israel's God is the one who makes a city a heap and a ruin, who destroys foreign palaces, who is a refuge to the poor and needy, a shelter from the rainstorm and a shade from the heat, who subdues oppressors and silences the ruthless (vv. 2–5). The image of the city as a heap and a ruin (v. 2) could refer to Babylon, but Walter Brueggemann suggests that "the city moves even beyond Babylon to be the ultimate city of wealth, arrogance, autonomous power, and exploitation. It is every city that is devoted to buying and selling, making money and abusing."[9] Isaiah sees God's decimating actions on this unnamed city and the cities of other ruthless nations as wonderful deeds that speak of God's ways and plans (v. 2). Because God has done wonderful deeds for those experiencing injustice and oppression (vv. 2, 4b–5), Isaiah is able to acknowledge that God is a refuge and a shelter to those in distress (v. 4a). The catalogue of God's wonderful deeds in verse 4a highlights a preferential option for the poor and needy on the part of God which Isaiah affirms by mentioning these deeds in his prayer.

Words of prayer, confession, and affirmation provide a segue into verses 6–8, a vision of a great celebration for all people and not just for the Israelites. The wine and good cheer that had once been flowing before it was dried up in Isa 24:6–9 is now once more flowing. This part of Isaiah's poem with its reference to the mountain as a gathering place for all peoples echoes Isa 2:1–4 and perhaps even provides a hint at what will take place when all the nations do stream to and arrive at the highest of mountains—God's holy mountain. This reference to the mountain also harks back to Isa 24:23. The inferred reference here is most likely to Mount Zion with all the implications of royal messianism included. The tradition upon which the poet drew for this description of the feast is probably Exod 24, a story that describes how seventy elders were invited with Moses, Aaron, and Aaron's sons to go to Mount Sinai and there see God and feast in God's presence. Notable in Isa 25:6–8 is the fact that God is no longer portrayed as warrior God. Israel's God has become the host of a

---

9. See Walter Brueggemann, *Isaiah 1–39* (Westminster Bible Companion; Louisville: Westminster John Knox, 1998), 197.

grand banquet. Images of warfare have given way to images of hospitality, because on God's holy mountain, swords are turned into plowshares and spears into pruning hooks. Nations no longer lift up swords against one another, and thus, people no longer have to train for war anymore (see Isa 2:4). The images of the shroud, the sheet, death, tears, and disgrace are all suggestive of sadness, but the destruction of the shroud and the sheet, the swallowing up of death forever, the wiping away of tears, and the taking away of disgrace (vv. 7–8) are images suggestive of renewal and transformation for all God's people who will be forever feasting at a rich banquet to be provided for them by their God—the God of the nations.

The poem closes with a statement of confidence. Here the prophet quotes imaginatively what the feasting people will say on the day of the banquet when they are all gathered on God's mountain. God's people are affirming and joyful. In verse 10a, the reference to God's hand resting on the mountain is an example of the use of anthropomorphism and metonym. Here God's hand symbolizes God's presence and fullness of power. God's hand once outstretched (Isa 14:27) has now found a place to rest.

Finally, a series of similes describes the Moabites and their fate (vv. 10a–12). The Moabites will be trodden down in their place "as straw is trodden down in a dung pit," and even though they spread their hands "like swimmers" for swimming, they will not be successful. As a conclusion to this last unit and to Isaiah's poem as a whole, these last verses serve as a reminder that transformation does not happen all at once and once and for all; it is a gradual process, one nation at a time as the Moabites exemplify.

3. Isaiah 26: A Song of Jubilation

The tone of jubilation continues in Isa 26. This song of jubilation is a song of praise that features several voices and is composed of two psalmic units (vv. 1–6 and vv. 7–19) and an appeal (vv. 20–21). Interestingly, Isa 25 opened with the prophet's personal reflective prayer (vv. 1–5), and now Isa 26 ends with the prophet's prayer (vv. 8–21). Isaiah 25 closed with words of certainty focused on salvation (vv. 6–12), and Isa 26 opens with a word of confidence that celebrates the strength of a city—Jerusalem—and the righteousness of a nation (vv. 1–2). Significant in this poem is the phrase "on that day" (v. 2), which is a reference to the Day of the Lord. In the ancient biblical world, the Day of the Lord was thought to be rooted in Israel's holy war experiences (see, e.g., Isa 5:26; Zeph 3:8; Zech 14:2). In the biblical text, one sees God personally intervening on the Day of the Lord (Isa 34:8; Ezek 24:25; Amos 3:14; Zeph 1:8; 2:2–3). The events of the Day of the Lord included raging fires (Isa 10:16; 38:22; Joel 2:30), whirlwinds and storms (Isa 28:2; 30:30; Jer 25:32; Ezek 38:22), the shaking of the heavens and the earth (Isa 2:10, 19; 13:13; 23:11; Ezek 38:19; Hag 2:21–22), floods (Isa 28:2; Jer 47:1–7), and the darkening of the sun and moon either by clouds, eclipses, or some other natural phenomenon (Isa 5;30; 13:10; 24:23; Ezek 32:7–8; Zeph 1:15). Finally, the Day of the Lord is not only a day of judgment (Isa 34:2–3; Jer 25:33; 49:26; Ezek 24:21) but also a day of deliverance, replenishment, refreshment, and rejoicing (Isa 29:18–19; Zeph 3:11–14, 16–20).

In Isa 26:1, the phrase "on that day" recalls Isa 24:21, where the day will be a day of punishment for the host of heaven and the kings of the earth. In Isa 25:9, however, the day will be a day of deliverance, and in Isa 26:1, the day will be one of joy and hope. Thus, the Day of the Lord implied in the phrase "on that day" establishes the eschatological nature of the poet's message and also paints a mixed theological portrait of Israel's God.

The first part of this song of jubilation is a song of praise for God's victory (vv. 1b–6). In these verses, the community acknowledges the greatness of God who has won a victory over an exalted enemy city (vv. 5–6). The image of the lofty city recalls the picture of the high and mighty ones who will be brought low (Isa 2:11–18). It also harks back to the image of the mighty king who will be brought down to Sheol (Isa 14:11). These images throughout the book of Isaiah, together with the one presented in verses 5–6, suggest that the city was guilty of oppressing the poor. The reference to the "strong city" in verse 1 is an allusion to Jerusalem. The "gates" in verse 2 are the city gates of Jerusalem. The community petitions God to open the gates so that the righteous nation that keeps faith may enter. Though the nation is not named, the most likely referent is the city's inhabitants. Though they are not perfect (v. 16a; 18), their strength lies in the fact that they keep faith, the central quality in maintaining right relationship with God. The gift that God bestows upon this people is peace (v. 3). Verses 4–5 are an exhortation that the community proclaims. Here people are being exhorted to trust in Israel's God because of what this God does. For the community that keeps faith, this God is an "everlasting rock" (v. 4), a metaphor typically associated with God. As a "rock," God's deeds are faultless (Deut 32:4), just (Ps 92:16), and powerful (Hab 1:12). God alone is a "rock" (2 Sam 22:32; Pss 18:32; 62:3, 7); no other "rock" exists besides God (Deut 32:31; Isa 44:8; 1 Sam 2:2; cf. Isa 26:13). Thus, this metaphor for

God not only reassures the people about their God, but it also establishes God's sovereignty among the people. Also included in these verses is a reversal of images. The poor and needy once in need of their God to help them (Isa 25:4) have now been strengthened by their God, which enables them to stomp on the lofty city (v. 6).

The second psalmic unit (vv. 7–19) is a continued celebration of God's strength and enduring love. Among the different literary forms and rhetorical devices featured in this unit is the vocative. Verses 7–19 contain two vocatives, "O Just One" (v. 7) and "O Lord" (vv. 8, 11, 12, 13, 15, 16, and 17). The repetitious use of "O Lord" establishes not only a sense of continuity and unity within the poem but also a sense of intimacy between God and the community and those who call upon God. The reference to the hand of God being lifted up in verse 11 recalls the image of God's hand heard in Isa 25:10 and is a reminder that the time has not yet come for God to rest God's hand on the mountain; work still needs to be done among the families of the earth (see vv. 10–11).

Verses 11–19 contrast the other lords that have ruled over Israel with the people of God. The other lords are dead and cannot rise. The allusion here is mostly to Babylon. The simile in verses 17–18 where the community is compared to a woman writhing with child and giving birth to the wind captures the reality that the Israelites have long labored in vain and have failed at achieving salvation until now when their dead shall live and their corpses shall rise (v. 19). Lastly, the image of dew and the earth giving birth to those long dead in verse 19b hints at what Blenkinsopp suggests is "the ultimate transformation of the natural order."[10]

Verses 20–21, an appeal, are the last unit of this poem. The speaker is mostly the prophet, who urges the people to take cover so as to avoid the experience of the wrath of God that is about to strike the inhabitants of the land for their iniquity. Here God is portrayed metaphorically as warrior God, the commander in chief of the heavenly hosts, who is leaving the holy abode to visit the earth (v. 21a). In verse 21b, earth is personified as a whistleblower that will no longer remain silent in the face iniquity. Earth will make known the violent crimes that have long been hidden and have long gone unpunished. The imagery in these two verses recalls Isa 24:1–13, but now, a land, a people, a nation once destined for destruction is destined for salvation but only after God has dealt with those sinners

---

10. See Blenkinsopp, *Isaiah 1–39*, 371.

among the righteous. Thus, the song of jubilation ends on a somber yet hopeful note.

4. Isaiah 27: Symbols, Songs, and Disputations

Isaiah's listeners having heard about God's imminent wrath in Isa 26:20–21, now see this divine wrath come into play (v. 1). They also hear about the promise of restoration for Israel. This poem is composed of three units: a message to Leviathan (v. 1), an allegory and its explanation (vv. 2–6), and a disputation speech (vv. 7–13).

The phrase "on that day" opens Isa 27. This phrase links Isa 27 with Isa 26 (see v. 1) and Isa 24 (see v. 21) and gives the opening verse an eschatological tone. In this opening verse, God is portrayed as a God of wrath. The recipient of God's wrath is Leviathan. This primordial dragon has been long associated with chaos[11] and enjoys a rich mythological history. In the ancient Near Eastern world, the battle between a god and a dragon symbolized the victory of life and order over chaos. In Canaanite mythology, Baal was the god who slew Leviathan and made civilized life a reality. As the biblical story evolved, God became the substitute for Baal, and God was the one who would slay Leviathan. In Isa 27:1, the phrase "on that day" followed by the future tense verb "will punish" implies that Leviathan has not yet been slain. In this poem, Leviathan symbolizes the last battle that needs to be won for the common good and the salvation of the world. Metaphorically, one could see the winning of this battle as a victory over sin and death. The adjectives used to describe Leviathan indicate the great strength of the animal: Leviathan, the "fleeing serpent"; Leviathan, "the twisting serpent." God's promise to slay Leviathan symbolizes God's calculated efforts at restoring order in the world (v. 1).

These images of primordial chaos and divine wrath quickly change to images of loveliness, gentleness, and peace embodied in the description of the vineyard in verses 2–5. This image of the vineyard harks back to Isa 5:1–7, where the vineyard was a disappointment to God. In Isa 27:2–5, however, the vineyard is a delight and is cared for by the divine gardener. By using the phrase "on that day," the poet points out that even the vineyard will be transformed, but only after Leviathan has been put to rest (v.

---

11. Leviathan, a mythic sea creature appears several places in the Hebrew Bible; see Job 3:8; 41:1; Pss 74:14; 104:26.

1). The repetition of "let them make peace with me" in verse 5 gives voice to God's heart's desire while indirectly casting a light on Israel's stubbornness.

In verse 6, the parable of the vineyard mentioned in verses 2–5 is now explained. The vineyard is Israel who, after being reconciled with God, will "blossom and put forth shoots, and fill the whole world with fruit" (v. 6). Read against the backdrop of Isa 5:1–7, the parable makes clear that Israel's God is a God who will never abandon God's people or creation. God is faithful gardener, forever returning to the vineyard to "till and to care for it" (see Gen 2:15).

A rhetorical question opens the poem's next and final unit, verses 7–13, a disputation speech. Isaiah uses an exhortation addressed to Israel to encourage the people to accept God's protection as they wait with anticipation for their restoration to Jerusalem. The poem closes with a double promise. Each promise begins with the phrase "on that day," which links these promises to those heard earlier in Isa 27:2; 26:1; and 24:21. These two promises offer the Israelite people a vision of hope. Thus, the prophet's last word is a word of hope. This final hopeful word is central to the prophetic office and mission (see, e.g., Isa 24:13–16; 26:9; 27:1–6, 12–13).

5. Concluding Comments

The poetry of Isa 24–27 reflects the hand of a skilled orator and rhetorician who knew how to manipulate and use language and images for the sake of inspiring, exhorting, instructing, and warning. The metaphorical language and literary techniques used in these four chapters shed light on God, Israel as a community, and Israel as a people living among other peoples. The poetics of the texts communicate a vision of justice that call people and nations to right relationship and speak of a God whose dream is to welcome all people to the holy mountain where feasting is a way of life and peace is the order of the day. If these texts are postexilic, then they offer the listeners of their day a word of caution and a word of hope as they begin to resettle and reshape their lives on the land. Isaiah 24–27 proclaim God's deep love for the people, God's sheer delight in them, and God's wonderful vision for them, but the texts also remind the people that what they dreamed might never happen to them did in fact happen and could happen again (Isa 24:1–13). God's final word, however, is a promise of salvation and redemption, one that is rooted in and flowing from God's great love and hospitality of heart for all ages.

With respect to whether Isa 24–27 functions as a unified block of material or is a loosely strewn together collection of texts, as Blenkinsopp has suggested, I offer the following remarks. First, although Isa 24–27 could be viewed as a group of texts strewn together with little or no logical ordering, I suggest that the texts' poetic sequence of events and the use of a variety of rhetorical elements both aid in developing an internal unity among the texts, which, in turn, helps to create a coherent picture of God's unfolding plan of salvation and the ways in which this divine plan is to be accomplished.

Second, the poetry of Isa 24–27 tells a story. The story begins in Isa 24. Here the poet focuses on cosmic annihilation for both the land and all its inhabitants without distinction. Everyone and everything is about to suffer God's punitive justice. In the midst of such bleakness, however, a glimmer of hope shines through (Isa 24:13–16, particularly v. 16).

This glimmer of hope unfolds in Isa 25, a chapter whose message stands in stark contrast to that of Isa 24. Isaiah 24 spoke of cosmic annihilation; Isa 25 speaks of the future deliverance and restoration of all God's people, Israel in particular. The partial vision of what the poet saw in 24:14–16—namely, God's glory and righteousness—comes into full view in 25:7–9 and unfolds throughout the rest of the poem.

Isaiah 26 picks up on the vision of salvation for all Israel and the nations and focuses on Judah. The prophet proclaims:

On that day this song will be sung in the land of Judah:
We have a strong city;
    he sets up victory
like walls and bulwarks. (26:1)

Isaiah 26 closes with a cosmic vision similar to the one announced in Isa 24:

For the Lord comes out from his place
    to punish the inhabitants of the earth for their iniquity;
the earth will disclose the blood shed on it,
    and will no longer cover its slain. (26:21)

Salvation for the nations and land restoration are promised, but before this happens, God's justice—God's judgments on all creation, the nations included—will come first to pave the way for God's universal salvation. Hence, the text of Isa 26 looks forward and backward, as Isa 27:1 continues the theme of punishment heard at the end of Isa 26:21. In that text, the prophet announces that God will punish the people of the earth for their transgressions; and now in Isa 27:1, the prophet announces that God will punish Leviathan, the mythological monster symbolic of power and chaos. The vision quickly turns, then, to the salvation of Israel with the image of a vineyard. The vineyard image recalls Isa 5:1–7. This passage describes a vineyard that produced bitter grapes. Later on it becomes transformed into a delightful vineyard that needs to be watched over and watered constantly, even with its thorns and thistles. This vineyard can never again be abandoned by its owner. The vineyard is where

> In days to come Jacob shall take root,
> Israel shall blossom and put forth shoots,
> and fill the whole world with fruit. (27:6)

Isaiah 27:12–13 speaks of the regathering of the Israelites on the holy mountain in Jerusalem—the mountain toward which, eventually, all nations will stream (Isa 2:1–4; cf. Mic 4:1–5). The agricultural imagery that runs throughout Isa 24–27 helps to develop the theme of divine punishment and divine redemption.

Thus, through the poetics of Hebrew poetry, Isa 24–27 conveys a story about destruction and salvation that is cosmic in scope, a story that includes all the nations with special attention drawn to Israel and Judah. "On that day" suggests a vision of annihilation and a vision of salvation. The defeat of the city of chaos (Isa 24:10) and the turning of a city into a heap (Isa 25:2) paves the way for the restoration of Jerusalem—a new city in Isa 27:1, the place of God's holy mountain—a home for all nations (Isa 2:2; cf. Mic 4:1–2).

When viewed in the context of Isa 13–23, Isa 24–27 makes two significant contributions. First, with its focus on God's impending judgment of the earth—a judgment that will have catastrophic effects on Israel and Judah, as well as the other nations—Isa 24–27 develops the theme of divine judgment conveyed in Isa 13–23, the proclamations concerning the nations. This theme of judgment continues throughout Isa 28–33 and begins with the prophet condemning the corrupt rulers, priests, and prophets of his day (Isa 28).

Second, with its focus on salvation and the coming of a new world order, Isa 24–27 develops the theme of promise contained in Isa 28–33, particularly in Isa 30:18–26 and 32:1–20. Isaiah 33 closes the first half of Isa 1–39. Both Isa 32 and 33 speak of the coming of a new king who will reign in righteousness (Isa 32:1–8) with peace as the fruit of God's reign through this new king of righteousness (Isa 32:16–20). The vision of a new world order that will emerge after the first one has passed—after God has come to judge the entire earth and all its inhabitants (Isa 13–31). This new world order will emerge when a new righteous king comes into power and God's peace reigns in the land.

Finally, in the context of Isa 1–39, Isa 24–27 develops the golden threads of judgment and salvation that run throughout all of Isa 1–39, while paving the way for the promise of salvation and a new servant-leader heard about in Isa 40–55, the heart of the book of Isaiah as a whole.

6. Hermeneutical Considerations

Before drawing this essay to a close, some points for critical hermeneutical reflection need to be raised. First, Isa 24–27 calls readers today to consider how the poet has presented the character of God in the text. The poet presents God as a powerful deity whose justice against transgression is portrayed as being quite punitive. God's justice, threatened and exercised in order to restore right relationship among all peoples, must be understood metaphorically and in light of both the Deuteronomistic theology of retribution that undergirds many of the prophetic texts and the prophet's and poet's religious, political, and social agenda and beliefs that contributed to the shaping of these texts as they appear in the biblical canon today. A new world order will come into being, but only after God completely destroys the old. The divine vision of salvation and restoration is a marvelous one, but the means to accomplish the vision, at least according to the text, needs more thought. How just is God and God's ways as both are portrayed by the text? Or, is the poet's and the text's portrayal of God and God's ways reflective of their respective times and culture?

Second, the vision of a sense of universal salvation embedded in Isa 24–27 invites contemporary readers of the biblical text to see how the message of the Hebrew Scriptures transcends itself to become good news for all people—the God of Israel is the God of the nations whose ultimate plan is salvation, restoration, and peace for all creation.

Lastly, the relationship between humankind's transgression and the suffering of the earth as suggested by Isa 24–27, particularly in Isa 24, is an important one. In its original context, the languishing and mourning of the earth is connected to warfare, invasions, and corruption among nations and among Israel and Judah, especially with the invasion of the Assyrians and Babylonians into Israel and Judah, respectively, an act attributed to God's justice. If one listens, however, to Isa 24 in a contemporary social location—one that has a global perspective—then texts like Isa 24 take on new understandings.

In closing, the poet of Isa 24–27 has crafted a unified, coherent, literary work of art that develops the major themes contained within the first part of the book of Isa 1–39 and within Isa 1–66 as a whole. The poet's artistry does not end, however, with the final word etched on an ancient parchment and preserved throughout generations. The text of Isa 24–27 now has a life of its own and beckons to readers and listeners of the text everywhere to understand the text first in its ancient context and then to hear it anew in new contexts as it continues to disturb us while inspiring us with hope. The word and vision of Isa 24–27 continues to go forth, and we who ponder the text are invited to be transfixed and transformed by it daily as we walk in the glorious tradition of Israel's poets and prophets of old.

BIBLIOGRAPHY

Ackroyd, Peter R. *Exile and Restoration: A Study of Hebrew Thought of the Sixth Century BC.* 5th ed. London: SCM, 1983.

Albright, William F. "More Light on the Canaanite Epic of Aleyân and Môt." *BASOR* 50 (1933): 13–20.

———. "The North-Canaanite Epic of ʾAlʾêyân Baʿal and Môt." *JPOS* 12 (1932): 185–208.

———. "Some Remarks on the Song of Moses in Deuteronomy XXXII." *VT* 9 (1959): 339–46.

Assmann, Jan. *Der Tod als Thema der Kulturtheorie: Todesbilder und Totenriten im Alten Ägypten: Mit einem Beitrag von Thomas Macho: Tod und Trauer im kulturwissenschaftlichen Vergleich.* Erbschaft unserer Zeit 7. Frankfurt: Suhrkamp, 2000.

Auvray, Paul. *Isaie 1–39.* SB. Paris: Gabalda, 1972.

Avigad, Nahman. "Hebrew Seals and Sealings and Their Significance for Biblical Research." Pages 7–16 in *Congress Volume: Jerusalem, 1986.* Edited by John A. Emerton. VTSup 40. Leiden: Brill, 1988.

Avishur, Yitzhak. *Stylistic Studies of Word-Pairs in Biblical and Ancient Semitic Literatures.* AOAT 210. Kevelaer: Butzon & Bercker, 1984.

Baltzer, Klaus. *Deutero-Isaiah: A Commentary on Isaiah 40–55.* Translated by Margaret Kohl. Hermeneia. Augsburg: Fortress, 2001.

Bautch, Richard. "Intertextuality in the Persian Period." Pages 25–35 in *Approaching Yehud: New Approaches to the Study of the Persian Period.* Edited by Jon L. Berquist. Atlanta: Society of Biblical Literature, 2007.

Berges, Ulrich F. *The Book of Isaiah: Its Composition and Final Form.* Translated by Millard C. Lind. Sheffield: Sheffield Phoenix, 2012.

———. *Das Buch Jesaja: Komposition und Endgestalt.* HBS 16. Freiburg: Herder, 1998.

Bergmann, Claudia D. *Childbirth as a Metaphor for Crisis: Evidence from the Ancient Near East, the Hebrew Bible, and 1QH XI, 1–18.* BZAW 382. Berlin: de Gruyter, 2008.

Berlejung, Angelika and Bernd Janowski eds. *Tod und Jenseits im alten Israel und in seiner Umwelt: Theologische, religionsgeschichtliche, archäologische und ikonographische Aspekte*. FAT 64. Tübingen: Mohr Siebeck, 2009.

Beuken, Willem A. M. "'Deine Toten werden leben' (Jes 26,19): 'Kindliche Vernunft' oder reifer Glaube?" Pages 139–52 in *Schriftauslegung in der Schrift: Festschrift für Odil Hannes Steck zu seinem 65. Geburtstag*. Edited by Reinhard G. Kratz, Thomas Krüger, and Konrad Schmid. BZAW 300. Berlin: de Gruyter, 2000.

———. *Jesaja*. 3 vols. PredOT. Nijkerk: Callenbach, 1979–89.

———. *Jesaja 13–27*. HTKAT. Freiburg: Herder, 2007.

———. "The Prophet Leads the Readers into Praise: Isaiah 25:1–10 in Connection with Isaiah 24:14–23 Seen against the Background of Isaiah 12." Pages 121–56 in *Studies in Isaiah 24–27: The Isaiah Workshop–De Jesaja Werkplaats*. Edited by Hendrick J. Bosman and Harm van Grol. OtSt 43. Leiden: Brill, 2000.

———. "Woe to Powers in Israel That Vie to Replace YHWH's Rule on Mount Zion! Isaiah Chapters 28–31 from the Perspective of Isaiah Chapters 24–27." Pages 25–43 in *Isaiah in Context: Studies in Honour of Arie van der Kooij on the Occasion of His Sixth-Fifth Birthday*. Edited by Michaël N. van der Meer, Percy S. F. van Keulen, Willem Th. van Peursen, Bas ter Haar Romeny. Leiden: Brill, 2010.

Bieberstein, Klaus. "Jenseits der Todesschwelle: Die Entstehung der Auferweckungshoffnungen in der alttestamentlich–frühjüdischen Literatur." Pages 423–46 in *Tod und Jenseits im alten Israel und in seiner Umwelt: Theologische, religionsgeschichtliche, archäologische und ikonographische Aspekte*. Edited by Angelika Berlejung and Bernd Janowski. FAT 64. Tübingen: Mohr Siebeck, 2009.

Blenkinsopp, Joseph. *Isaiah 1–39: A New Translation with Introduction and Commentary*. AB 19. New York: Doubleday, 2000.

———. *Isaiah 56–66*. AB 19B. New York: Doubleday, 2003.

Bonatz, Dominik. "Ashurbanipal's Headhunt: An Anthropological Perspective." *Iraq* 66 (2004): 93–101.

Bormann, Franz-Josef and Gian D. Borasio, eds. *Sterben: Dimensionen eines anthropologischen Grundphänomens*. Berlin: de Gruyter, 2012.

Bosman, Hendrik Jan. "Syntactic Cohesion in Isaiah 24–27." Pages 19–50 in *Studies in Isaiah 24–27: The Isaiah Workshop–De Jesaja Werkplaats*. Edited by Hendrick J. Bosman and Harm van Grol. OtSt 43. Leiden: Brill, 2000.

Bosman, Hendrik Jan, and Harm van Grol, eds. "Annotated Translation of Isaiah 24–27." Pages 3–18 in *Studies in Isaiah 24–27: The Isaiah Workshop–De Jesaja Werkplaats*. Edited by Hendrick J. Bosman and Harm van Grol. OtSt 43. Leiden: Brill, 2000.

———. *Studies in Isaiah 24–27: The Isaiah Workshop–De Jesaja Werkplaats.* OtSt 43. Leiden: Brill, 2000.

Bosshard-Nepustil, Erich. *Vor uns die Sintflut: Studien ze Text, Kontexten und Rezeption der Fluterzählung Genesis 6–9.* BWA(N)T 5. Stuttgart: Kohlhammer, 2005.

Briant, Pierre. *From Cyrus to Alexander: A History of the Persian Empire.* Winona Lake, Ind: Eisenbrauns, 2002.

Bright, John. *A History of Israel.* 4th ed. Louisville: Westminster John Knox, 2000.

Brueggemann, Walter. *Isaiah 1–39.* Westminster Bible Companion. Louisville: Westminster John Knox, 1998.

Bullinger, Ethelbert William. *Figures of Speech Used in the Bible.* London: Eyre and Spottiswoode, 1898.

Burkes, Shannon. *Death and Qoheleth and Egyptian Biographies of the Late Period.* SBLDS 170. Atlanta: Society of Biblical Literature, 1999.

Calvin, John. *Commentary on the Prophet Isaiah.* Translated by William Pringle. Grand Rapids: Baker, 2003.

Caquot, André. "Remarques sur le 'Banquet des Nations' en Esaïe 25, 6–8." *RHPR* 69 (1989): 109–19.

Carr, David M. "Reading Isaiah from Beginning (Isaiah 1) to End (Isaiah 65–66): Multiple Modern Possibilities." Pages 188–218 in *New Visions of Isaiah.* Edited by Roy F. Melugin and Marvin A. Sweeney. JSOTSup 214. Sheffield: Sheffield Academic Press, 1996.

Cassuto, Umberto. "Baal and Mot in the Ugaritic Texts." *IEJ* 12 (1962): 77–86.

Cheyne, Thomas Kelly. *Introduction to the Book of Isaiah.* London: A&C Black, 1895.

———. *Prophecies of Isaiah.* London: Kegan Paul, 1886.

Childs, Brevard S. *Isaiah.* OTL. Louisville: Westminster John Knox, 2001.

Chilton, Bruce D. *The Isaiah Targum: Introduction, Translation, Apparatus, and Notes.* ArBib 11. Wilmington, Del.: Michael Glazier, 1987.

———. *The Isaiah Targum: Introduction, Translation, Apparatus, and Notes.* ArBib 11. Collegeville, Minn.: Liturgical Press, 1990.

Clements, Ronald E. *Isaiah 1–39.* NCB. Grand Rapids: Eerdmans, 1980.

Clifford, Richard J. *The Cosmic Mountain in Canaan and the Old Testament.* HSM 4. Cambridge: Harvard University Press, 1972.

———. "Isaiah 55: Invitation to a Feast." Pages 27–35 in *The Word of the Lord Shall Go Forth: Essays in Honor of David N. Freedman in Celebration of His Sixtieth Birthday.* Edited by Carol L. Meyers and Michael O'Connor. Winona Lake, Ind.: Eisenbrauns, 1983.

Coggins, Richard J. "The Problem of Isaiah 24–27." *ExpTim* 90 (1978–1979): 328–33.

Collins, John J. *Daniel*. Hermeneia. Minneapolis: Fortress, 1993.

Cook, Stephen L. "The Fecundity of Fair Zion: Beauty and Fruitfulness as Spiritual Fulfillment." Pages 77–100 in *Daughter Zion: Her Portrait, Her Response*. Edited by Mark J. Boda, Carol J. Dempsey, and LeAnn S. Flesher. SBLAIL 13. Atlanta: Society of Biblical Literature, 2012.

Cunha, Wilson de A. "A Brief Discussion of MT Isaiah 24,14–16." *Bib* 90 (2009): 530–44.

Davies, Jon. *Death, Burial, and Rebirth in the Religions of Antiquity*. London: Routledge, 1999.

Day, John. "A Case of Inner Scriptural Interpretation: The Dependence of Isaiah XXVI.13 XXVII.11 on Hos XIII.4–XIV.10 (Eng. 9) and its Relevance to Some Theories of the Redaction of the 'Isaiah Apocalypse.'" *JTS* 31 (1980): 309–19.

———. "The Dependence of Isaiah 26.13–27.11 on Hosea 13.4–14.10 and Its Relevance to Some Theories of the Redaction of the «Isaiah Apocalypse»," Pages 357–68 in *Writing and Reading the Scroll of Isaiah: Studies of an Interpretive Tradition*. Edited by Craig C. Broyles and Craig A. Evans. VTSup 70. Leiden: Brill, 1997.

———. *God's Conflict with the Dragon and the Sea: Echoes of a Canaanite Myth in the Old Testament*. UCOP 35. Cambridge: Cambridge University Press, 1985.

———. "Leviathan." Pages 295–96 in vol. 4 of *The Anchor Bible Dictionary*. Edited by David Noel Freedman. 6 vols. New York: Doubleday, 1992.

———. "טל אורת in Isaiah 26 19." *ZAW* 90 (1978): 265–69.

———. "Ugarit and the Bible: Do They Presuppose the Same Canaanite Mythology and Religion?" Pages 35–52 in *Ugarit and the Bible: Proceedings of the International Symposium on Ugarit and the Bible, Manchester, September 1992*. Edited by George J. Brooke, Adrian H. W. Curtis, and John F. Healey. UBL 11. Münster: Ugarit-Verlag, 1994.

———. *Yahweh and the Gods and Goddesses of Canaan*. JSOTSup 265. Sheffield: Sheffield Academic Press, 2000.

Delcor, Mathias. *Études Bibliques et Orientales de Religions Comparées*. Leiden: Brill, 1979.

———. "Le festin d'immortalité sur la Montagne de Sion à l'ère eschatologique en Is. 25, 6–9, à la lumière de la literature Ugaritique." Pages 122–31 in *Études Bibliques et Orientales de Religions Comparées*. Leiden: Brill, 1979.

Delitzsch, Franz. *Commentar über das Buch Jesaja*. Edited by Carl F. Keil and Franz Delitzsch. Biblischer Commentar. Leipzig: Dörffling & Franke, 1889.

———. *Commentary on the Song of Songs and Ecclesiastes*. Leipzig: Dorffling & Franke, 1875. Repr., Edinburgh: Clark, 1877. Repr., Grand Rapids: Eerdmans, 1982.

Dempsey, Carol J. *Isaiah: God's Poet of Light*. St. Louis: Chalice, 2010.

Dietler, Michael. "Theorizing the Feast: Rituals of Consumption, Commensal Politics, and Power in African Contexts." Pages 65–114 in *Feasts: Archaeological and Ethnographical Perspectives on Food, Politics, and Power*. Edited by Michael Dietler and Brian Hayden. Tuscaloosa, Ala.: University of Alabama Press, 2001.

Dietler, Michael, and Brian Hayden. "Digesting the Feast: Good to Eat, Good to Drink, Good to Think: An Introduction." Pages 1–22 in *Feasts: Archaeological and Ethnographical Perspectives on Food, Politics, and Power*. Edited by Michael Dietler and Brian Hayden. Tuscaloosa, Ala.: The University of Alabama Press, 2001.

Dietrich, Manfried, and Oswald Loretz. "Der Tod Baals als Rache Mots für die Vernichtung Leviathans." *UF* 12 (1980): 404–7.

Dietrich, Manfried, Oswald Loretz, and Joaquin Sanmartín, ed. *Die keilalphabetischen Texte aus Ugarit*. AOAT 24.1. Neukirchen-Vluyn: Neukirchener, 1976

Doyle, Brian. *The Apocalypse of Isaiah Metaphorically Speaking: A Study of the Use, Function and Significance of Metaphors in Isaiah 24–27*. BETL 151. Leuven: Leuven University Press, 2000.

———. "Fertility and Infertility in Isaiah 24–27." Pages 77–88 in *The New Things: Eschatology in Old Testament Prophecy: Festschrift for Henk Leene*. Edited by Ferenc Postma, Klaas Spronk, and Eep Talstra. ACEBTSup 3. Maastricht: Shaker, 2002.

———. "How Do Single Isotopes Meet? 'Lord it' (b'l) or 'Eat it' (bl'): A Rare Word Play Metaphor in Isaiah 25." Pages 153–84 in *The Bible through Metaphor and Translation: A Cognitive Semantic Perspective*. Edited by Kurt Feyaerts. New York: Lang, 2003.

———. "A Literary Analysis of Isaiah 24,10a." Pages 173–93 in *Studies in the Book of Isaiah: Festschrift Willem A.M. Beuken*. Edited by Jacques van Ruiten and Marc Vervenne. BETL 132. Leuven: Leuven University Press, 1997.

Duhm, Bernhard. *Das Buch Jesaia: Übersetzt und erklärt*. HKAT 3.1. Göttingen: Vandenhoeck & Ruprecht, 1892.

———. *Das Buch Jesaia: Übersetzt und erklärt*. 3rd ed. HKAT 3.1. Göttingen: Vandenkoeck & Ruprecht, 1914.

———. *Das Buch Jesaia. Übersetzt und erklärt*. 4th ed. HKAT 3.1. Göttingen: Vandenhoeck & Ruprecht, 1922.

Eberhardt, Gönke. "Die Gottesferne der Unterwelt in der JHWH-Religion." Pages 373–95 in *Tod und Jenseits im alten Israel und in seiner Umwelt: Theologische, religionsgeschichtliche, archäologische und ikonographische Aspekte*. Edited by Angelika Berlejung and Bernd Janowski. FAT 64. Tübingen: Mohr Siebeck, 2009.

———. *JHWH und die Unterwelt: Spuren einer Kompetenzausweitung JHWHs im Alten Testament.* FAT 2/23. Tübingen: Mohr Siebeck, 2007.

Ehrensvärd, Martin. "Linguistic Dating of Biblical Texts." Pages 175–77 in *Biblical Hebrew: Studies in Chronology and Typology.* Edited by Ian Young. London: T&T Clark, 2003.

Eidevall, Goran. *Prophecy and Propaganda: Images of Enemies in the Book of Isaiah.* ConBOT 56. Winona Lake, Ind.: Eisenbrauns, 2009.

Eissfeldt, Otto. *Baal Zaphon, Zeus Kasios und der Durchzug der Israeliten durchs Meer.* BRGA 1. Halle: Niemeyer, 1932.

Everson, A. Joseph, and Hyun Chul Paul Kim, eds. *The Desert Will Bloom: Poetic Visions of Isaiah.* SBLAIL 4. Atlanta: Society of Biblical Literature, 2009.

Fieldhouse, Paul. *Food and Nutrition: Customs and Culture.* London: Croom Helm, 1986.

Fischer, Johann. *Kapiten 1–39.* Vol. 1 of *Das Buch Isaias.* HSAT 7.1. Bonn: Hanstein, 1937.

Fisher, Loren R. ed. *Ras Shamra Parallels: The Texts from Ugarit and the Hebrew Bible.* Vol. 1. AnOr 49. Rome: Pontificium Institutum Biblicum, 1972.

Fu, Janling. "The Archaeological Signature of Feasting: Theoretical and Methodological Aspects." Paper presented at the annual meeting of the American Schools of Oriental Research. San Francisco, November 2011.

Galvin, Garrett. *Egypt as a Place of Refuge.* FAT 2/51. Tübingen: Mohr Siebeck, 2011.

Gaster, Theodor H. *Thespis: Ritual, Myth, and Drama in the Ancient Near East.* Rev ed. New York: Harper & Row, 1961.

Gertz, Jan Christian, Jan Christian Gertz, Angelica Berlejung, Konrad Schmid, and Markus Witte. *T&T Clark Handbook of the Old Testament: An Introduction to the Literature, Religion, and History of the Old Testament.* London: T&T Clark, 2012.

Gesenius, Wilhelm. *Philologisch–kritischer und historischer Commentar über den Jesaia.* 2 vols. Leipzig: Vogel, 1821.

Goldziher, Ignác. *Der Mythos bei den Hebräern und seine geschichtliche Entwickelung.* Leipzig: Brockhaus, 1876.

Gray, George Buchanan. *A Critical and Exegetical Commentary on the Book of Isaiah, I–XXXIX.* ICC. New York: Scribner's Sons, 1912.

Gray, John. *The Biblical Doctrine of the Reign of God.* Edinburgh: T&T Clark, 1979.

Grogan, Geoffrey W. "Isaiah." Pages 433–864 in *Isaiah-Ezekiel.* Edited by Frank E. Gaebelein and Richard P Polcyn. EBC 6. Grand Rapids: Zondervan, 1986.

Grol, Harm van. "An Analysis of the Verse Structure of Isaiah 24–27." Pages 51–80 in *Studies in Isaiah 24–27: The Isaiah Workshop–De Jesaja Werkplaats*. Edited by Hendrick J. Bosman and Harm van Grol. OtSt 43. Leiden: Brill, 2000.

Gross, Walter. "Zum alttestamentlich-jüdischen Verständnis von Sterben und Tod." Pages 465–80 in *Sterben: Dimensionen eines anthropologischen Grundphänomens*. Edited by Franz-Josef Bormann and Gian D. Borasio. Berlin: de Gruyter, 2012.

Grottanelli, Cristiano. "The Roles of the Guest in the Epic Banquet." Pages 272–332 in *Production and Consumption in the Ancient Near East*. Edited by Carlo Zaccagnini. Budapest: University of Budapest, 1989.

Hagelia, Hallvard. "Meal on Mount Zion: Does Isa 25:6–8 Describe a Covenant Meal?" *SEÅ* 68 (2003): 73–93.

Halpern, Baruch, and David S. Vanderhooft. "The Editions of Kings in the 7th–6th Centuries B.C.E." *HUCA* 62 (1991): 179–244.

Hanson, Paul D. *The Dawn of Apocalyptic: The Historical and Sociological Roots of Jewish Apocalyptic Eschatology*. Rev. ed. Philadelphia: Fortress, 1979.

Hasel, Gerhard F. *The Remnant: The History and Theology of the Remnant Idea from Genesis to Isaiah*. AUM 5. Berrien Springs, Mich.: Andrews University Press, 1974.

Hayden, Brian. "Fabulous Feats: A Prolegomenon to the Importance of Feasting." Pages 23–64 in *Feasts: Archaeological and Ethnographical Perspectives on Food, Politics, and Power*. Edited by Michael Dietler and Brian Hayden. Tuscaloosa, Ala.: The University of Alabama Press, 2001.

Hayes, John H. and Stuart A. Irvine. *Isaiah: The Eighth-Century Prophet: His Times and His Preaching*. Nashville: Abingdon, 1987.

Hayes, Katherine M. *"The Earth Mourns": Prophetic Metaphor and Oral Aesthetic*. Atlanta: Society of Biblical Literature, 2002.

Hays, Christopher B. "Damming Egypt / Damning Egypt: The Paronomasia of *skr* and the Unity of Isa 19:1–15." *ZAW* 120 (2008): 612–16.

———. *Death in the Iron Age II and in First Isaiah*. FAT 79. Tübingen: Mohr Siebeck, 2011.

Healey, John F. "Burning the Corn: New Light on the Killing of Mōtu." *Or* 52 (1983): 248–51.

———. "Death, Underworld and Afterlife in the Ugaritic Texts." Ph.D. diss., University of London, 1977.

———. "Dew." Pages 249–50 in *Dictionary of Deities and Demons in the Bible*. Edited by Karel van der Toorn, Bob Becking, and Pieter W. van der Horst. 2nd ed. Leiden: Brill, 1999.

————. "MOT מות." Pages 598–603 in *Dictionary of Deities and Demons in the Bible*. Edited by Karel van der Toorn, Bob Becking, and Pieter W. van der Horst. 2nd ed. Leiden: Brill, 1999.

Heider, George C. *The Cult of Molek: A Reassessment*. JSOTSup 43. Sheffield: JSOT Press, 1985.

Hendel, Ronald. "Unhistorical Hebrew Linguistics: A Cautionary Tale." Online: www.bibleinterp.com/opeds/hen358022.shtml.

Henkelman, Wouter F. M. "'Consumed before the King.' The Table of Darius, that of Irdabama and Irtaštuna, and that of His Satrap, Karkiš." Pages 667–775 in *Der Achämenidenhof: Akten des 2. Internationalen Kolloquiums zum Thema "Vorderasien im Spannungsfeld klassischer und altorientalischer Überlieferungen," Landgut Castelen bei Basel, 23.–25. Mai 2007*. Edited by Bruno Jacobs and Robert Rollinger. Classica et Orientalia 2. Wiesbaden: Herrassowitz, 2010.

————. "Parnakka's Feast: Šip in Pārsa and Elam." Pages 89–166 in *Elam and Persia*. Edited by Javier Álvarez-Mon. Winona Lake, Ind.: Eisenbrauns, 2011.

Henry, Marie Louise. *Glaubenskrise und Glaubensbewährung in den Dichtungen der Jesajaapokalypse: Versuch einer Deutung der literarischen Komposition von Jes. 24-27 aus sem Zusammenhang ihrer religiösen Motivbildungen*. BWA(N)T 86. Stuttgart: Kohlhammer, 1967.

Herdner, Andrée. *Corpus des tablettes en cunéiformes alphabétiques découvertes à Ras Shamra-Ugarit de 1929 à 1939*. Mission de Ras Shamra 10. Paris, 1963.

Herrmann, Wolfram. "Jahwes Triumph über Mot." *UF* 11 (1979): 371–77.

————. "Die Implikationen von Jes 25,8aα." *BN* 104 (2000): 26–30.

Hibbard, J. Todd. *Intertextuality in Isaiah 24–27: The Reuse and Evocation of Earlier Texts and Traditions*. FAT 2/16. Tübingen: Mohr Siebeck, 2006.

Hieke, Thomas. "'Er verschlingt den Tod für immer' (Jes 25,8a). Eine nerfüllte Verheissung im Alten und Neuen Testament." *BZ* 50 (2006): 31–50.

Holmstedt, Robert. "Historical Linguistics and Biblical Hebrew." Pages 97–125 in *Diachrony in Biblical Hebrew*. Edited by Cynthia Miller-Naudé and Ziony Zevit. Winona Lake, Ind.: Eisenbrauns, 2012.

Hunt, Patrick N. "Mount Saphon in Myth and Fact." Pages 103–15 in *Phoenicia and the Bible: Proceedings of the Conference Held at the University of Leuven on the 15th and 16th of March 1990*. Edited by Edward Lipiński. Studia Phoenicia XI. Leuven: Uitgeverij Peeters, 1991.

Hurvitz, Avi. "Originals and Imitations in Biblical Poetry: A Comparative Examination of I Sam 2:1–10 and Ps 113:5–9." Pages 115–21 in *Biblical and Related Studies Presented to Samuel Iwry*. Edited by Ann Kort and Scott Morschauser. Winona Lake, Ind.: Eisenbrauns, 1986.

Irwin, William H. "'The Smooth Stones of the Wadi'? Isaiah 57:6." *CBQ* 29 (1967): 31–40.

James, Edwin O. *The Tree of Life: An Archaeological Study.* SHR 11. Leiden: Brill, 1966.

Janowski, Bernd. *Der Gott des Lebens.* Vol. 3 of *Beiträge zur Theologie des Alten Testaments.* Neukirchen: Neukirchener, 2003.

———. "JHWH und die Toten: Zur Geschichte des Todes im Alten Israel." Pages 447–77 in *Tod und Jenseits im alten Israel und in seiner Umwelt: Theologische, religionsgeschichtliche, archäologische und ikonographische Aspekte.* Edited by Angelika Berlejung and Bernd Janowski. FAT 64. Tübingen: Mohr Siebeck, 2009.

Jastrow, Marcus. *A Dictionary of the Targumim, the Talmud Babli and Yerushalmi, and the Midrashic Literature.* New York: Judaica, 1996.

Jensen, Joseph. *Isaiah 1–39.* OTM 8. Wilmington, Del.: Michael Glazier, 1984.

Jindo, Job Y. *Biblical Metaphor Reconsidered: A Cognitive Approach to Poetic Prophecy in Jeremiah 1–24.* HSM 64. Winona Lake, Ind.: Eisenbrauns, 2010.

———. "On Myth and History in Prophetic and Apocalyptic Eschatology." *VT* 55 (2005): 412–15.

Johnson, Aubrey R. *Sacral Kingship in Ancient Israel.* 2nd ed. Cardiff: University of Wales Press, 1967.

Johnson, Benjamin J. M. "'Whoever Gives Me Thorns and Thistles': Rhetorical Ambiguity and the Use of *my ytn* in Isaiah 27.2–6." *JSOT* 36 (2011): 105–26.

Johnson, Dan G. *From Chaos to Restoration: An Integrative Reading of Isaiah 24–27.* JSOTSup 61. Sheffield: JSOT Press, 1988.

Johnston, Philip S. *Shades of Sheol: Death and Afterlife in the Old Testament.* Downers Grove, Ill.: InterVarsity Press, 2002.

Joosten, Jan. "The Knowledge and Use of Hebrew in the Hellenistic Period Qumran and Septuagint." Pages 115–30 n *Diggers at the Well: Proceedings of a Third International Symposium on the Hebrew of the Dead Sea Scrolls and Ben Sira.* Edited by Takamitsu Muraoka and John F. Elwolde. Leiden: Brill, 2000.

Kaiser, Otto. *Isaiah 13–39.* Translated by R. A. Wilson. OTL. Louisville: Knox, 1974.

———. *Der Prophet Jesaja: Kapitel 13–39.* ATD 18. Göttingen : Vandenhoeck & Ruprecht, 1973.

Kessler, Martin. *Battle of the Gods: The God of Israel Versus Marduk of Babylon: A Literary/Theological Interpretation of Jeremiah 50–51.* Assen: Van Gorcum, 2003.

Kim, Hyun Chul Paul. "Isaiah 22: A Crux or a Clue in Isaiah 13–23?" In *Declare*

Ye among the Nations: Oracles against the Nations in Isaiah, Jeremiah, and Ezekiel. Edited by Else K. Holt, Hyun Chul Paul Kim, and Andrew Mein. London: T&T Clark, forthcoming.

———. "Little Highs, Little Lows: Tracing Key Themes in Isaiah." In *"A Light to the Nations": Essays Honoring Joseph Blenkinsopp and His Contribution to the Study of Isaiah.* Edited by Richard Bautch and J. Todd Hibbard. Grand Rapids: Eerdmans, forthcoming.

Kissane, Edward J. *The Book of Isaiah: Translated from a Critically Revised Hebrew Text with Commentary.* 2 vols. Dublin: Richview, 1960.

Kooij, Arie van der. "The Teacher Messiah and Worldwide Peace. Some Comments on Symmachus' Version of Isaiah 25:7–8." *JNSL* 24 (1998): 75–82.

Kratz, Reinhard G. "Rewriting Isaiah: The Case of Isaiah 28–31." Pages 245–66 in *Prophecy and Prophets in Ancient Israel: Proceedings of the Oxford Old Testament Seminar.* Edited by John Day. New York: T&T Clark, 2010.

Kuhrt, Amélie. "Ancient Near Eastern History: The Case of Cyrus the Great of Persia." Pages 107–27 in *Understanding the History of Ancient Israel.* Edited by Hugh G. M. Williamson. Oxford: Oxford University Press, 2007.

Lelli, Fabrizio. "Stars." Pages 809–15 in *Dictionary of Deities and Demons in the Bible.* Edited by Karel van der Toorn, Bob Becking, and Pieter W. van der Horst. 2nd ed. Leiden: Brill, 1999.

Lemaire, Andre. "Amon, Moab, Edom, à l'âge du Fer en Jordanie." Pages 60–65 in *La Jordanie de l'âge de la pierre à l'époque Byzantine.* Paris: Ecole du Louvre, 1987.

Lete, Gregorio del Olmo. "The Ugaritic Ritual Texts: A New Edition and Commentary: A Critical Assessment." *UF* 36 (2004): 539–648.

Levenson, Jon D. *Resurrection and the Restoration of Israel: The Ultimate Victory of the God of Life.* New Haven: Yale University Press, 2006.

———. *Sinai and Zion: An Entry into the Jewish Bible.* NVBS. New York: HarperCollins, 1985.

Levin, Christoph. Review of Richard M. Wright, *Linguistic Evidence for the Pre-exilic Date of the Yahwistic Source. RBL* (2006). Online: http://www.bookreviews.org/pdf/4860_5055.pdf.

Lewis, Theodore J. *Cults of the Dead in Ancient Israel and Ugarit.* HSM 39. Atlanta: Scholars Press, 1989.

Liess, Kathrin. "'Hast du die Tore der Finsternis gesehen?' (Ijob 38,17): Zur Lokalisierung des Totenreiches im Alten Testament." Pages 397–422 in *Tod und Jenseits im alten Israel und in seiner Umwelt: Theologische, religionsgeschichtliche, archäologische und ikonographische Aspekte.* Edited by Angelika Berlejung and Bernd Janowski. FAT 64. Tübingen: Mohr Siebeck, 2009.

Lindblom, Johannes. *Die Jesaja-Apokalypse: Jes. 24–27.* LUÅ 34.3. Lund: Gleerup, 1938.

Lipschitz, Oded, and Oren Tal. "The Settlement Archaeology of the Province of Judah: A Case Study." Pages 33–52 in *Judah and the Judeans in the Fourth Cenutry B.C.E.* Edited by Oded Lipschits, Gary N. Knoppers, and Rainer Albertz. Winona Lake, Ind.: Eisenbrauns, 2007.

Liwak, Rüdiger. "רפאים." Pages 607–11 in vol. 13 of *Theological Wordbook of the Old Testament.* Edited by R. Laird Harris and Gleason L. Archer Jr. 2 vols. Chicago: Moody, 1980.

Lloyd, Jeffery B. "The Banquet Theme in Ugaritic Narrative." *UF* 22 (1990): 169–93.

Loewenstamm, Samuel E. "The Killing of Mot in Ugaritic Myth." *Or* 41 (1972): 378–82.

Ma, John. "City as Memory." Pages 248–59 in *The Oxford Handbook of Hellenic Studies.* Edited by George Boys-Stones, Barbara Graziosi, and Phiroze Vasunia. Oxford: Oxford University Press, 2009.

MacDonald, Nathan. *Not Bread Alone: The Uses of Food in the Old Testament.* Oxford: Oxford University Press, 2008.

Madigan, Kevin J. and Jon D. Levenson. *Resurrection: The Power of God for Christians and Jews.* New Haven: Yale University Press, 2008.

Manfried Mietrich, Oswald Loretz, and Joaquín Sanmartín. *The Cuneiform Alphabetic Texts from Ugarit, Ras Ibn Hani and Other Places (KTU).* Münster: Ugarit-Verlag, 1995.

March, Wallace E. "A Study of Two Prophetic Compositions in Isaiah 24:1–27:1." Ph.D. diss., Union Theological Seminary, 1966.

Margulis, Baruch. "Weltbaum and Weltberg in Ugaritic Literature: Notes and Observations on RŠ 24.245." *ZAW* 86 (2009): 1–23.

Marti, Karl. *Das Buch Jesaja: Erklärt.* KHC 10. Tübingen: Mohr Siebeck, 1900.

Martin-Achard, Robert. *From Death to Life: A Study of the Development of the Doctrine of the Resurrection in the Old Testament.* Translated by John P. Smith. Edinburgh: Oliver and Boyd, 1960.

Mason, Steven D. "Another Flood? Genesis 9 and Isaiah's Broken Eternal Covenant." *JSOT* 32 (2007): 177–98.

Mathewson, Dan. *Death and Survival in the Book of Job: Desymbolization and Traumatic Experience.* New York: T&T Clark, 2006.

Mazzini, Giovanni. "The Torture of Mot for a Reading of KTU 1.6 V 30–35." *SEL* 14 (1997): 23–28.

McGinnis, Claire Mathews, and Patricia K. Tull, eds. *"As Those Who are Taught": The Interpretation of Isaiah from the LXX to the SBL.* SBLSymS 27. Atlanta: Society of Biblical Literature, 2006.

Meier, Samuel A. *Speaking of Speaking: Marking Direct Discourse in the Hebrew Bible*. VTSup 46. Leiden: Brill, 1992.

Melugin, Roy F., and Marvin A. Sweeney. *New Visions of Isaiah*. JSOTSup 214. Sheffield: Sheffield Academic Press, 1996.

Middlemas, Jill. "Trito-Isaiah's Intra- and Internationalization: Identity Markers in the Second Temple Period." Pages 105–25 in *Judah and the Judeans in the Achaemenid Period: Negotiating Identity in an International Context*. Edited by Oded Lipschitz, Gary Knoppers, and Manfred Oeming. Winona Lake, Ind.: Eisenbrauns, 2011.

Millar, William R. *Isaiah 24–27 and the Origin of Apocalyptic*. HSM 11. Missoula, Mont.: Scholars Press, 1976.

Miller, Glenn. "Isaiah 25:6–9: God's Banquet." *Int* 49 (1995): 175–78.

Miller, Patrick D. *The Divine Warrior in Early Israel*. Cambridge: Harvard University Press, 1973. Repr., Atlanta: Society of Biblical Literature, 2006.

Motyer, J. Alec. *The Prophecy of Isaiah: An Introduction and Commentary*. Downers Grove, Ill.: InterVarsity Press, 1993.

Mowinckel, Sigmund. *The Psalms in Israel's Worship*. Translated by Dafydd R. Ap-Thomas. 2 vols. The Biblical Resources Series. Grand Rapids: Eerdmans, 2004.

Neiman, David. "Gihon and Pishon: Mythological Antecedents of the Two Enigmatic Rivers of Eden." Pages 321–28 in *Proceedings of the Sixth World Congress of Jewish Studies, Held at the Hebrew University of Jerusalem, 13–19 August, 1973, under the Auspices of the Israel Academy of Sciences and Humanities*. Vol. 1. Edited by Avigdor Shinan. Jerusalem: World Union of Jewish Studies, 1977.

Nicholson, Ernest W. "The Antiquity of the Tradition in Exodus XXIV 9–11." *VT* 25 (1975): 69–79.

———. "The Interpretation of Exodus XXIV 9–11." *VT* 24 (1974): 77–97.

Nickelsburg, George W. E. *Resurrection, Immortality, and Eternal Life in Intertestamental Judaism*. Exp. ed. HTS 56. Cambridge: Harvard University Press, 2006.

Nihan, Christophe. "Ethnicity and Identity in Isaiah 56–66." Pages 67–104 in *Judah and the Judeans in the Achaemenid Period*. Edited by Oded Lipschitz, Gary Knoppers, and Manfred Oeming. Winona Lake, Ind.: Eisenbrauns, 2011.

Nissinen, Marti. "City as Lofty as Heaven: Arbela and Other Cities in Neo-Assyrian Prophecy." Pages 174–239 in *'Every City Shall Be Forsaken': Urbanism and Prophecy in Ancient Israel and the Near East*. Edited by Lester L. Grabbe and Robert D. Haak. JSOTSup 330. Sheffield: Sheffield Academic Press, 2001.

Nitsche, Stefan A. *Jesaja 24–27: Ein dramatischer Text: Die Frage nach den Genres prophetischer Literatur des Alten Testaments und die Textgraphik der grossen Jesajarolle aus Qumran.* BWA(N)T 166. Stuttgart: Kohlhammer, 2006.

Noegel, Scott B. "Dialect and Politics in Isaiah 24–27." *AuOr* 12 (1994): 177–92.

Oswalt, John N. *The Book of Isaiah 1–39.* NICOT. Grand Rapids: Eerdmans, 1986.

Otzen, Benedikt. "Traditions and Structures of Isaiah XXIV–XXVII." *VT* 24 (1974): 196–206.

Paul, Shalom. *Isaiah 40–66: Translation and Commentary.* ECC. Grand Rapids: Eerdmans, 2012.

———. "Signs of Late Hebrew in Isaiah 40–66." Pages 293–300 in *Diachrony in Biblical Hebrew.* Edited by Cynthia Miller-Naudé and Ziony Zevit. Winona Lake, Ind.: Eisenbrauns, 2012.

Pietersma, Albert, and Benjamin G. Wright, eds. *A New English Translation of the Septuagint and Other Greek Translations Traditionally Included under that Title.* New York: Oxford University Press, 2007.

Pinnock, Frances. "Considerations on the 'Banquet Theme' in the Figurative Art of Mesopotamia and Syria." Pages 15–26 in *Drinking in Ancient Societies: History and Culture of Drinks in the Ancient Near East: Papers of a Symposium Held in Rome, May 17–19, 1990.* Edited by Lucio Milano. Padova: Sargon, 1994.

Plöger, Otto. *Theocracy and Eschatology.* Translated by Stanley Rudman. 2nd ed. Richmond: Knox, 1968.

Podella, Thomas. "Totenrituale und Jenseitsbeschreibungen: Zur anamnetischen Struktur der Religionsgeschichte Israels." Pages 530–61 in *Tod, Jenseits und Identität: Perspektiven einer kulturwissenschaftlichen Thanatologie.* Edited by Jan Assmann and Rolf Trauzettel. VIHA 7. Freiburg: Alber, 2002.

Polak, Frank. "Sociolinguistics: A Key to the Typology and the Social Background of Biblical Hebrew." *HS* 47 (2006): 115–62.

Polaski, Donald C. *Authorizing an End: The Isaiah Apocalypse and Intertextuality.* BibInt 50. Leiden: Brill, 2001.

———. "Reflections on a Mosaic Covenant: The Eternal Covenant (Isaiah 24.5) and Intertextuality." *JSOT* 77 (1998): 55–73.

Pritchard, James B. *The Ancient Near East: Supplementary Texts and Pictures Relating to the Old Testament.* 2nd ed. Princeton: Princeton University Press, 1969.

———. *Ancient Near Eastern Texts Relating to the Old Testament.* 3rd ed. Princeton: Princeton University Press, 1969.

Procksch, Otto. *Jesaja: Übersetzt und erklärt*. KAT 9.1. Leipzig: Deichertsche, 1930.

Redditt, Paul L. "Isaiah 24–27: A Form Critical Analysis." Ph.D. diss., Vanderbilt University, 1972.

———. "Isaiah 26." *RevExp* 88 (1991): 195–99.

Rendsburg, Gary A. "A Comprehensive Guide to Israelian Hebrew: Grammar and Lexicon." *Orient* 38 (2003): 5–35.

———. "Late Biblical Hebrew in the Book of Haggai." Pages 329–44 in *Language and Nature: Papers Presented to John Huehnergard on the Occasion of his 60th Birthday*. Edited by Rebecca Hasselbach and Na'ama Pat-El. SAOC 67. Chicago: Oriental Institute, 2012.

Rendtorff, Rolf. *Canon and Theology: Overtures to an Old Testament Theology*. Translated by Margaret Kohl. Minneapolis: Fortress, 1993.

Ribichini, Sergio. "Adonis." Pages 7–10 in *Dictionary of Deities and Demons in the Bible*. Edited by Karel van der Toorn, Bob Becking, and Pieter W. van der Horst. 2nd ed. Leiden: Brill, 1999.

Richards, Kent Harold. "Death." Pages 108–10 in vol. 2 of *The Anchor Bible Dictionary*. Edited by David Noel Freedman. 6 vols. New York: Doubleday, 1992.

Ridderbos, Jan. "Jahwah Malak." *VT* 4 (1954): 87–89.

Ringgren, Helmer. "לבן lbn." Pages 451–54 in vol. 4 of *Theologisches Wörterbuch zum Alten Testament*. Edited by Gerhard J. Botterweck and Heinz-Josef Ringgren. Stuttgart:Kohlhammer, 1984.

Roberts, Jimmy Jack McBee. "Double Entendre in First Isaiah." *CBQ* 54 (1992): 39–48.

Rohland, Edzard. "Die Bedeutung der Erwählungstraditionen Israels für die Eschatologie der alttestamentlichen Propheten." Ph.D. diss., Heidelberg, 1956.

Rooker, Mark. *Biblical Hebrew in Transition: The Language of the Book of Ezekiel*. Sheffield: JSOT Press, 1990.

Routledge, Bruce. "Learning to Love the King: Urbanism and the State in Iron Age Moab." Pages 130–44 in *Urbanism in Antiquity, From Mesopotamia to Crete*. Edited by Walter E. Aufrecht, Neil A. Mirau, and Steven W. Gauley. JSOTSup 244. Sheffield: Sheffield Academic Press, 1997.

———. *Moab in the Iron Age, Hegemony, Polity, Archaeology*. Philadelphia: University of Pennsylvania Press, 2004.

Rudman, Dominic. "Midrash in the Isaiah Apocalypse." *ZAW* 112 (2000): 404–8.

Rudolph, Wilhelm. *Jesaja 24–27*. BWA(N)T 62. Stuttgart: Kohlhammer, 1933.

Schmidt, Brian B. "Memory as Immortality: Countering the Dreaded 'Death After Death' in Ancient Israelite Society." Pages 87–100 in *Death, Life-*

after-Death, Resurrection and the World to Come in the Judaisms of Antiquity. Vol. 4 of *Judaism in Late Antiquity.* Edited by Alan J. Avery-Peck and Jacob Neusner. HO 55. Leiden: Brill, 2000.

Schmitz, Philip C. "The Grammar of Resurrection in Isaiah 26:19a–c." *JBL* 122 (2003): 145–49.

Schniedewind, William S. *How the Bible Became a Book.* Cambridge: Cambridge University Press, 2004.

———. "Steps and Missteps in the Linguistic Dating of Biblical Hebrew." *HS* 46 (2005): 377–84.

Schnocks, Johannes. "Konzeptionen der Übergänge vom Leben zum Tod und vom Tod zum Leben." Pages 317–31 in *Biblische Anthropologie: Neue Einsichten aus dem Alten Testament.* Edited by Christian Frevel. QD 237. Freiburg: Herder, 2010.

Scholl, Reinhard. *Die Elenden in Gottes Thronrat: Stilistisch-kompositorische Untersuchungen zu Jesaja 24–27.* BZAW 274. Berlin: de Gruyter, 2000.

Schoors, Antoon. *Jesaja: uit de grondtekst vertaald en uitgelegd.* Bussum: Unieboek, 1972.

Schramm, Brooks. *The Opponents of Third Isaiah: Reconstructing the Cultic History of the Restoration.* JSOTSup 193. Sheffield: Sheffield Academic Press, 1995.

Seitz, Christopher R. *Isaiah 1–39.* Interpretation. Louisville: Knox, 1993.

———. *Isaiah 1–39.* Interpretation. Louisville: Knox, 1996.

Seow, Choon L. *A Grammar of Biblical Hebrew.* Nashville: Abingdon, 1995.

Shin, Seoung-Yun. "A Lexical Study on the Language of Haggai-Zechariah-Malachi and Its Place in the History of Biblical Hebrew." Ph.D. diss., Hebrew University, 2007.

Skinner, John. *The Book of the Prophet Isaiah.* 2 vols. Rev. ed. CBSC. Cambridge: Cambridge University Press, 1897.

———. *The Book of the Prophet Isaiah.* 2 vols. CBSC. Cambridge: Cambridge University Press, 1917.

Smend, Rudolf. "Anmerkungen zu Jes. 24–27." *ZAW* 4 (1884): 161–224.

Smit, Peter-Ben. "Appetite for Destruction: A Note on Isa 25:8a." *BN* 111 (2002): 44–47.

Smith, Mark. S. "The Baal Cycle." Pages 81–180 in *Ugaritic Narrative Poetry.* Edited by Simon B. Parker. SBLWAW 9; Atlanta: Scholars Press, 1997.

———. *The Early History of God: Yahweh and the Other Deities in Ancient Israel.* 2nd ed. Grand Rapids: Eerdmans, 2002.

———. "Mythology and Myth-making in Ugaritic and Israelite Literatures." Pages 293–341 in *Ugarit and the Bible: Proceedings of the International Symposium on Ugarit and the Bible, Manchester, September 1992.* Edited by George J. Brooke, Adrian H. W. Curtis, and John F. Healey. UBL 11. Münster: Ugarit-Verlag, 1994.

———. *The Origins of Biblical Monotheism: Israel's Polytheistic Background and the Ugaritic Texts*. New York: Oxford University Press, 2001.

———. *The Rituals and Myths of the Feast of the Goodly Gods of KTU/CAT 1.23: Royal Constructions of Opposition, Intersection, Integration, and Domination*. SBLRBS 51. Atlanta: Society of Biblical Literature, 2006.

———. *The Ugaritic Baal Cycle I: Introduction with Text, Translation and Commentary of KTU 1.1–1.2*. VTSup 55. Leiden: Brill, 1994.

Smith, Mark S. and Wayne T. Pitard, *The Ugaritic Baal Cycle II: Introduction with Text, Translation and Commentary of KTU/CAT 1.3–1.4*. VTSup 114. Leiden: Brill, 2009.

Snoek, Hans. "(Dis)Continuity between Present and Future in Isaiah 26:7–21." Pages 211–18 in *The New Things: Eschatology in Old Testament Prophecy: Festschrift for Henk Leene*. Edited by Ferenc Postma, Klaas Spronk, and Eep Talstra. ACEBTSup 3. Maastricht: Uitgeverij Shaker, 2002.

Sokoloff, Michael. *A Dictionary of Jewish Babylonian Aramaic of the Talmudic and Geonic Periods*. Ramat-Gan: Bar Ilan University Press, 2002.

Sommer, Benjamin D. *A Prophet Reads Scripture: Allusion in Isaiah 40–66*. Stanford: Stanford University Press, 1998.

Speiser, Ephraim A. *Genesis: Introduction, Translation and Notes*. AB 1. New York: Doubleday, 1964.

Spronk, Klaus. *Beatific Afterlife in Ancient Israel and in the Ancient Near East*. AOAT 219. Neukirchen-Vluyn: Neukirchener, 1986.

Stavrakopoulou, Francesca. *Land of our Fathers: The Roles of Ancestor Veneration in Biblical Land Claims*. LHBOTS 473. New York: T&T Clark, 2010.

Steck, Odil Hannes. *Studien zu Tritojesaja*. BZAW 203. Berlin: de Gruyter, 1991.

Steiner, Richard C. "The Aramaic Text in Demotic Script." Pages 309–27 in *Canonical Compositions from the Biblical World*. Vol. 1 of *The Context of Scripture*. Edited by William W. Hallo and K. Lawson Younger. 3 vols. Leiden: Brill, 1997.

Stern, Ephraim. *The Assyrian, Babylonian, and Persian Periods (732–332 B.C.E.)*. Vol. 2 of *Archaeology of the Land of the Bible*. ABRL. New York: Doubleday, 2001.

Stolz, Fritz. "בושׁ *bōš* zuschanden werden." Pages 269–72 in vol. 1 of *Theologisches Handwörterbuch zum Alten Testament*. Edited by Ernst Jenni and Claus Westermann. 2 vols. Zürich: Theologischer Verlag 1978.

Stordalen, Terje. *Echoes of Eden: Genesis 2–3 and Symbolism of the Eden Garden in Biblical Hebrew Literature*. CBET 25. Leuven: Peeters, 2000.

Stromberg, Jacob. *Isaiah after Exile: The Author of Third Isaiah as Reader and Redactor of the Book.* Oxford: Oxford University Press, 2011.

———. "The Second Temple and the Isaianic Afterlife of the חסדי דוד (Isa 55,3–5)." *ZAW* 121 (2009): 242–55.

Stronach, David. "The Imagery of the Wine Bowl: Wine in Assyria in the Early First Millennium B.C." Pages 175–95 in *The Origins and Ancient History of Wine.* Edited by Patrick E. McGovern, Stuart J. Fleming, and Solomon H. Katz. London: Routledge, 1995.

Suriano, Matthew J. *The Politics of Dead Kings: Dynastic Ancestors in the Book of Kings and Ancient Israel.* FAT 2/48. Tübingen: Mohr Siebeck, 2010.

Sweeney, Marvin A. *Form and Intertextuality in Prophetic and Apocalyptic Literature.* FAT 45. Tübingen: Mohr Siebeck, 2005.

———. *Isaiah 1–39 with an Introduction to Prophetic Literature.* FOTL 16. Grand Rapids: Eerdmans, 1996.

———. "New Gleanings from an Old Vineyard: Isaiah 27 Reconsidered." Pages 51–66 in *Early Jewish and Christian Exegesis: Studies in Memory of William Hugh Brownlee.* Edited by Craig A. Evans and William F. Stinespring. Atlanta: Scholars, 1987.

———. "Textual Citations in Isaiah 24–27: Toward an Understanding of the Redactional Function of Chapters 24–27 in the Book of Isaiah." *JBL* 107 (1988): 39–52.

Tiemeyer, Lena-Sofia. *Priestly Rites and Prophetic Rage: Post-exilic Prophetic Critique of the Priesthood.* FAT 2/19. Tübingen: Mohr Siebeck, 2006.

Toorn, Karel van der. "Echoes of Judaean Necromancy in Isaiah 28, 7–22." *ZAW* 100 (1988): 199–217.

———. *Family Religion in Babylonia, Ugarit, and Israel: Continuity and Changes in the Forms of Religious Life.* SHCANE 7. Leiden: Brill, 1996.

Tournay, Raymond J. "Les Psaumes Complexes: Les Psaumes 7 et 82: Structure et Attaches Litteraires." *RB* 56 (1949): 37–60.

Tromp, Nicholas J. *Primitive Conceptions of Death and the Nether World in the Old Testament.* Rome: Pontifical Biblical Institute, 1969.

Tucker, Gene M. "The Book of Isaiah 1–39: Introduction, Commentary, and Reflections." Pages 25–305 in *The New Interpreter's Bible* 6. Edited by Leander E. Keck. 12 vols. Nashville: Abingdon, 2001.Tull, Patricia K. *Isaiah 1–39.* Macon, Ga.: Smyth & Helwys, 2010.

Ulfgard, Håkan. *The Story of Sukkot: The Setting, Shaping, and Sequel of the Biblical Feast of Tabernacles.* BGBE 34. Tübingen: Mohr Siebeck, 1998.

Ussishkin, David. "The Borders and De Facto Size of Jerusalem in the Persian Period." Pages 147–66 in *Judah and the Judeans in the Persian Period.* Edited by Oded Lipschits and Manfred Oeming. Winona Lake, Ind.: Eisenbrauns, 2006.

Van Zyl, A. H. "Isaiah 24–27: Their Date of Origin." Pages 44–57 in *New Light on Some Old Problems: Papers Read at the 5th Meeting Held at the University of South Africa, Pretoria 30 January –2 February 1962*. Edited by A. H. can Zyl. Potchefstroom : Pro Rege, 1962.

Veen, Peter van der. "'The Seven Dots' on Mesopotamian and Southern Levantine Seals: An Overview." Pages 11–22 in *Die Zahl Sieben im Alten Orient: The Number Seven in the Ancient Near East*. Edited by Gotthard G. G. Reinhold. Frankfurt: Lang, 2008.

Vermeylen, Jacques. "La composition littéraire de L'apocalypse d'Isaïe (Is. XXIV–XXVII)." *ETL* 50 (1974): 5–38.

———. *Du prophète Isaïe à l'apocalytique: Isaïe, I–XXXV, miroir d'un demi millénaire d'expérience religieuse en Israël*. 2 vols. EBib. Paris: Gabalda, 1977–1978.

Wallace, Howard N. *The Eden Narrative*. HSM 32. Atlanta: Scholars Press, 1985.

Watson, Paul Layton. "The Death of 'Death' in the Ugaritic Texts." *JAOS* 92 (1972): 60–64.

———. "Mot, the God of Death, at Ugarit and in the Old Testament." Ph.D. diss., Yale University, 1971.

Watts, John D. W. *Isaiah 1–33*. WBC 24. Waco, Tex.: Word, 1985.

———. *Isaiah 1–33*. WBC 24. Rev. ed. Nashville: Nelson, 2005.

Welten, Peter. "Die Vernichtung des Todes und die Königsherrschaft Gottes: Eine traditionsgeschichtliche Studie zu Jes 25,6–8; 24,21–33 und Ex 24,9–11." *TZ* 38 (1982): 129–46.

Wensinck, Arent J. *The Ideas of the Western Semites Concerning the Navel of the Earth*. Verhandelingen der Koninklijke Akademie van Wetenschappen te Amsterdam 17. Amsterdam: Müller, 1916.

Weren, Wim. *Uit stof en as: Bijbelse beelden van Gods relatie met de doden: Rede ter gelegenheid van zijn afscheid als hoogleraar in de Bijbelwetenschappen (Nieuwe Testament) aan de Universiteit van Tilburg op vrijdag 27 mei 2011*. Tilburg: Tilburg University, 2011.

Werlitz, Jürgen. "Scheol und sonst nichts? Zu den alttestamentlichen 'Jenseits'-Vorstellungen." Pages 41–61 in *Das Jenseits: Perspektiven christlicher Theologie*. Edited by Stefan Schreiber and Stefan Siemons. Darmstadt: Wissenschaftliche Buchgesellschaft, 2003.

Wieringen, Archibald L. H. M. van. "Assur and Babel against Jerusalem: The Reader-Oriented Position of Babel and Assur within the Framework of Isaiah 1–39." Pages 49–62 in *'Enlarge the Site of Your Tent': The City as Unifying Theme in Isaiah: The Isaiah Workshop–De Jesaja Werkplaats*. Edited by Archibald van Wieringen and Annemarieke van der Woude. OtSt 58. Leiden: Brill, 2011.

——. "'I' and 'We' before 'Your' Face: A Communication Analysis of Isaiah 26:7–21." Pages 239–51 in *Studies in Isaiah 24–27: The Isaiah Workshop–De Jesaja Werkplaats*. Edited by Hendrick J. Bosman and Harm van Grol. OtSt 43. Leiden: Brill, 2000.

——. *Jesaja*. Belichting van het bijbelboek. Leuven: Vlaamse Bijbelstichting, 2009.

——. *The Reader-Oriented Unity of the Book Isaiah*. ACEBTSup 6. Vught: Skandalon, 2006.

Wildberger, Hans. "Das Freudenmahl auf dem Zion: Erwägungen zu Jes. 25, 6–8." *TZ* 6 (1977): 373–83.

——. *Isaiah 13–27*. Translated by Thomas H. Trapp. CC. Minneapolis: Fortress, 1991.

——. *Isaiah 13–27*. Translated by Thomas H. Trapp. CC. Minneapolis: Fortress, 1997.

——. *Jesaja 13–27*. BKAT 10.2. Neukirchen-Vluyn: Neukirchener, 1978.

Williamson, Hugh G. M. *The Book Called Isaiah: Deutero-Isaiah's Role in Composition and Redaction*. Oxford: Clarendon, 1994.

——. "The Formation of Isaiah 2.6–22." Pages 57–67 in *Biblical and Near Eastern Essays: Studies in Honour of Kevin J. Cathcart*. Edited by Carmel McCarthy and John F. Healey. JSOTSup 375. London: T&T Clark, 2004.

Winter, Irene J. "The King and the Cup: Iconography of the Royal Presentation Scene on Ur III Seals." Pages 253–68 in *Insight through Images: Studies in Honor of Edith Porada*. Edited by Marilyn Kelly-Buccellati, Paolo Matthiae, and Maurits Van Loon. BMes 21. Malibu: Undena Publications, 1986.

Wiseman, D. J. "A New Stele of Assur-nasir-pal." *Iraq* 14 (1952): 24–44.

Wodecki, Bernard. "The Religious Universalism of the Pericope Is 25:6–9." Pages 35–47 in *Goldene Äpfel in silbernen Schalen: Collected Communications to the XIIIth Congress of the International Organization for the Study of the Old Testament, Leuven 1989*. Edited by Klaus-Dietrich Schunck and Matthias Augustin. Frankfurt: Lang, 1992.

Wyatt, Nicholas. "Killing and Cosmogony in Canaanite and Biblical Thought." *UF* 17 (1986): 375–81.

——. *Religious Texts from Ugarit: The Words of Ilimilku and His Colleagues*. 2nd ed. The Biblical Seminar 53. London: Sheffield Academic Press, 2002.

Xella, Paolo. *Il mito di Šhr e Šlm: Saggio sulla mitologia ugaritica*. Studi Semitici 44. Rome: Istituto di Studi del vicino oriente, Università di Roma, 1973.

Young, Ian and Robert Rezetko. *Linguistic Dating of Biblical Texts*. Bible World. 2 vols. London: Equinox, 2008.

Zevit, Ziony. "Not So Random Thoughts Concerning Linguistic Dating and Diachrony in Biblical Hebrew." Pages 455–88 in *Diachrony in Biblical*

Hebrew. Edited by Cynthia Miller-Naudé and Ziony Zevit. Winona Lake, Ind.: Eisenbrauns, 2012.

———. "Symposium Discussion Session: An Edited Transcription." *HS* 46 (2005): 371–76.

Ziffer, Irit. "From Acemhöyük to Megiddo: The Banquet Scene in the Art of the Levant in the Second Millennium BCE." *TA* 32 (2005): 133–67.

Contributors

Micaël Bürki is completing his Ph.D. at Collège de France in Paris, France.

Paul Kang-Kul Cho is Assistant Professor of Hebrew Bible at Wesley Theological Seminary, Washington, D.C.

Stephen L. Cook is Catherine N. McBurney Professor of Old Testament Language and Literature at Virginia Theological Seminary, Alexandria, Virginia.

Wilson de A. Cunha is Assistant Professor of Hebrew and Old Testament Studies at LeTourneau University, Longview, Texas.

Carol J. Dempsey, OP, is Professor of Biblical Studies at the University of Portland, Oregon.

Janling Fu is completing his Ph.D. at Harvard University, Cambridge, Massachusetts.

Christopher B. Hays is D. Wilson Moore Associate Professor of Ancient Near Eastern Studies at Fuller Theological Seminary, Pasadena, California.

J. Todd Hibbard is Assistant Professor of Religious Studies at University of Detroit Mercy, Detroit, Michigan.

Hyun Chul Paul Kim is Harold B. Williams Professor of Hebrew Bible at Methodist Theological School in Ohio, Delaware, Ohio.

Beth Steiner is completing her D.Phil. at Oxford University, Oxford, United Kingdom.

John T. Willis is Professor of Old Testament at Abilene Christian University, Abilene, Texas.

Archibald L. H. M.van Wieringen is Professor of Old Testament at School of Catholic Theology, Tilburg University, the Netherlands.

Annemarieke van der Woude is a biblical scholar and theologian residing in the Netherlands.

Index of Ancient Sources

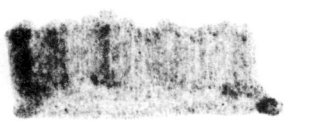

DATE DUE